WAITING FOR DEMOCRACY

A Citizen's Journal

Rick Salutin

VIKING

VIKING
Published by the Penguin Group
Penguin Books Canada Ltd, 2801 John Street, Markham, Ontario,
Canada L3R 1B4
Penguin Books Ltd, 27 Wrights Lane, London W8 5TZ, England
Viking Penguin Inc., 40 West 23rd Street, New York, New York 10010,
USA
Penguin Books Australia Ltd, Ringwood, Victoria, Australia
Penguin Books (NZ) Ltd, 182-190 Wairau Road, Auckland 10, New
Zealand

Penguin Books Ltd, Registered Offices: Harmondsworth, Middlesex,
England

First published 1989

1 3 5 7 9 10 8 6 4 2

Copyright © Rick Salutin, 1989

Printed and bound in Canada

Canadian Cataloguing in Publication Data
Salutin, Rick, 1942–
   Waiting for democracy

ISBN 0-670-82284-1

1. Canada. Parliament – Elections, 1988.*
2. Canada – Politics and government – 1984-
I. Title.

JL193.S25 1989   324.971'0647   C89-094848

for Kathleen O'Hara and Wren Montgomery

When they rises up, they gets confused.

The Adventures of Faustus Bidgood
Faustus Bidgood Productions,
Newfoundland, 1986

WAITING FOR DEMOCRACY

CONTENTS

ACKNOWLEDGEMENTS

My thanks to Joyce Wayne, who propelled this project out of the realm of mere idea; Morty Mint and Cynthia Good of Penguin Books, who were enthusiastic about the idea, and tolerant when it altered quite a lot; Kathryn Dean for her perceptive copy editing; David Kilgour, editor, for indispensable help in turning an experience into a book; Gregory Bryce, Rachel Cox, Dawn McKeigan, and Merrily Weisbord for their help as I travelled; all the Canadians with whom I talked, from political leaders to innocent bystanders, whose names or thoughts or sometimes just inspiration, appear within; Terry Mosher and Ron Kaplansky for the privilege of working with them on *What's the Big Deal?*; the members of the coalitions against free trade, and especially among them: Tony Clarke, Marjorie Cohen, Susan Feldman, Michael Lewis, Peggy Nash, Laurell Ritchie, Scott Sinclair and Ken Traynor — with whom I had the indescribable pleasure of working and battling for three amazing years.

Life before Voting

I

This is a book about the difference between politics and elections. It began with the election of Billy Cass as president of the student council at my high school in 1959. Or perhaps it began the year before, when the slick and superficial campaign of Steve Levy routed the principled forces behind Syd Goldenberg. I know, I worked for Syd, I worked my heart out. Nothing I have observed in politics ever since has perplexed and affected me as those elections did — but the Canadian election of 1988 came close.

Those early campaigns were a shock to my frail adolescent system of values. Billy should never have won, nor should Steve. Michael Landauer should have beaten Billy and Syd should have clobbered Steve. Syd made a great speech — brilliant really. I recall an image we worked on together: the school had ceased to move ahead, it carried on inertially, like a slow muddy river, but he — Syd —

1

promised to deepen the channel, alter the course and get it flowing again! What eloquence, what intellect.

Steve, against whom Syd ran, was quarterback of the school team, the Falcons. He was in an academically inferior class. He and his buddies belonged to a crass high school frat. They entered the election as a lark, I was sure. Their methods were heavy-handed. Norm "Pooch" Freedman, a guard on the basketball team, meandered into our classroom — we were the "brain" class — during lunch hour on voting day, and slumped on top of a desk, as though he often dropped by. He'd been dispatched, clearly, by Michael Firestone, the strategist of the Levy camp, much as others were often sent by Tory high command to spy on journalists aboard the campaign buses of 1988.

Yet the voters of Forest Hill Collegiate opted for Steve Levy, who became Steve Young when his quarterbacking was done, moved to Hollywood, appeared in a few films, including one with George C. Scott, then returned to Toronto, where I occasionally see him on TV playing celebrity charades.

He beat Syd, and I was inconsolable. I reeled home along Vesta Drive, rode the creaky elevator to our sixth-floor apartment and took up pen to pour out my sorrow, rage and — especially — incomprehension.

It went something like this: "The people are stupid. Democracy is idiotic. The people can't be trusted with judgements about the future or with choosing their own leaders. They don't think, they are perverse, they make choices which are exactly opposed to their real interests. Politics is too important to be left to them."

I had come to these conclusions on my own, and probably, I felt, for the first time in human history. Democracy was not a thing to castigate lightly. I felt let down and lonely. I didn't know I was in a crowded tradition, along with Plato, Aristotle, Burke. . . .

The next year, my last in high school, the experience repeated, only worse, when Billy Cass beat Michael Landauer. Mike, who was undoubtedly going to become

the first Jewish prime minister, crunched by the electorate. It was twenty years till I voted in another election.

I was out of Canada for the next ten of those years, studying or teaching at various universities and seminaries,
mostly in the United States. I discovered politics on the
way out of theology. At that time in the U.S. — the sixties,
as the years between 1968 and 1972 are called — there
was much political activity in the form of marching, pro-
testing or streetfighting; many of us found little interest in
the electoral form of politics, which threw up titans like
Hubert Humphrey and Richard Nixon for consideration.
As a Canadian down there, I couldn't have voted if I'd
wanted to, and I didn't want to. Maybe I was still put out
over Steve Levy and Billy Cass.
    When I moved back to Canada in late 1970, I still didn't
vote. Not for years. It is hard for me to convey how irrelevant and piddling electoral politics seemed to me then.
Politics, I felt, was about basically changing society, not
dithering over a superficial balloting process. Yet a
strange thing began to happen in my writing — an activity
I began at that time.
    My first stage play was called *Fanshen*, a dramatization
of William Hinton's book about the Chinese Revolution
sweeping through a village in 1948. The play had an election scene: Canadian actors as Chinese peasants voting for
the first time in their lives. In my next play, *1837*, about
the failed rebellion in Upper Canada that year, another
election scene appeared. In *I.W.A.*, a play about a woodworkers' strike that I worked on in Newfoundland, there
was a big strike vote. In a TV drama, *Maria*, the central
event was a vote by workers in a factory on whether to join
a union. In the play *Les Canadiens*, all of Act II centred on
a hockey game played at the Montreal Forum on election
night, 1976, when vote results usurped game results!
These scripts contained campaigning, electioneering, voting — savoured far too much by someone as dubious

about electoral politics as I claimed to be. Why did it happen?

Voting has a hold on us. I felt it everywhere I travelled in Canada during the election of 1988. People cherish their vote, even when they don't use it or when they use it irresponsibly, as they often say themselves, without "paying enough attention" to the issues. This devotion to voting has been instilled in us since schooldays and through the education we receive outside school as well. Winston Churchill's words — that democracy is the worst form of government except for all the others — stick in our minds. Churchill didn't say what he meant by democracy. He just assumed, as we all usually do, that it's a matter of voting for representatives in a British or American electoral system.

Our commitment to voting in elections goes deeper than a learned habit, though, and it raises questions about elections themselves. We want to feel we have some power over the forces that shape our society and so control our lives. We want to feel this is *our* society and that being a citizen in it means more than paying taxes and holding a passport. Whether elections achieve this is up for discussion.

We live in an age of elections. Within weeks during November 1988, national elections were held in Canada, the U.S. and Israel. Elsewhere in the world — in Central American countries as different as Guatemala and Nicaragua, in the Soviet bloc and in the U.S.S.R. itself — elections are now a dominant feature of politics. They are pervasive, yet the more you see of them the more you wonder about them. Perhaps you cannot have real politics without elections, but it is possible to have elections without much real politics. In its unique way, the Canadian election of 1988 raised such issues.

Once upon a time, citizenship was considered that thing which most defined a human being. It was not something you chose or shopped and paid for as people now sometimes do; it more or less chose you, and you felt privileged to receive it. To the ancient Greeks, for instance, a person's role as citizen was the essential thing about them. What you did as a citizen — participating in public debate, taking on civic responsibilities — determined who you were *in the most personal sense*. All the things *we* consider personal — idiosyncrasies, neuroses, private passions and tastes — would have been in the realm of the trivial and impersonal for the Greeks. A human being truly existed only as a citizen.

This attitude is just about the reverse of our own. Espousing a view like that in our society can make you feel eccentric or just crazy. If anything seems like a leisure option today, it's politics. The odd individual enjoys it, the way some like snorkelling and others spend time with their kids.

Such people, we sometimes say, are "political," or political animals. We mean they have a peculiar obsession with politics. You hear this usage often when you spend time around political parties. "I'm a political animal," people say proudly — or sheepishly. Left-wing people often display a similar mindset. They talk about being "political," though they leave out "animal." They say that most people in this society are not political, they are "apolitical." These uses of "political" or "political animal" are the opposite of what Aristotle, who first used the term, meant by it.

He was an obsessive categorizer, who slotted whatever passed under his gaze. He assumed human beings were animals and shared qualities like locomotion with other animals. When he wanted to establish the quality that distinguished humans from all other animals, he did not cite possession of a soul. He felt that something like a soul characterized other animals as well. Nor did he pick love, creativity, sinfulness, the ability to learn or the capacity to make tools. Aristotle concluded that it was their political character that made humans unique. We were the *zoon politikon*.

What did Aristotle mean by "political"? It was not a matter of joining some stupid party, stuffing envelopes, chanting "Bri-an, Bri-an" or "Tur-ner, Tur-ner," at a "leadership" convention, or yearning for an election victory in the hope of being appointed to some board.

"Which life is more desirable, the life of participation in the work of the state and the constitution, or one like a foreigner's, cut off from the association of the state?" he wrote in his book *Politics*. It's a question he didn't even bother answering, to him the answer was evident — participate in the work of the state and constitution, of course. For Aristotle, an apolitical man — literally a cityless man, since *polis*, the root of "politics," means "city" — was like a "solitary piece in checkers." Such a person couldn't have any fun because he couldn't play the game. It was obvious that "in the best state, it is bound to be the case that the virtue of a man and of a citizen are identical." Being the best you could be meant being the best *citizen* you could be.

If anything, Aristotle was more restrained on this subject than most citizens of Athens. I. F. Stone writes that being *apolis*, cityless, "already denoted a tragic fate in Sophocles and Herodotus, a century before Aristotle." The *polis* was never just a geographic notion; it always implied a "political" community. Pericles, the greatest Athenian statesman and democrat, said, "A man may at the same time look after his own affairs and those of the state. . . We consider anyone who does not share the life of the city not as minding his own business but as useless." Hannah Arendt wrote that, according to the Greeks, "a life spent in the privacy of "one's own" (*idion*), outside the world of the common, is 'idiotic' by definition."

This kind of Greek thinking must sound like Swahili to many of my own fellow citizens. How to explain why it makes such sense to me — that the essence of being human means being a citizen, a *polites*, the member of a *polis*, or city, or state, or political community, or nation for that matter. That being human is all about being *political*, as Aristotle said. That the "virtue" of a human being and of a citizen really are "identical." A human being at his best is, simply put, a citizen. It sounds so . . . *boring*.

That we really are essentially connected seems to me obvious — and silly to deny. No infant would survive without a whole social infrastructure, without other human beings and all the supports the entire society has put in place. How would you come into the world? Where? The hospital or home in which you are born was built, literally, by the hands of a person probably long dead, whom you never knew, but to whom you are indebted. The milk formula you imbibe is the result of millenia of agricultural development. The heating systems and water supply that make survival possible are the end of an almost interminable and practically untraceable chain of technological development and construction.

There's language. The interhuman communication that makes possible technology, social complexity, even the acquisition of a sense of self — I am speaking about levels of speech infinitely beneath literary expression — is the bequest of all human civilization and all human beings who ever lived, and *each* of us acquires *all* of it. We are, no way around it, dependent on the human collectivity past and present at every breath we take. Eliminate social connections and none of us would be — or last.

(I step out onto the deck which the clever design of someone who lived here before me has allowed me to use without leaving my third floor workroom. I walk about it in the bright sunlight, the boards creaking beneath my feet in the intense cold. I move swiftly back indoors, through the sliding double-glazed panels, and am greeted by the thick warmth of the radiators. I am indebted to all the crews on the prairies who drill natural gas, those who built the pipelines and maintain them, and who repair the mains here in Toronto, and also the offices full of people who bill me, and collect and process my payments, to redistribute to those crews up the pipelines on the wells out west, and I think of the money I pay them with, which I receive from those who pay me to write books, plays, magazine articles, which I hope at least occasionally find their way into the hands of those who are keeping me warm so that I can write these things.)

In contrast to the way these connections with others help make us what we are, our "individual" characteristics — the personal qualities that cannot be derived from or connected to the efforts of others — seem pretty minimal, though often lovable. Even the achievement of a great artist, of a Shakespeare, is small compared to the achievement of the human race in inventing and cultivating language, including the English language. We are indebted to Shakespeare, but he is indebted to us.

Why should there be a conflict between the "personal" and the collective? We can acknowledge our bond to others *and* make our own distinctive contributions to the ongoing effort. That's politics. Politics is the realm of our lives in which we human beings acknowledge the fact of our interconnectedness and attempt to take charge of its effects. It is how we try to organize our unavoidable interconnectedness. It is the way in which we do our best to seize conscious control of that interconnectedness. It is not just because human beings are interconnected, but because we try to *do something* about that connectedness, that we are political animals. More than any other activity, politics is what we do about what we really are.

And yet, if politics is so central to what we are, why does it often seem so peripheral in people's lives? Because for most of us, politics means casting a vote once every few years for a representative, or the leader of a party and not much else. That is not how politics looked, for example, in ancient Athens.

Democracy there was direct. Citizens did not vote for members who represented them; they were expected to participate themselves in the major political decisions that affected them. At least forty times a year and often more frequently the citizens of Athens met in assembly, debated and chose their future course. This was a much smaller political community than our own, but it was not tiny. In Pericles' time, the number of citizens was 35,000 or 40,000 out of a total population of perhaps a quarter-million in the city and the surrounding countryside. The system included typical atrocities: women did not have the rights of citizens, nor did foreigners, and the whole structure rested on slave labour. But for those who were citizens, it was a remarkably participatory process.

The assembly was simply a big open-air meeting on a hill called the Pnyx. A proposal would be put forward — it might be an administrative or tax issue or a major matter of foreign policy like declaring war — then be debated and voted on, usually on the same day. Citizens participated not only in making the decisions, but in carrying them out. As Aristotle wrote, "What effectively distinguishes the citizen proper from all others is his participation in giving judgement and in holding office." There were a large number of officials and a council of five hundred, *all of whom* were chosen by lot — like our jury system — and restricted to one or two one-year terms. Elections, says Aristotle, were considered undemocratic, because they did not treat everyone as equal for purposes of office holding, although a small number of positions, like generals, were elected. Leadership was not expressed through holding high office, but rather through playing a leading role in democratic debate.

This is a long way from our kind of democracy, and makes our version look a little pale. The Athenians met, deliberated and voted on the issues almost once a week for two centuries! As Sir Moses Finley wrote, "There is a vast difference between voting on infrequent occasions for a man or a party on the one hand, and on the other hand voting every few days directly on the issues themselves." This looks like an example of the difference I mentioned between elections and politics. And yet for long moments the Canadian election of 1988 felt strangely Athenian, because the people kept trying to vote on issues rather than candidates, and to enter the fray directly themselves, even as the custodians of political realism strove mightily to shift them back to their traditional role as mere voters for leaders and parties. We went to an election, and politics kept breaking out. This book is about the difference between elections and politics, but it is also about the connections between them.

II

The vote of 1988 became an election unlike all others because of the explosion of the free trade issue within it. This need not have been. The fate of the free trade agreement did not have to be decided in an election — it could have been settled separately, between elections, as the Conservative government had originally hoped. Nor did it have to become the central fact of that particular election. It became so, largely because of incessant agitation against the agreement over a period of years by many Canadians well outside the official party and electoral process. That activity drew into a national political debate people who rarely if ever participated in electoral politics. The two streams met in the election of fall 1988. I should add that I was one of those drawn into the debate, and therefore eventually into the election, in a way I had never anticipated when I originally decided to write a book about what I anticipated would be a typical federal election.

The impetus for a free trade agreement with the United States probably began with the Business Council on National Issues, made up of the heads of the 150 largest corporations in Canada. It is certainly the most powerful single organization in the country, measured by success in getting its way. Since at least 1981, the BCNI had lobbied for a new trade arrangement with the United States. Many of its member corporations appeared before the Royal Commission on the Economic Union and Development Prospects for Canada headed by Donald Macdonald, a former Liberal finance minister, and argued in favour of the proposal. Even before the commission concluded its report, Macdonald announced his commitment to a "leap of faith" into a free trade agreement with the United States.

Before that recommendation was made, the Conservative party leadership had disavowed any free trade initiative. Both during his campaign for the Tory leadership and in the House of Commons, Brian Mulroney had explicitly rejected a free trade agreement, in categorical terms. After his election, however, he and his government came under strong pressure from business on the trade issue. At his "Shamrock Summit" with American president Ronald Reagan in Quebec in March 1985, Mulroney reversed his position in a joint declaration of intention with Reagan about a new trade agreement. By September of that year, after the Macdonald Commission issued its final report and blessed the concept, Mulroney announced in the House that his government had officially asked the United States to enter negotiations. At this point — still early, in the sense that there was no specific agreement to react to, but late in the sense that business had spent years laying the groundwork for free trade — reactions from beyond the normal frame of political power and corporate wealth began.

In early December 1985, a meeting was called in Toronto. (I take this case because I am familiar with it. Other such meetings were held elsewhere in the country.) The Toronto gathering was initiated through a raft of phone calls made by Laurell Ritchie. She was president of a union of textile workers, mostly immigrant women. Their operation was scruffy but scrappy, and about as scaled-down as a union can get. It didn't belong to the big Canadian Labour Congress; instead it was part of a small umbrella group called the Confederation of Canadian Unions, an amalgam of independent unions, none very large, most of which had broken away from "internationals" — that is, unions with their headquarters in the States. There was scant affection at the time between unions like Laurell's and their counterparts in the Canadian Labour Congress.

Laurell always seemed to be doing almost everything along with the endless work of running her union. She'd be selling tickets for a benefit or preparing a brief for the women's movement or rushing off to an anti-anti-abortion demonstration or guiding around a visiting labour organizer from Bolivia or attending a memorial concert or reading for someone like Milton Acorn or Stan Rogers.

Then she'd get up at 6:00 A.M. to leaflet outside one of the plants. She said the meeting would include a lot of people from different organizations who were worried about the free trade thing.

It was tense in the untidy office of the National Action Committee on the Status of Women. Maybe thirty people were present. They came from labour, the women's movement, agriculture, social service groups, some of the churches, the universities, publishing and the arts. The air of suspicion was thick. There were people who didn't often work together, from organizations that had probably never been found in the same room.

Discussion moved around the table and everyone spoke on what concerned them and their members about free trade. By halfway round, people were relaxing. It was so *interesting*. Each group opposed free trade, or at least worried about it — but for many different reasons. The farmers said Canada has a short growing season and if we're going to provide our own food, we need the protection of marketing boards. The churches worried about the moral implications of absorption into the U.S. market and losing touch with the poor nations of the Third World. The artists said the U.S. has never acknowledged our right to protect our own voices in our country. People got so wrapped up in what others were saying that they stopped fretting about rivalries and touchy feelings.

Some worried about being seen as simply negative. Others said, Maybe so, but it would be difficult to find positive positions shared by everyone present. What's wrong with being negative said someone else — if it's in a good cause, like saving your country and the things you value about your society? The group decided to continue meeting and to call itself, rather directly, the Coalition against Free Trade. Since it was based in Toronto, it included a number of national organizations with headquarters in that city. In coming months, as similar coalitions were created in every province, it became known as the "Toronto Coalition."

On the first anniversary of the Shamrock Summit, in March 1986, the new Coalition tested its cause by staging an Against Free Trade Revue at Massey Hall in Toronto. People were turned away for lack of seats. As the audience poured in, the press and media stood at the front and mused, People really seem to *care* about this thing. They hadn't expected the powerful hold of free trade on Canadians. Looking at the crowd myself that night, I felt almost as if I believed in a collective memory: free trade connects Canadians to their past. They react to it instinctively.

The program for the night was based on that first coalition meeting, the trip around the table. There were speakers from each constituency, with actors, comics and musicians in between. Walter Gordon, the grand old man of Canadian nationalism, spoke first. He ran past his allotted two minutes. Someone urged the stage manager to blink a warning light on the speaker's podium at Gordon. She looked up — a jaded veteran who has run stages like the Stratford Festival — and said angrily, "Blink Walter Gordon?" Marjorie Cohen, economist and vice-president of NAC, the women's organization, talked about free trade and women. "This is macho economics," she said. Bob White, head of the Canadian Auto Workers union, said that even if the agreement contained an exemption for the Autopact, he would oppose it, because it was bad for *Canada*. White got the strongest response of the night when he said Canadians didn't want any part of the American war against Nicaragua. The Roman Catholic bishop of Victoria, Remi de Roo, spoke like a prophet, and Clarke MacDonald, a former moderator of the United Church, got the Hall chanting "NO" to questions about the deal's effects. The night's biggest hit was actor Eric Peterson, who recited "The Cremation of Sam McGee," with a running interpretation of the poem as a warning about what happens when you make deals with Americans. Think of the poem's central image, he said: a well-intentioned Canadian, lumbered with an American corpse he must cart forever around the Arctic wastes, *because he gave his word.*

The odd mix of politics and culture, speeches and performance, seemed normal, as though one had seen it often. It worked because the "cultural" element was not mere filler; it was at the heart of the issue. In a way free trade was *all* about culture, in that the distinctive nature of Canadian society was endangered by Americanization. For the first time in Canadian history, culture was at the centre of a debate about politics and economics. The government understood this; they swore culture was not "on the table" and later claimed it received an exemption from the terms of the deal. This did not sway artists, who massively opposed the agreement and intervened more directly in politics than they ever had.

As artists and their organizations were drawn into politics, others in the anti-free trade movement were drawn into culture. At another Massey Hall rally a year and a half later, the Clichettes performed: three women wearing billowing wigs and chiffon dresses who lipsynch songs from the fifties. They "sang" "You Don't Own Me." Gord Wilson, president of the Ontario Federation of Labour, sitting transfixed in the audience, almost missed his turn to speak. As he was led backstage, he kept muttering, "Extraordinary. Extraordinary. . . ." Wilson, a relatively conservative labour leader, had never seen anything like the Clichettes. The anti-free trade movement had this capacity to mould different constituencies into a political force. It was unlike other coalitions, which centre on a single issue like daycare or missile testing. It was, in its way, about *all* issues: a way of life.

During the next eighteen months, it frequently seemed that little was happening. It was the time of the Phoney War over free trade. Events like the Massey Hall rallies took place across the country, with that distinctive blend of politics and culture. Coalitions formed in every province, and proliferated so that there were local as well as provincial bodies. Many, like the Toronto Coalition, were made up of organizations, though individuals could participate. Other groups like the Council of Canadians and Citizens against Free Trade, were composed of individuals. Gradually these bodies formed links, and a national umbrella organization called the Pro-Canada Network emerged.

Most of the activity was organizational, though there were exceptions. Marjorie Cohen, for example, was on the road nearly every weekend for four years, responding to invitations from public health workers in Edmonton, environmentalists in the B.C. interior, teachers, nurses, daycare workers, immigrant women's groups — to speak about the effects of free trade on women. She pointed to the service sector as one of the keys to the agreement, long before negotiations were finished. She debated and wrote. It would be wrong to say she was single-handedly responsible for the gender gap on free trade, but she had more to do with it than anyone else.

It was difficult, though, to keep the fight going in the absence of much real information about the negotiations that were taking place. Many academic experts opposed to free trade were convinced no deal would be made, because the Americans would never grant guaranteed access to their market or surrender the right to invoke retaliatory trade laws — conditions the Mulroney government had declared essential. Others said there might be a "cosmetic" deal to save the government's face. Those who proposed such theories expected the Americans, in one way or another, to protect us from ourselves.

There was another reason for this period of lull. It was part of the government's plan. A secret "communications strategy" on the free trade initiative, obtained by the *Toronto Star* from the Prime Minister's Office in September 1985, was clear. What the government sought from citizens was, in their words, "benign neglect."

"The strategy," according to the document, "should rely less on educating the general public than on getting across the message that the trade initiative is a good idea. In other words, a selling job.

"The public support generated should be recognized as extremely soft and likely to evaporate rapidly if the debate is allowed to get out of control so as to erode the central focus of the message. At the same time a substantial majority of the public may be willing to leave the issue in the hands of the government and other interested groups if the government maintains communications control of the situation. Benign neglect from a majority of Canadians may be the realistic outcome of a well executed communications program."

In these words, the government clearly acknowledged that they were planning to minimize discussion about free trade, because if informed, Canadians would probably oppose the deal. "It is likely that the higher the profile the issue attains, the lower the degree of public approval will be," said the document. In the years that followed, they did not waver from this strategy. When they spoke of their deal, it was as part of a "selling job" over which they could "maintain communications control."

The use by press and media of this memo is instructive. It was reported, then coverage continued as if no secret strategy had ever surfaced. The government proceeded to do as they said they would: conceal significant information and avoid debate while making a sales pitch. The press reported the sales pitch as though it was genuine information. Each time anyone called for more debate and discussion on free trade, the government said the issue had been well discussed. The press reported these statements with no asides to inform readers and viewers that such claims were contradicted by the government itself, which had admitted it did not *want* Canadians well informed. Numerous polls taken before, during and after the election, confirmed the strategy's success. People always felt ill-informed on the issue.

It is interesting that the government strategy anticipated that the main opposition to its free trade policy would come not from the Opposition parties, but from outside the formal political process. "The strategy is designed to defuse negative arguments," the document said, "and to head off the development of a major coalition on the negative side of the issue." The government had located its two main enemies: open discussion, and popular opposition in the form of a coalition.

This set of conflicts probably doomed one of the few exciting ideas to emerge during the Phoney War: a major debate about free trade. In March 1987, Donald Macdonald and former Alberta premier Peter Lougheed announced the formation of a national pro-free trade organization, the Canadian Alliance for Trade and Job Opportunities, perhaps in response to the dreaded "development of a major coalition on the negative side." The Alliance was the Business Council on National Issues under another name; even its address and executive director, Thomas d'Aquino, were the same. The Coalition against Free Trade wired a challenge to debate. D'Aquino "welcomed" the opportunity.

A date, a locale — the historic St. Lawrence Hall in downtown Toronto — and a format were agreed on. Both sides named their teams. For the deal: Macdonald, Lougheed, Alcan head David Culver and economist Richard Lipsey. They had earlier listed Jacques Parizeau of the Parti Québécois, but reconsidered when Parizeau said he supported free trade because it would lead to the break-up of Canada. The Coalition named Bob White, Marjorie Cohen, writer Margaret Atwood and Quebec Bishop Adolphe Proulx.

This could have been a truly democratic moment. The Hall would be dressed with bunting and banners, maybe with bands too — celebrating a long tradition of public debate on this very issue. Television wasn't included, but surely the media would pick it up. Perhaps it would become a model for vital discussion across the country. Then the Alliance added a condition: they would drop out unless the debate was nationally televised. With time short, this demand was impossible to meet, although most networks showed interest. Only the CBC declined to even consider the matter. An executive explained it could not cut American programming from its schedule for a free trade debate because it would lose ad revenue. "Isn't that ironic?" he said. The Alliance cancelled.

Perhaps they wanted a way out, for reasons similar to those expressed in the government's communications strategy. Yet the idea had developed a momentum of its own. It was like the Flying Dutchman: it couldn't go anywhere, but it couldn't stop. Global TV scheduled an October date for the same debate. By October, when negotiations were over and the terms of the deal were known, the president of Global said they had changed their minds because "nothing would be gained at this point" by having "an acrimonious debate" on the subject.

A stripped-down version of the debate finally happened on Toronto's tacky, gutsy CITY-TV in November 1987. When Tory minister Barbara McDougall refused to debate anyone but other politicians, CITY compliantly disinvited Bob White and Marjorie Cohen, replacing them with a Liberal and an NDPer. This late change may have been the most significant part of the belated event.

Why? The free trade debate had by then mobilized a unique confrontation of social forces. In favour was most of the business community, with rare exceptions, and a few others: American-based construction unions, red meat farmers and the Canadian Consumers' Association, though the latter eventually withdrew their support. Against the deal were the vast majority of women's organizations, churches, labour unions, artists, farmers, environmentalists and seniors. I am speaking of organized forces; polled individually, Canadians were more or less split. The debate was not so much about sovereignty in an abstract sense, as about two visions of Canadian society, represented by different sections of that society. There had been no line-up of this sort — business against almost everyone else — since the 1930s. The debate as originally planned would have displayed this division. Instead, when the debate aired on CITY, it looked like an internal dispute among politicians. The real social cleavage did not become apparent in the press and media until the final weeks of the election campaign of 1988, when things previously impossible started to happen.

By summer 1987, Canadian and American negotiating teams had been meeting secretly for almost two years. The deadline for concluding a trade deal, imposed by the U.S. Congress, was October 1, 1987. The coalitions opposing the deal were nonpartisan and had worked mostly outside the formal political process to this point, but as the deadline approached, contacts with the official political level increased. It seemed unavoidable.

In Manitoba, for example, the provincial coalition met with representatives of the NDP government, urging them to take a clear position opposing a deal in principle. The response was ambiguous. In Toronto, the coalition arranged to meet with the Ontario government. The Liberals were governing as a minority at the time, propped up by the NDP. In the past, Premier David Peterson had appeared to oppose a deal, but recently he'd said little. He claimed he was reserving judgement. He did not attend the meeting but Herschell Ezrin, Peterson's chief aide, did. Ezrin was asked if Peterson was being quiet about free trade because he wanted to become prime minister. Ezrin vigorously denied it. He said he would set up a meeting with Peterson and representatives of the Toronto Coalition. At the meeting, Peterson asked for advice and lingered long past the scheduled time to hear it. Those who claimed to understand such things said this was an important sign.

A delegation also met with Bob Rae, leader of the provincial NDP. Rae said he did not intend to campaign primarily on the free trade issue in the coming provincial election. He strongly opposed free trade, but feared that if it became the central issue, it would draw votes to the Liberals. Instead, the NDP would campaign on its own chosen winner: public auto insurance.

In August 1987, Peterson called a provincial election. He ran, more or less, on opposition to free trade. He spoke to voters about the future of their country while Rae promised to save them a few dollars on their cars. A big Liberal win was probably foreordained, and it happened, but the NDP's role was self-defeating and ominous.

These early contacts with the world of "real" politics were frustrating and often inscrutable, especially compared with the directness and exhilaration of other coalition activities. I, for instance, had a brief and mystifying dalliance with Ezrin, Peterson's aide. It began when I put in a call one day and he returned it. Those of greater experience said this was significant. Then Ezrin returned another call. Then he called, uncalled. This, I was told, was serious. Ezrin even called from the airport on the way to a federal-provincial conference. Yet I had no idea of the value of those contacts. Whenever I suggested ideas for the Ontario government, Ezrin had anticipated them and often already acted on them. Was this a chance for us to use or were we being used? Did anyone know, even Ezrin?

Then, in the middle of the provincial election campaign, I fell from grace. I received some materials from Ezrin that seemed unintended for me, yet surely someone playing the game at his level did not make simple mistakes. It was a sign, or I was being tested. It didn't occur to me to simply ask what was going on. Instead I devised a subtle system of countersigns, met with Ezrin and signalled frantically. After that he never returned a call. I was off his list. I felt like Falstaff when the king passed him by saying, "I know thee not, old man, fall to thy prayers." I had gone from virgin to discard.

In the aftermath of the provincial election, Peterson did not endorse the deal, but gradually backed away from opposing it. By the time of the federal election almost a year later, he played a relatively small role. Ezrin by then had left Peterson's office. He was working on the federal Liberal campaign team and getting ready to become communications vice-president for Molson's, where one of his first acts was to announce a mighty merger with Carling O'Keefe, in the name of the new competitiveness under free trade.

On a Wednesday afternoon in late September 1987, Canada's chief trade negotiator, Simon Reisman, broke off talks and left Washington for Ottawa. He said it really was finished, there would be no deal. Bob White of the Canadian Auto Workers immediately called Reisman's move a negotiating ploy. The deadline for negotiations was ten days off.

The suspense was great — for those who were involved. For others, life went on. People kept saying, What do you think's gonna happen? And, By this weekend, we'll know. Much of the time, at least in Toronto, they meant the outcome of the final week of the pennant race in the American League, where the Blue Jays were in a tight contest with the Detroit Tigers.

Friday morning's headlines proclaimed that Reisman was back in Washington, accompanied by a Cabinet team. The "success" of free trade negotiations between Canada and the United States was announced at midnight on Saturday. The waiting was over.

The deal revealed was more drastic, by far, than the most extreme predictions that had been made about it. The Canadian side got not even the bare minimum for which, we had been told, we entered negotiations. There was no guaranteed access for Canadian products to the U.S. market. All American trade remedy laws would continue to apply, and the Americans could make new ones as well. Canadian exports would remain completely vulnerable. The Canada-U.S. disputes panel established would merely judge whether existing laws had been correctly applied. In return, Canada gave up more than had ever been hinted at during two years of secret talks. For example, the U.S. was guaranteed access to all Canadian energy resources forever, on the same terms as Canadians. Most U.S. investment could enter Canada with no right of screening or requirement that it benefit

Canadians. Health and product standards were to be "harmonized" (i.e., Americanized). The service sector, the economy's biggest employer by far, was opened wide to free trade — far more comprehensively than had ever been granted by any country anywhere. Jobs in services, especially women's jobs, would certainly flow south. Only a summary of the deal was available — the final wording was unknown for months — but the implications for health care, social services, culture and the environment were severe. In addition, Canada was committed to *years* more of bargaining over what constituted unfair government subsidies. There would be continuing American pressure to give up social, regional and cultural support programs, and far less to bargain with in order to save them. In many ways, the agreement was a sort of Trojan Horse concealing a right-wing agenda that the government would have had great difficulty implementing more directly.

From the standpoint of the opposition to free trade, the deal announced was actually so bad that its weakness became a problem. Many Canadians found it difficult to believe their own government could propose something so unbalanced. Weren't governments there to serve the people? They might make mistakes, but this deal seemed beyond simple error or stupidity. It looked too bad to be true.

The conclusion of the agreement put the free trade debate firmly on the agenda of federal politics. The provinces which had previously played an important role, became less significant. It was far from certain, however, that a federal election would ever be fought on the issue. The deal was scheduled to come into effect on January 1, 1989, within the current government's mandate. They could simply wait it out. Much would depend on the attitude of the Opposition parties, and it was unclear what stand they would take — particularly the Liberals under John Turner. Still, as Marjorie Cohen said, "In other countries if the government tried to put over something like this without even consulting the people, they would have a revolution. The least we can do is have an election."

On Monday, October 5, 1987, the day after the deal was made public, John Turner was transformed. It was an astounding reversal. Turner had returned to federal politics as leader of his party in 1984, following nine years in the intimate embrace of big business as a corporate lawyer and board member of both Canadian and multinational firms. He came back explicitly to move his party to the right and in a business direction. During the election that year, Mulroney had positioned himself — successfully — to the left of Turner. During his disastrous years as leader, under constant attack within his own party and caucus, Turner had not indicated any significant alteration in his viewpoint. As for the free trade initiative, he had expressed reservations, but never principled opposition. The NDP had been far more committed to fighting it.

Now Turner stood on the floor of the House and made the issue his own. Within minutes, it seemed, he had digested the agreement and all its implications. He waved the summary of the text as though it was growing from his palm. He seemed reborn. No more stammers, confident, on solid ground. He seemed to have mastered the issue overnight, and taken an implacable position. This had the sound of more than a standard Opposition reaction.

How did it happen? Was it sheer accident? Did his handlers let him get out of sight just when the copy of the deal arrived? Did he wander off in the halls of Parliament with it and settle in an unoccupied committee room while they suddenly noticed with horror that he was gone, absconded with the deal and no one knew what might happen if the two were alone together for any length of time? While they scoured the corridors and private clubs, did he read through it like the lawyer and businessman he was, wide-eyed, saying to himself, or aloud although no one was there: This deal stinks! Then it was too late, the deed was done, the relationship struck. By the time they caught up to him, or the pair of them — Turner and the deal — they were bound in an inseparable relationship of antipathy. From then till the election of 1988, he always seemed to have a copy of it in his hand or pocket. You felt he read it through every night before he went to bed, reassuring himself of its awfulness and refuelling himself for what he rightly called his crusade against it. He clung furiously to that deal, as if it made sense of the world: how golden John was treated like refuse by life, politics, friends — till the meaning of it all came clear: he was put here for a purpose, to fight this thing and expose it to his fellow citizens.

Two days later a delegation from the anti-free trade movement met with Ed Broadbent in a corner room of the House of Commons. It was early evening, and although it was just the beginning of October, night seemed to lower quickly. Broadbent appeared dozy, so much that someone asked if he was really serious about stopping the deal. He looked a bit hurt and said that if it went through he doubted there would be a Canada at all twenty-five years into the future. At the end of the meeting, someone mentioned how different things would be if Broadbent were in power. "That could happen," he said almost wistfully, as though thoughts of power were on his mind. Perhaps they'd been there since the Gallup polls of mid-1985 showed the NDP at 44 percent in public opinion, leading the other two parties for the first time since 1943.

The popular opposition to free trade seemed to begin all over again. The coalitions and organizations already active increased their activity; the unions, the National Action Committee on the Status of Women and the churches sent literature to their members. More public meetings were held, and days were set aside for protest, some local and some national. Graphic artist Michael Cavanaugh designed an anti-free trade logo: a corner of an American flag with a small maple leaf in it and the Words,

"No, Eh." On buttons and T-shirts, it was picked up across the country. The money raised allowed the Toronto Coalition to double its paid staff — to two.

The real explosion came in local activity. New coalitions sprang up spontaneously, then found their way into setting up connections with already established groups. In Mississauga, Ontario, for instance, nurse Alice Kolisnyk called a friend, businessman Jim Currie. They organized a public forum with speakers from sectors like farming, oil and business, signed up those who came and founded the Mississauga Coalition against Free Trade with one hundred members. "From then on we did event after event till it was over," said Kolisnyk. They dropped 24,000 leaflets and other publications on how the deal would affect their community, picketed their Tory MP, wrote all four hundred members of the U.S. Congress and attended government-sponsored sessions promoting free trade to business whenever they could afford it. They "dressed up looking very nice and smart," according to Kolisnyk, and raised hard questions for trade minister John Crosbie or whoever else was there. Local coalitions wrote briefs and urged their municipal councils to declare opposition to the agreement. Similar activities were generated by workers in local unions, women's groups, churches, seniors and environmentalists.

A sort of frenzy of activity took over people's lives and did not let up until a year later when the election was over. Many had rarely or never been involved in public issues — artists and writers I knew, for instance, some of whom could probably not have named the political parties. For myself, I became incapable of writing about anything without mentioning the trade debate. The editor of a literary journal asked if I would contribute to an issue on "Male Desire"; I said yes, if I could call it Male Desire and Free Trade.

Most of this work, throughout the country, was volunteered and unpaid. It was as though people simply assumed a second life, their lives as opponents of free trade, for the duration. The money raised went back into publications, leaflets, posters. The Pro-Canada Network, the coordinating body in Ottawa which by now included most anti-free trade forces, had at most one staff person until the election was called, then added another. Meanwhile, the federal government was spending $30 million to sell the agreement. It printed more than ten million pieces of literature on the deal, almost all glossy and expensive, including 245,000 copies of the full legal text and thirteen "issue brochures" on consumer aspects, the auto industry and the like. When these publications were found indigestible by reader surveys, the remainder were pulped and re-issued as other booklets and brochures. A phone bank in Toronto stood by full-time to answer queries about the deal, free, from anywhere in the country. Business forces were also spending actively in favour of the deal, though on a much smaller scale than during the final weeks of the coming election.

The emergence of the national popular movement of opposition to the free trade deal went nearly unreported in the Canadian press and media. When particular events were covered, they were not put in the context of a developing pattern. In fact, within weeks of the deal being signed in October 1987, reporters were talking about "free-trade fatigue," as if this was a problem for ordinary citizens, rather than journalists. They tended to describe the debate in simplistic dualities, like overheated nationalist emotion versus cool economic logic, or big business versus big labour. I don't know how many times I saw particular protests and demonstrations referred to as the last gasp of the anti-free trade movement. Perhaps this ineptitude was connected to the general support, explicit and implicit, provided by the press and media for the government's trade policy. Yet even the *Toronto Star*, really the only major source of information in the country consistently critical of free trade, also failed to report the emergence of coalitions and popular opposition. The media were apparently incapable of dealing with a political and economic story occurring outside the framework of conventional parliamentary and electoral politics. So when the free trade issue finally took over the election of 1988 and when party support swung wildly during the latter half of the campaign, the media mistakenly attributed these developments solely to John Turner's performance in the televised debates.

Contacts continued between the coalition movement and the Opposition parties, with a view to stiffening their resolve and forcing an election on the issue. In March, for example, Turner met with the Toronto Coalition. He had been avoiding the meeting for months, as if he suspected that a labour-NDP ambush had been laid for him.

He said that, unlike the coalition, he was not against free trade itself, just this deal. He acknowledged that he'd been spending most of his time meeting with business groups in order to convince them that the deal was bad for them. He was told there were other people out there, with reason to oppose the thing, just waiting for someone to give them concrete reasons why — and he was wasting his effort on the one constituency that would never come around. He said he was certain he could at least "neutralize" business. "Give me thirty minutes with any group in Canada," he said. His wife, Geills, jumped in to say, "Listen to them, John; they're right and you're wrong." He seemed at ease with this, as though she frequently expressed her own ideas. It was surprising in the light of Turner's bum patting during the 1984 campaign, and the many old-fashioned jock qualities he had. There were surprises in him. He was urged to focus on areas like social programs and the environment that were affected by the deal, rather than dwelling on the business and trade elements he was clearly most comfortable with. He said he was serenely confident the battle against free trade would be won. He sounded like he lived in a fool's paradise, but perhaps it kept him going.

On May 25, the leaders of thirty-five organizations representing more than ten million Canadians gathered in a large room in the west block of the House of Commons. They were there to meet with the leaders of the

Opposition parties on the subject of free trade. There had never been an assembly like it. Quebec, supposedly solidly for free trade, sent an impressive delegation. Even the environmental movement, notorious for its diversity and disagreements, was speaking with unity for the first time anyone could recall.

Turner was first. Again, he did not come across as crazed, the way he almost always seemed on television. He said he was serenely confident. Even some of the labour people who, as they say, have NDP branded on their backsides, were surprised.

Broadbent was more complicated. He was asked about strong rumours that the NDP did not want an election on the deal and that if one came, they intended to soft-pedal the issue, for fear it would hand votes to the Liberals. If that was their strategy, he was told, it was a mistake that could only land the federal NDP where the same calculation had landed their Ontario branch — far from power. He was also asked if the NDP was reluctant to work with the coalitions because they split loyalties between the NDP and themselves, and also because the NDP feared Liberal influence in them, just as the Liberals feared the reverse.

Broadbent denied anything nefarious was afoot and said the NDP could make free trade their own issue, since the *kind* of Canada menaced by the trade deal was precisely a social democratic society, which the NDP had largely been responsible for, through inspiration and legislation. It was a natural issue to claim as their own, he insisted, and they could take it away from the Liberals.

Madeleine Parent, representing the Quebec organization, Solidarité Populaire, said to Broadbent in careful French that the NDP had an extraordinary opportunity to claim the nationalist vote in Quebec. She pointed out that the Tories were committed to the deal and therefore to the U.S., that the federal Liberals were hopelessly anti-nationalist in Quebec because of the Trudeau legacy and that the Parti Québécois had undermined its own nationalist credibility by backing a free trade deal that could submerge Quebec in the United States. She explained that the key to Quebec had always been nationalism — Québécois, not Canadian — and Broadbent now had a wonderful opportunity to don that mantle. It seemed impossible not to grasp the sense she was making. She was laying out an ideal strategy for his party in Quebec.

A press conference followed, which was well attended, but that night and next day virtually nothing appeared in the news about the historic meetings. Any industrial sales show or dentists' convention would have received more coverage.

By spring 1988, the fight about free trade had turned into a fight about democracy as well. Would the issue be settled in a national election? Would the Canadian people be able to decide by vote?

The arguments for an election were clear. The government had not been elected with a mandate to implement what was, by their own proud acknowledgement, the greatest change in Canadian history. In fact, they had explicitly opposed free trade when they were in Opposition. Besides, they were in the fourth year of their five-year term, the traditional time to go to the country. From the pro-free trade viewpoint, the reasons to avoid an election were also clear. According to the polls, the government did not have enough support to form a majority — no one did — and in any minority scenario the trade deal was doomed. The deal was scheduled to come into force on January 1, 1989. If an election could be postponed till after that, Canadians were more likely to respond to arguments about giving it a chance and not offending the United States, and anyway look, the sky isn't falling. Even if the Tories lost a post-deal election it would be much harder for a Liberal or an NDP government to cancel an agreement that was already in force than to reject it beforehand.

In a truly bizarre twist, it became clear that the only route to the democratic solution, that is, an election on free trade, was by way of that most undemocratic institution, the Canadian Senate. The Senate was overwhelmingly Liberal, and could, if it desired, block free trade legislation until an election was held. Most people in the coalitions, many of them profoundly opposed to the mere existence of the Senate, held their noses and began to lobby senators.

For my own part, I talked with Royce Frith, one of the Liberal party's power brokers past years. We'd met through his daughter Valerie, a publisher. He'd said then that he favoured free trade. He added now that he opposed this particular deal, just as his party's leader did. But he didn't know about forcing an election and doubted his colleagues would take that stand. Either they were in favour of the deal, like the businessmen and party contributors they were, or they didn't want the heat of being called anti-democratic.

I got most deeply involved, however, in the project of the cartoon booklet or, as it was sometimes called, the comic book. Coalitions everywhere in the country had been requesting something accessible that could explain the issue to people. The previous February, I had asked Terry Mosher — the cartoonist Aislin, who lived in Montreal — if he knew anyone who could draw an anti-free trade comic book. I knew he didn't do comics himself and that over the years he had often allowed his cartoons to be used for various causes but did not do special work. He said he'd like to be involved.

That's like Gretzky saying he's available for your hockey team. You don't say, "Sorry, we already have a centre"; you change your plans. We talked about an alternate approach, maybe a sixteen-page booklet, with text and caricatures on facing pages, and possibly some colour. I promised a text by early March. Then I broke my leg, then other deadlines arose. The booklet looked like another good idea that would never be, like the national televised debate.

In June I asked Terry if he'd still do it. He asked when he could have a text, and I said two weeks. I read through the considerable literature I had on the deal and tried to condense the arguments. I was troubled by the matter of form. We live in a society in which people don't read much, yet there seemed no way to cover free trade without many words. A comic book might work — people read comic books, supposedly because of the pictures — but we weren't doing a comic book. Yet it's not just pictures that draw people into comics; it's conversations. People also sit through words on television, radio and in movies — because they're placed in characters' mouths. We could do the thing in dialogue.

I began writing a conversation between two Canadians: one a man with lots of questions about the deal, the other a woman who had looked into it and informed herself. it came out quite long, about twenty-four pages, one topic per page. I sent it to Terry on the fourth of July, with a typical writer's confidence: he would be disgusted, he'd say it was incompetent and useless, there was nothing he or anyone could do to salvage this crap — but I'd be off the hook.

A few days later I received a large package. Terry had taken the text, cut it into chunks, and attached cartoons to each chunk, many of which he had fully coloured. There were cartoons on each page, in some cases two, and a striking variety of layouts. And the colours! You'd look at these drawings, almost all of which originally ran on the editorial page of the Montreal *Gazette*, and think — surely these were never meant as mere black and white drawings; the originals were just sketches for these final coloured versions. "What we've got now is a concept," he said.

People in the coalitions who saw the mockups all did the same thing: they leafed through the cartoons, laughed, then languidly returned to the text, drawn back by the drawings. I reworked the text and whittled it down. Terry's wife, Carole, said I should think about housewives getting it at the supermarket in Saskatoon. Why supermarkets? At that point our theory of distribution was to have members of the women's movement give it out at shopping plazas.

I sent the text back and in days received a fully coloured cartoon booklet. Then we got excited. "We're going to change some minds," said Terry on the phone. Bob White of the Auto Workers looked at it in the lobby of a downtown hotel and asked how much it would cost. I had no idea. I said, a couple of hundred thousand dollars. He winced and said, "Well, we've got to try and do it." Peggy Nash, communications director for the Auto Workers, suggested a designer they used, and said the union would cover his costs and whatever was needed to get the booklet print-ready—maybe ten thousand dollars. Peggy also said she thought giving it out at supermarkets wouldn't be effective. It had to go right into the daily papers, she said, so that it came to people with the full authority of a Loblaws shopper's newsletter or a Canadian Tire insert.

The designer, Ron Kaplansky, said since Terry and I were not being paid, he'd also work free of charge. He was as professional at his end as Mosher. At first he wanted to expand the size of the booklet to "let the thing breathe" then relented because of costs. Meanwhile, the text was out to various readers for suggestions.

All we still needed, when the project was costed, was $800,000. Eight Hundred Thousand Dollars. To print and insert it in a respectable number of daily papers across Canada. It was ludicrous. Yet it happened, because no one ever acknowledged that it was ludicrous. Nobody actually blurted out, "You're all crazy, you're talking about raising *eight hundred thousand dollars!*"

The Toronto Coalition had recently hired a second office person, to work alongside Scott Sinclair, a graduate student in economics who'd been its sole employee, at $500 a week. Ken Traynor had travelled all over Canada raising money and support for South African trade unions. He moved into the office with Scott. Not an office actually: they sat at two desks, facing each other in the middle of the floor at the Ontario Teachers' Federation building on Bay Street in Toronto. That was it, the operation a CBC executive warned her producers about, lest they be manipulated by it, since, according to her, it was much more articulate and better organized than the pro-free trade forces. Ken took on the booklet.

The unions had been at the heart of fundraising for two and a half years, but many had overspent and were nearly tapped out. We showed the project to Margaret Atwood. She asked what it needed and we said about a hundred thousand to get it going. She said she and other writers would take responsibility for that much, and was confident it could be done. Atwood recruited publisher and broadcaster Adrienne Clarkson and they spent about three weeks each on the phone, raising money. When unions heard how much writers were raising, they felt less put upon and more receptive. Provincial and local coalitions began fundraising to cover the costs of inserting the booklet in newspapers in their area — about $120,000 in total. Traynor prepared various kits. Nothing worked like seeing the layouts; people seemed to know it would have an effect. A certain amount even came in from business.

I didn't really believe it would happen. Why not? Because of the money and the size of the project, but mostly because of my feeling that we were attempting too direct an intervention. I have always felt marginal to the formal political process: the parties, the elections, the campaigning. My role has been to stand on the periphery, where almost everyone except those with wealth and power are, and provide some perspective. But to speak from inside, on the same ground as politicians and mass retailers? I couldn't really imagine it. Then the issue of the hooker cartoon exploded.

Mosher's best cartoon in the booklet was called "Two Great Canadians." It had three panels. In the first, John A. Macdonald stands in front of Mrs. Macdonald, protecting her and saying, "Canada Is Not for Sale." In the second, Diefenbaker stands beside his wife, also defending her and saying the same thing. In the third panel stands Mulroney in purple sport coat, dark glasses and sloping hat, pushing a blonde prostitute ahead of him and saying, "Get Busy." It was brilliant and powerful, with a sense of history, and an internal critique of Toryism that could affect even those in the party. It had a visceral strength nothing else in the booklet had. People would look at that cartoon, I felt sure, and never again see Mulroney in the same way.

At a meeting of the Pro-Canada Network, someone asked, "Do you think we'll be able to get that cartoon by the feminists?" This became a huge battle. To me it reeked of censorship, self-righteous leftism and an urge to self-destruct. There was nothing sexist in the cartoon as far as Terry and I were concerned. Why let leftists and feminists, just to prove their correctness to themselves and each other, ruin the single most powerful moment of the project? When I told Terry, he was outraged. He said he wouldn't let his own editors or the government or the right censor him, and he wouldn't take it from the left either. The issue festered. Conversations about it ended in total hostility. Very reluctantly, we agreed to allow the cartoon to be replaced, rather than endanger the project. But I was furious, maybe more than Terry. I spoke to the people involved — we'd worked together so closely and happily — and decided to leave the coalition. Kathleen, with whom I lived, said I shouldn't do it. I asked her to give me one reason why not. "Save the country?" she said.

By then the project had been scaled back. Eight hundred thousand was out of reach but six or seven was possible, and that money could print 2.2 million copies and put them in one newspaper in every major city in English Canada — home deliveries only. There wasn't money for newsstand sales as well. We aimed for a Tuesday in early October. We didn't know whether there would be a fall election or when, but that didn't seem to matter.

One Friday in August Royce Frith said, "This guy is absolutely immovable on this thing." He meant Turner, and free trade. The party, including its leaders in the Senate, had tried to convince Turner to let the deal go through, get it out of the way, then run against the Tories on sleaze, competence or anything but free trade. Turner wouldn't budge, and in the end, he was their leader, they were appointees of the party he led. A few days later Turner announced he had instructed the Senate to hold up enabling legislation until an election had been held to "let the people decide." The senators agreed. For the first time, it looked like the country would actually go to the barricades over the free trade deal.

Mulroney said it was undemocratic, but he didn't look all that democratic himself. He'd been ready to bulldoze through a deal he had rejected during his run for the leadership in 1983 and which hadn't even been mentioned in his campaign of 1984. And suddenly Turner was looking decisive, even prime ministerial.

Broadbent said little in the first few days after Turner's announcement. Then, after lengthy consideration, he exploded in spontaneous outrage. Turner's action was undemocratic, he said, sounding much like Mulroney, even using some of Mulroney's phrases. It was the first time we saw Broadbent lining up with Mulroney against Turner, a teaming which became decisive for the outcome of the election.

The Tories campaigned hard and unopposed all summer and into September 1988. They made announcements, spent huge amounts of money on projects and megaprojects throughout the country and talked about everything except free trade. When they finally called the election on October 1, they were far ahead in the polls. It looked like it was over before it had happened.

I had decided to write a book about the next federal election in the summer of 1987, before the free trade deal had been made. Most informed opinion at the time said the effort would fail, there would be no deal and therefore no free trade election. The big political news then concerned the possibility of an NDP breakthrough, even an NDP government.

In the book I planned to write, I wanted to explore the meaning of politics for members of this society. I intended to travel across Canada and ask people how they felt about politics, using the election as an occasion to elicit their opinions. I wanted to test Aristotle's notion that human beings are *political* animals, in the context of my own society. *Waiting for Democracy* was my title because I thought of elections as something that happened while we were waiting for the real thing.

This was still my agenda when the election began. I covered the country on my own, asking people what politics meant to them and what they thought of the election. I checked in with local riding contests and candidates, but I didn't restrict myself to the election. I was looking for politics in a broader sense.

Yet early on, it became clear that my original plan would not quite work. Because of this election and because of me. There was politics in the broad sense, the old Greek sense, right in the middle of the election of 1988. In a way it was the election that proved the rule. It dealt with the way citizens felt about their society — to a greater extent than any election I have seen in my lifetime and perhaps in Canadian history. Even the familiar electoral process and its components — parties, leaders, campaigns built on empty slogans and on a search for the lowest common denominator — all started to wither and something else flared briefly: a national discussion about the nature and future of our society, in which people got involved as more than just voters. As citizens.

This had everything to do with the free trade debate. It seems to me that debate transformed the election because it raised the most basic questions of citizenship for large numbers of Canadians. While the popular movement against the deal was responsible for pressing the issue on Canadians, it was the issue itself to which the country responded. What was it about this issue that impassioned citizens and relegated the well-constructed agendas of political professionals to irrelevance? One voter reflected on it this way: "You started by thinking about what you might lose. And then you moved on to think about what you had that you cared about. And then you thought about what it was you would like to have." By the end of that process, voters had arrived at a way of thinking through the most basic questions about politics and the responsibilities of citizenship. Free trade became the Canadian way of asking the fundamental question of Greek political philosophy: What is the good society? This drove the political pros crazy. It was simply not reducible to the kinds of issues they could poll on in order to plan a typical party campaign. On every such poll, free trade led all other "issues" by so much that it was hardly on the same chart. Because it was not just another issue. Nor was it just an issue that included almost every other issue within it — though that was true as well. It was the issue of citizenship, of democracy, of politics in the large sense, because it raised the question, What kind of society do we want to inhabit? Once it became the centre of the election, it inevitably stretched the boundaries of ordinary electoral politics. It became the testing ground for the relationship between politics and elections.

My personal dilemma, as I travelled and wrote, was that I could not maintain the relatively detached role of writer that I had imagined for myself. Though I never intended to be neutral, I did think I would function primarily as a writer and observer while I covered the election. I would have had my own views, certainly, but they would have placed me at a critical distance from all three parties and from the usual stew of muddled issues. Instead, because of the free trade debate and my activities connected with it, I became far more involved than I had anticipated. I cared — tremendously. I was implicated. It would have been foolish, in this account, to pretend that a personal involvement did not exist; it would have slipped through anyhow, in all those ways by which writers let their feelings show, despite their most earnest efforts. Besides, my unexpected involvement was not so different from what happened to many Canadians in the election of 1988. I have tried to use it, rather than suppress it, in order to illuminate the kinds of experiences that characterized the event.

The free trade issue, then, figures inevitably in the

account that follows. It is not, however, the object of discussion; it is instead the main prism through which the hoary questions of politics, citizenship and democracy are glimpsed during the amazing campaign that it shaped. It is, in my opinion, aspects of those larger concerns and not the raging debate over free trade that made the election of 1988 unique and even inspiring.

The Election of 1988

Week One

Saturday, October 1

Toronto. Some people I know are making a film about Stan Rogers. It won't air till next summer. Whenever I ask my students in the Canadian Culture course at the University of Toronto about Rogers, few have heard of him. He is, I'd say, the greatest singer and songwriter we ever had. He was thirty-three when he died in an Air Canada disaster five years ago and he left dozens of wonderful songs. There's no knowing what he'd have done by now. I've thought a lot about Rogers as this election approaches. It seems to me that he and his legacy are what the campaign should be about. Like his song, "Northwest Passage," which some have called our real national anthem, in which he sings, "Tracing one warm line through a land so wide and savage. . . ." Just one warm line, and the land still so wide and savage. It's been hard building a country here, never yet quite achieved — a tiny nation in a huge country, as poet Milton Acorn once said. Rogers wrote about the people: fishermen, oil rig workers, ranch wives, minor league hockey coaches, their obsessions and tragedies. As I leave, the film crew are talking comparisons: with Lightfoot, with Stompin' Tom Connors. Really, Rogers was Shakespearean in his breadth and passion. He took this country so seriously.

Back home, I meet with a photographer who's come to shoot a picture for a review of a novel, my first, about a Jew who flees Nazi Germany and spends the rest of his life in Canada. We walk up the street to the little synagogue on the corner. I don't go there much, so I stand away from it and the photographer gets it in the shot. He mentions that his mother, now dead, was Margaret Laurence, the dean, you might say, of Canadian novelists. She covered so much in her books: the new role of women, the sense of culture, the connection to native peoples. She wrote little in her last ten years; instead she devoted herself to the fight for a peaceful world. He says he and his sister are having problems with publishers concerning his mother's literary legacy. It's complicated because publishing houses are suddenly being sold and swallowed into huge conglomerates. In a few years, as an agent said, there'll be five publishers and twenty writers — in the world. What artists like Rogers and Laurence have begun to give us is a sense of what our country and its inhabitants are about, a hard thing to know for most people, who are busy just living their lives. Normally such broad views of society aren't relevant to ordinary politics and elections, but this time may be different.

I stop by Atwood's to pick up some of the cheques she's collected, mostly from writers, for the cartoon booklet. The contributions are all in small lumps: five hundred, a thousand, the most has been five thousand — none of it tax-deductible. When the businesspeople give as they have in the millions to promote the trade deal — and as they will in even greater amounts toward the end of this election — they write it off as a business expense.

At night I go the Westbury Hotel, where the Confederation of Canadian Unions executive board is meeting this weekend. The doughty little labour organization is down to some thirty-two thousand members, and since the huge unions, led by the Auto Workers, have accepted the principle of Canadian independence, there are troubling questions about the continued existence of the CCU, even though they've made a big difference in this country. The guys from the Pulp, Paper and Woodworkers union in B.C., who like to strike once a year whether they need it or not, have lots of ideas about culture and the deal. When I'm around these people, we usually end up talking more about books than unions. I leave early. Tomorrow I fly west to finish the business of one book and begin another.

Sometime during this day full of culture, Mulroney visited the governor general, and announced there will be an election on November 21, seven weeks from now. It seems like it's been with us a long time already.

Sunday, October 2

I join Merri Armstrong, a bartender and single parent, for breakfast at a restaurant on Bloor Street.

"I never have any ideas about politics, you know that," she says. "I don't pay much attention to politics and I suppose I should. Because this election's pretty important. Because if Mulroney gets in again, I think we're sunk. Because I don't believe in free trade. Sounds to me like we're giving the Americans a great deal of stuff and we're not getting anything back."

I ask what bothers her about the free trade deal, and she refers to "the water thing. Or the controls we won't be able to put on the companies that come in. Stuff like that. Or the Americans can start setting up their own medical clinics." This is fairly specific information from someone who apologizes for being uninformed. It is typical of people I meet.

"I don't read the papers very much," she says. "I listen to CBC in the morning. 'As It Happens' at night. What I can't understand is if Mulroney was so opposed to free trade four years ago, how can he turn around and push it now? It makes me wonder how long-term his view is. What's gonna happen five years from now? If he's changed his mind that quickly." This, too, is typical. She knows the history of Mulroney's position on free trade, but she does not draw an ungenerous conclusion: that he lies, or is for sale. She draws the most magnanimous conclusion she can from the evidence: that our prime minister is short-sighted — a bad quality in a leader, but not morally reprehensible. People like Merri prefer a charitable interpretation of the behaviour of others. She'd rather think of them as she thinks of herself, conducting life as decently as possible. She'd like the same generosity extended to her when she fails or falls short.

"My vote?" says Merri. "I guess Broadbent. Turner can't even manage his own party, so how can he manage the country?" Does this mean she is soft on socialism? "I don't know how I feel about socialism. One part of me is terribly capitalistic. I truly believe people have to work their own way. I've never asked for UIC. I tell the truth on my income tax. So the thought of socialism — I don't believe in free this and free that. It's wrong. It's my WASP upbringing. I've always believe you work for what you get. But I believe we have to take care of the elderly. . . ."

Or people with AIDS. When I met Merri, she was tending bar at a Bloor Street hangout, and her brother Ross, a star athlete, was dying of AIDS. She took him into her home, to live with her and her four-year-old son, and nursed him till he died.

She thought about finding a shrink to help deal with the aftermath, but didn't. She's not the sort of person who routinely treats her own experience as something worthy of professional attention. Instead she now works two or three nights a week at Casey House, an AIDS hospice.

She's at the bar till one, then Casey House from two till
four, hours of the night when dying people wake up
scared and need someone. She's started to feel less guilty
about her brother's death and more confident that she did
as much as she could have. She knows the workings of our
society better than many who write about it and explain it.
She knows about power and pain. If she is apolitical, it's in
the narrow sense. She has a sense of social solidarity.

"I don't mind paying for OHIP," she says of the provincial medical plan, "even though I only go to a doctor
about once a year." Why doesn't she lie on her taxes? "I
don't know. If I'd declared $200 a year less last year, I'd
have gotten assistance for dependents, because I'm a single parent. But I can make it on my own. If I can, I'm
going to. Take my friend. He'll use any scam in the book
— UIC, income tax, welfare, deductions for income tax —
but everybody knows it's wrong. I figure if you can pay
your own way in life, you should. That's just normal." You
could call this classical socialism — from each according to
his ability, to each according to his needs — but Merri
doesn't see it that way. In fact, socialism to her is about
people trying to take advantage of others and looking for
a free ride. It's strange: from the time of ancient Greece
to this century, ruling elites opposed giving the vote to the
majority for fear the mass of people would use their political power to level economic differences. It never
happened. Instead, people like Merri called on their own
sense of social responsibility to justify keeping things
more or less as they were.

"Every year it's the same," says Merri. "Who's the least
worst candidate? It seems insane to me. Nobody's voting
for a party because they believe in it, but because they
don't like all the others. That's how they do it. I always
vote myself. I used to vote just to counter the vote of the
guy I lived with. He always voted Conservative. I haven't
missed once since I turned voting age." *Why* does she
vote? "So when I get somebody saying to me, You're not
doing anything, so why do you bitch? I can say, I voted!"
This commitment to voting is widespread. People take

their right to vote seriously; they tend to treat it more as an obligation than as a right. They fret about exercising it responsibly. Merri is a responsible person. People sense it in her. When she cuts rowdies off at the bar, they accept her authority.

Sometimes she thinks about larger questions of public policy. "When Ross was trying to get the experimental drugs that they wouldn't allow into Canada, it made me mad. But it's like one time they cut off my phone and all I said I'd do about it was that I'd write to "Star Probe." I just get mad and don't do anything. I'm candy-assed — but, Rick, I have so much on my plate that I have to deal with. So I counteract it with . . . something else. Like working at Casey House." She sees this as a sort of political act, which "counteracts" her lack of effect in the political realm proper. How does Casey House function as politics?

"Not for me. But because of Ross." She does it so that his memory does not fade. She is carrying his meaning into the world through her work with others who are in the same grim and unjust situation he found himself in. It is an act of solidarity with the human condition. It is politics in the true sense: action taken in combination with other human beings to deal with conditions that affect everyone and with which we can only deal collectively, if at all.

We return to free trade and I say Mulroney may try to avoid the subject in the TV debates — which have yet to be negotiated. "How come?" she asks. "Wouldn't the TV stations be able to make him debate it? I'm surprised because you always expect the government to be looking out for us and not keeping us ignorant." That generosity again. She'd find it very difficult to believe the government would willingly suppress information. I describe the secret communications strategy of September 1985. "It seems very . . . very . . . Russian!" she says. "Keeping the people ignorant? In Canada?"

I ask if she's ever worked for a candidate or knows anyone who has. She doesn't even answer; she simply shakes her head.

"I'm pretty uninformed," she says. "Except on free trade. And the environment. They're things I care about. But there's a whole spectrum of issues, like childcare, I don't have any opinion about." Like most people I talk to, she blames herself for being uninformed. Yet it's hard to have opinions on "issues" if, for instance, all the politicians sound as if they're saying the same thing. Everyone in this election is for childcare — so how's an ordinary person to choose between them? That's why, for most people, political choices often come down to deciding whom they trust. The issues are impenetrable, so you try to look the candidates in the eye and say, Do I believe that one?

In this respect, our present election is unique. There is a clear division on free trade. One party is for it, two are against; they're not all fudging by saying the same thing. You can tell how unusual this clear division is by how uncomfortable it seems to make the main players.

On the plane to Vancouver, I sit beside a pleasant woman on her way to see her father who lives up the B.C. coast. He's in bad health, she says. She's not sure about free trade. Beside her is a business student, very keen to get in there and compete with the Americans. They're happy to talk politics, but the election is still a long way off for most Canadians.

According to the newspaper reports on yesterday's campaigning, Mulroney said the election is about who can best "manage change." There's a risky slogan. Broadbent said this one is about "the future of ordinary Canadians." It sounds as if he attacked Turner with more verve than he went after Mulroney. "You can't change your spots in this life of ours. You can't produce budgets as he did favouring the corporate sector, you can't spend half your life on the forty-second floor of the executive suites, and abandon the conservative ideology," he said. That seems a pretty dour view of human nature, especially for a socialist. Turner, the corporate leopard, sounds like he's on a different planet. He said the election is about "an independent and sovereign Canada, which has never been so threatened as it is by the Mulroney trade deal." He went into detail about the deal and said, "I'm not going to allow Mr. Mulroney to sell out our birthright, I'm not going to let him destroy a great 120-year-old dream called Canada. This is more than an election, this is your future."

Stan Persky rescues me about an hour after I book into the hotel in Vancouver. It's still mid-afternoon, thanks to three hours' worth of time zones. We walk along English Bay. I think of Stan as one of the most upbeat people of our time. He came here from San Francisco in the sixties and was acclaimed mayor of Gastown by the hippies who lived there then. He was a founder of the alternate paper the *Georgia Straight*. He writes cheerfully about everything: Eastern Europe, gay rights, B.C. politics. You name it, it absorbs, engages and often delights him. He is an activist but also, as long as I've known him, an optimist. Yet he's depressed about this election which has barely begun.

It has to do with B.C. Out here people elect the Socreds again and again after deciding in the middle of each term to dump them. Politicians like Reagan, Thatcher and Vander Zalm seem to have discovered the secret of winning elections, no matter how badly they piss on voters between times. Once a writ is dropped, they recite the spell and walk back in. Then they behave arrogantly, contradict all they promised during the campaign, lay waste various aspects of their societies and call and win another election. The Tories seem to be on a roll like that. Or maybe not. It's easy to fashion fanciful thoughts in Lotusland. Maybe Canadians wanted an election on free trade, so they just *told* pollsters they'd vote Tory so an election would be called. It is gorgeous along the sea wall. It is like summer. People are in shorts, sunning, jogging — throngs of them.

We stop at a bistro for cappuccino in a styrofoam cup and sit in the window. A copy of the *Province* is lying on the counter. "B.C. Votes May Change It All," says the headline. Canadian elections are almost always settled before they arrive out here, but the people of B.C. live in hope that one election night what they do will matter to the rest of us. What a country, what a huge, odd country.

The editorial is headed, "Only one issue in the election." What is it? The deficit! "Social programs will have to be reassessed with a hard heart and probably made less universal. . . ." It seems like an irrelevant and wrongheaded analysis at the time, though months later, following the Tory victory, when the government is slashing exuberantly at the deficit, I wonder about the prescience of the *Province*.

There's also a column on the editorial page, by Eric Nicol. I've been a Nicol fan since I was eleven years old, sick in bed, and read a funny collection of his columns called *Twice Over Lightly*. Here he still is, bleak and blasted after many decades, long since given up on the country, retreated for the most part into cynicism and bitter humour. His column is about free trade, the other "only one issue" of this election. "Furl that fool maple-leaf flag, junior, before you jinx your daddy's job prospects," it says bitterly. Yet a wan yearning still subsists in Nicol. As if he tries to stop hoping, but still secretly hopes. It is betrayed by his anger, a more determined emotion than despair. "It is probably accurate to assume that the Mulroney government," he writes, "with the blessing of Canadian big business, has judged that it is too late to put in the diaphragm. The free trade deal will give the rape the semblance of a planned honeymoon."

Evening. The cabbie is a journalism student at a community college, has studied political science and uses terms like "bicameral legislature." He says he's delighted we're going to have an election that amounts to a referendum on free trade. This is a real citizen's attitude, in the classical sense. For professionals and activists, the focus of an election is its outcome. Not this fellow. He doesn't know where he stands on the issue, but he's looking forward to the action.

In today's *New York Times*, Flora Lewis says that "liberal" has replaced "reactionary" as the worst thing to be in American politics today. We are different, aren't we? We even have a Liberal Party of Canada. We must be the only country left in the world in which the songs of Gilbert and Sullivan still make sense: "For every boy and every girl / That's born into this world alive / Is either a little Liberal / Or else a little Conservative."

Monday, October 3

From now on, I'll awake each morning, read the papers, watch "Canada AM" and listen to the news. This is the first time, but it already feels like an unshakable ritual. It creates an odd dissonance. The press treats this election as if it sprang full-grown from the forehead of the governor general. In the press, the election barrels along: everyone knows his role and plays it heartily. That's politics in the press, so different from the tentative, subtle echoes of politics in the lives of people I talk to, like Merri the bartender and last night's cab driver. The two versions seem so far apart. Will they come any nearer during the course of this election?

The Gallup poll has the Tories way ahead at 43 percent. The Liberals are at 33 and the NDP at 22. Mulroney is the most popular leader, but free trade is seen as the most important issue. There's the dissonance, right there. It's as though people are confused because a debate about an issue is trying to happen in the midst of an election campaign, where leaders and non-issues tend to take over. It's like a referendum and an election in a jumble. Will they sort it out? Will they treat this election in the end as a referendum on free trade or will the Tories get away with ignoring the issue and running on their ability to "manage change"?

Judging from the papers, the NDP is running for Official Opposition. There's little sense of urgency in their rhetoric. They stress their competence and responsibility, and getting aboard "Ed's team," with a strong emphasis on Broadbent as a really nice guy. This has a strange effect. Even if Broadbent is the nicest guy in the race, the moment he starts playing on that, he's using it manipulatively, so he's not such a nice guy anymore. A lot of this emphasis must come from Vic Fingerhut, their American pollster. He invented the "fairness for average Canadians" strategy, which the NDP believe saved them in the last election and led to the brief heyday of the "Ed Scare" in 1985 when they hit 44 percent and led the national polls. But that was mid-mandate, marked by a double vacuum of leadership in the two main parties and no clear issues. Once the deal emerged, there was an issue; once there's an issue you can't pretend it's not there and continue to operate on the vague elements of image. Or can you? They seem entranced by polling, and so far it's worked. At their heady Montreal convention in 1985, they were asked if they'd done extensive surveys on their decision to use the term, "average Canadians" versus "ordinary Canadians." It seemed like a little joke. They said soberly, Of course we have.

And Turner? He simply does not have what it takes. He comes across, people keep saying, as crazed. Not nastily insane, just manic. People may even sympathize with what he says — they often do — but they look at him and see coconuts. It's complex. He does not appear psycho in person — just tense, earnest and klutzy. He tries too hard, not a quality that bothers you much in direct contact, but it's painful in public or on TV.

There seems no question that he cares about the deal and aches for its effects on the country. He yearns for a public debate with Mulroney on the subject. He says over and again that this has made his hellish return to public life worthwhile. In some ways he is a frightening and revealing sight. A conventional pol, an Establishment Man, suddenly discovering his soul. He and his wife Geills are a matched pair — a bit larger than life, born to rule, to have a good time, uncomprehending of why fate has dealt them this hard hand, yet plucky enough in that upper

crust way to carry on rather than whine or quit. I keep
thinking, "John and Geills went up to the Hill. . . ."

I am into it now: the parties, the personalties, the wives,
the gossip, the backroom boys. Welcome to the world of
conventional politics.

Tuesday, October 4

Calgary. Around noon, I am sitting in a car listening to a
CBC phone-in show on the car radio. The question of the
day is, What issue will listeners base their vote on? Out
here, people of all kinds seem to listen to CBC. In
Ontario, the listeners would be less varied. Right-wingers
call in, they're concerned about the unborn. There's a lot
of support for the Reform party, a new conservative challenger to the Tories. There's much talk about western
alienation, as if it functions as an insecurity blanket almost
everyone can huddle under. And there's a fair amount on
free trade. A political scientist is the studio guest; he keeps
getting in the way, interrupting the informative flow coming from the listeners, but what are experts for?

There's another poll today. By the end of this campaign
there will have been only two or three days that saw no
polls. The current Angus Reid has the Tories at 45 percent, the NDP at 27 and the Liberals at 26. A columnist I
know, who's been writing about the deal and its dangers
for a right-wing pro-deal paper out here, says, "When are
these bastards going to peak?"

Wednesday, October 5

Winnipeg. Noon. A bird sanctuary off a dusty road on the
outskirts of the city. Jake Epp, minister of health, is here.
This is pretty pure, as media events go. There's no real
excuse for it, no access by the public to this remote spot.
There are invited guests and reporters. The purpose,
presumably, is to show government concern about the en-

vironment, which their polls show is a high concern among voters. All the parties are scrambling to show how much they care. In the States, George Bush is running as the reincarnation of Teddy Roosevelt, the conservation president. Epp makes some general remarks and tries to take the edge off the anger people out here still feel about a Tory decision to give a fighter repair contract to Montreal, despite a better bid from Manitoba. After his remarks, the invited guests descend on tables of crustless sandwiches, and the cameras follow Epp out to the pond. He chats with officials and gestures toward the ducks and birds, moving deftly to allow the cameras a better shot, while never acknowledging them.

Thursday, October 6

Tonight the NDP are nominating Manitoba ex-premier Howard Pawley for the East Selkirk riding, near here. Broadbent will attend. The event will start early, to make national news coverage. Fred Gudmundson has agreed to drive me out. He says it's been a while since he subjected himself to a party event, and he's getting out of shape.

Fred was a CCF stalwart when he was a farmer in Saskatchewan back in the forties and fifties. He was the youngest member of the provincial executive. He knew Tommy Douglas well, and Hazen Argue. He participated in the debates about the transformation of the CCF into the NDP and was active in the National Farmers' Union in its most radical days. In recent years, since he and the family have lived in Winnipeg, he's worked mostly as a consultant to native groups, especially the Dene.

We meet at the hotel and talk about the defeat of the Pawley government last March. They fell because they didn't anticipate the defection of one of their members on a vote of confidence. Then they lost a provincial election. As we get in the car I say, "Pawley really blew it, eh?" Fred is in the driver's seat. "Just dumb," he says affectionately, as if that's not the worst trait a politician can have. He thinks Broadbent is much nastier and more ruthless than Pawley, altogether a better man for the leadership of a political party.

"I was in that fucking party for forty fucking years," he says as we drive, "and all it ever gave me was grief and took I don't know how many years off my life. Now," he goes on with a sigh, "I don't have any problems with them because I don't have any expectations. They're just a bunch of grubby opportunists. Not slick opportunists like the Liberals or Conservatives. Grubby opportunists, like the guys who follow garbage trucks."

I tell him what my friend John Saul, an Africa expert familiar with liberation movements there, once said about the NDP. "I look at their leaders," said John, "and I see the faces of the men who murdered Rosa Luxemburg." He means the German social democrats at the end of the First World War, who betrayed Luxemburg, a radical Marxist, to right-wing militarists who had seized power. It's a chilling thought. "I have that problem," says Fred, driving along placidly.

We pull into the Happy Thought High School in Selkirk, an apt place to nominate dumb, decent Howard Pawley. There are some anti-NDP demonstrators in the parking lot, and inside the gym is packed. Pawley is working the crowd with the delight of a born campaigner. He gives Fred a big welcome, as do others. They must be wondering what his appearance here, like the ghost of Christmas past, portends.

There are farmers and working people and little of the urban look you find at NDP gatherings in Toronto, Halifax or Vancouver. Onstage is a scrubbed-looking fellow with a boyish grin. He seems familiar. I think maybe he's a TV reporter — one of the new, cute ones. No, Fred says, it's Gary Doer, the current leader of the provincial party, whom they chose to replace Pawley and lead them out of the wilderness with his yuppie good looks.

They have a fine old time speech making, and Pawley comes onstage, having a little trouble because he tries a door onto the platform that's locked. He says there must be Tories on the other side, since the NDP always has an open door. It's one of those comments reporters refer to as a quip, so readers will know a joke was intended. He talks about the trade deal and his unsatisfying experiences with Brian Mulroney. There are no other candidates and he is duly acclaimed.

It is time for Broadbent. The press from his tour bus have been buzzing around for the last few minutes, crowding in the entrance near the stage, settling at a table well equipped for their presence. Some are recognizable from the tube, others look around as though they expect to be recognized. There's Hugh Winsor of the *Globe*, checking out the crowd. But no Ed. Then suddenly at the rear door — a stir, a rising hum, the lights go down, a P.A. system blares a rousing song, a gorgeous shower of light near the entrance, a phalanx moving in backwards, cameras held high above their heads, and Here's Ed — the first time I witness the Triumphal Entry.

He moves like a regal wave through this high school gym. It's not just him, he is an entourage: there are cameramen, advance men, security men and then coming on, straight into the space they clear, separated from the adoring crowd, Ed himself, tanned like a movie star. Everything about him says Star. It's like the time I watched a National Ballet class, and somehow Veronica Tennant stood out from the rest. She had an aura, a "presence" the dancers said, which she could turn on and off. He is not of this crowd in the way that Pawley and Doer are. I guess this is the professionalism of the NDP campaign that the press have been mentioning with approval. I don't like it much.

Quite suddenly the music stops, Ed is up on the platform and all is still — because the excitement was actually coming out of the sound system, it was artificial, the crowd was fairly passive as it happened around them. The speech he delivers is ordinary. He uses some set lines I've read in the papers, the so-called stump speech. Or maybe it's just that after the entrance, whatever follows must seem secondary. The important point has been made: the centrality of this person.

Afterwards, in front of some lockers but separated by a door from the masses, he holds a scrum, the inconsequential ritual that has replaced press conferences. Pawley lingers after Broadbent is gone to answer a few questions himself. The press herd obediently back to their buses, one for smokers and one for non. Winsor is on a pay phone beside the pop machine in the school corridor calling in his story. The Broadbent tour wagonmaster, a frazzled woman with frazzled hair, is impatiently telling him the buses are ready to depart, but he is cool as water; he says if she rushes him his story will miss the national edition. She seethes, but he is the *Globe*, and he wins. As Fred and I drive back, I say I didn't really like the triumphal entry. Tommy Douglas started that nonsense, says Fred. He remembers that when Woodrow Lloyd was leader of the Saskatchewan NDP, he would sit up on the platform like everyone else, waiting his turn.

Why does the NDP evoke such a strong reaction from people like Fred? I don't think it's just a matter of personal frustration. Fred was a prairie farmer; he knows how to live with frustration. It's less private than that. It's because the NDP represents many of the riddles of Canadian politics in our time. For instance: how has it managed to do so badly over the years, even though in many ways it seems like a natural governing party.

That may be considered a minority view, but there's evidence to support it. The NDP's forerunner, the CCF, was founded in 1932; by 1943 it was leading all the political parties in the polls and nearly formed a provincial government in Ontario that year. In 1944 it was elected in Saskatchewan. Much of its "progressive" program has been consciously and blatantly swiped by the other parties. Its populism, social conscience, grass roots orientation, mixed approach to the economy, selective nationalization — a socialism that is strongly democratic — all seem appropriate to Canadian political culture. It looks as if it represents the aspirations of most citizens —

far more than the other parties, which are so closely aligned to the elites. It has had electoral successes in three different provinces, but far less than you might expect.

Business and its political allies have certainly been aware of the CCF/NDP potential and have made a major effort to forestall it. Their main vehicle for doing this has been the Liberal party, which accounts for the fact that much of the twentieth century has belonged not to Canada, as Laurier predicted, but to the Canadian Liberal party, which he led. A businessman once explained to me that people like him contribute to the two main parties because "if both these parties don't maintain their position, there is a danger of getting something much more radical in office." Such people are usually circumlocutory on this subject, but Ian Sinclair, chairman of Canadian Pacific, gave the game away after the Tory victory of 1984 in a speech to the Chamber of Commerce in Toronto. He urged his fellow businessmen to continue contributing to the enfeebled Liberals "to ensure we have a free-enter-prise party in Opposition." One corporate lawyer, a former Tory MP, told me he was irked by Sinclair's openness. "I'd have just said, 'to preserve the present two-party system.' People would have understood what he meant." The former MP always belittled the NDP when he was campaigning himself. "That's just politics," he said. "You're not going to *admit* you're worried about them." A whiff of the old fear surfaced in 1985 when polls suggested the NDP might win the next election and a stock market newsletter said, "The readership to which these words are directed might well tremble at such a prospect." Of course, it's not the NDP in itself that occasionally makes business tremble; it's what it represents: a challenge to business's pre-eminence, along with a socialist instead of a capitalist vision.

What's irksome to people like Fred is that the NDP usually seems to contribute to its own marginalization by undercutting precisely what makes it different from the other parties. Its predecessor, the CCF, ran in its first elections in 1934 and 1935, and by 1936 was embroiled in debates over whether to compromise its program for electoral appeal. That year the Saskatchewan party dropped the word "socialism" from its platform so as not to offend voters. They've never shunned power for the sake of their ideals. They just haven't been very successful at acquiring it.

As this election unfolds, they again seem poised to take their logical place as a major force on the political scene because the Liberals are botching things relentlessly. Today Turner announced a national daycare program and was immediately mired in contradictions about what it'll cost. He looks like a fuck-up again.

Back in the hotel lobby I see Ray Aboud, CBC radio. Ray will never be recognized in public, partly because he's radio and partly because he's not a star. He's a working stiff among reporters. He's exhausted already. He has to file reports for "Canada at Five," "The World at Six" and "World Report" in the morning when he can, hourly newscasts when possible, plus a weekly "question-and-answer" for the program "The House."

Ray says I'm not missing anything by not being on the campaign planes. "They keep you in the dark and they feed you bullshit," he says — a zingier phrase than will ever find its way into an on-air report. I decide then and there to avoid the campaign planes and buses, though I had wondered about it till now. Maybe I'll join them for the final week, and I'll check in with them if they happen to cross my path as I travel, just as I'll pay some attention to local campaigning. But the rest of the time I'll stay out here on my own, with everyone else.

Friday, October 7

The election has been on less than a week, and I feel I've been pursuing something not yet really there. The leaders are involved and so is the press. But the people — they'll drop in at differing rates over the next six weeks, some

earlier and some later, depending on where they live and
what else is on their plates. The system gives them a maxi-
mum seven weeks of "politics" every four years or so.
How they feel and how they'll vote will hang on when they
get in, among other things.

The Maltese cabby in Toronto who drives me in from
the airport today has five kids. He's been driving for four
years. Before that he was "in the hotel business." But they
don't want old people there, he says. I ask how he feels
about this country, compared to other places he's seen.
"Look at the Americans," he says. "They send up the shuttle bus" — he means the space shuttle — "it costs them a
hundred million dollars, but you go to Buffalo, you can't
go into the streets because of the crime. They should
spend less on the shuttle bus, maybe 25 million. They
should keep up the research, but they should spend the
rest for some force to keep the people in Buffalo safe."
This is a *mélange* of insight and illogic. It is what comes of
the scraps of information and misinformation that whiz
by people in headlines, radio newscasts, overheard conversations, and with which they try to construct a
meaningful version of a political reality in which they are
treated as incidental players at best. Everywhere I go in
the country, I hear people trying their best to put it together with little basic material in the form of facts and
information and virtually nothing by way of analytical or
interpretive tools. If you could penetrate the key or code
they use, I don't know what you could do with it, but
you'd begin to understand how this society exists in the
heads of its vast majority.

I feel like The Fugitive from the old TV show, in restless search of a witness who could free him, but he doesn't
know where to look, or even if the witness really exists.
Except I'm looking for politics. As one campaign manager
said, "If you find it, let me know."

Week Two

Saturday, October 8

I call PC headquarters in Toronto to inquire about campaign events and wait for one of the press people to pick up the phone. It sounds like a men's club: deep voices, raucous. The smell of cigars comes right through the phone. A voice says, "They must've had to get the strangest camera angle to make it look like there was anyone there at all." These people are involved in every microscopic moment of the campaign, even though it's just begun. They're political junkies, they'd say themselves. They sound so cocky — there's no edginess, as there is at Liberal headquarters when you phone. When are these bastards going to peak?

I find the pros, like Norm Atkins, chairman of the Tory campaign, the most distasteful players on the political scene. For them politics has so little to do with . . . politics, in the old Greek sense. They don't seem to care about issues, or if they do, they don't let that affect them. Sometimes they even disagree with party policies. I ran into one on a plane and he said he was "uncomfortable" with free trade. A week later he was in the paper singing its praises. They put their skills at the service of the party and the interests that control the party. They're hired guns, or they're there for the action, the public interest never comes into it. At least a caveman like Tory minister Harvie Andre believes that what he is doing is right. He's a sincere ideologue, there's some morality to it for him. Not so the pros . . . .

Driving up to the Armenian Community Centre for a Turner campaign event, I wonder if you can get away with running a Bill Davis campaign when there's a burning issue. That's what the Tories are trying, the kind Atkins ran time after time here in Ontario. Those Atkins-Davis campaigns depended on the absence of an issue;

one year their campaign song was, "Come on people /
Let's keep the promise / Davis can do it / He'll keep the
promise." Those phrases were all over radio and TV. A
twelve-year-old kid stopped me on Bloor Street during
that election. "What promise?" he asked. "How stupid can
you get?" Now they float an empty slogan about their ability to "manage change."

    In 1985, an issue finally happened into an Ontario cam-
paign — separate school funding — and the Tories
couldn't play it their way anymore. They continued to ply
feelgood politics and lost for the first time in forty-two
years. When something is tearing people apart, if you try
and hover above it, you just look callous and arrogant. In
this election the issue could be free trade. But is it tearing
people apart?

The Armenian Community Centre is off Consumers
Road, up in the northern reaches where most of Toronto
lives. The people in this hall speak Armenian, so it's hard
to eavesdrop. They're fluent in as many as four languages
each. Sarkis Assadourian is their Liberal candidate. They
say proudly that Sarkis is the first Armenian Canadian
ever to run for office, or maybe just Parliament. He beat
Mike Smith for the nomination. Many of the Liberal riding contests around Toronto were chaotic; some,
stridently racist. As they unravelled, through the spring
and summer of '87, it looked like more Turner incompe-
tence. It's kind of admirable, though, even if Assadourian
won't play as well as Smith on the lawn signs. The Liberal
policy of multiculturalism — invented in the Trudeau
years as a way of beating down Quebec nationalism —
comes home to roost. Later, at a reception, another Liberal candidate, Yasmin Ratansi, says, "I remember when
multiculturalism meant nervous politicians tasting strange
foods."

    As for Turner, present at this event, flashing and light-
ing like a pinball machine as the kids in an Armenian
choir sing militant songs, he is a far more complex human
being than either of the other leaders. Mask upon mask in

the sense of Greek drama. Mulroney is make-up: there is nothing under his mask, he is sheer surface, he is the mask itself. Broadbent is relatively simple: tough and ambitious. Turner, though, wears that manic grin, the expression that makes people think he's crazy: it's like a tension between selves, a person torn in different directions, a face like a TV screen that shows everything passing behind it. A promising kid, but with a lot of insecurity, raised by a widowed mother, who rose high in the civil service when women didn't do that sort of thing. Then she remarried, connecting him to wealth and power and setting him on the perfect course. Taken over by the business class to become one of them, embracing them in return, placed as prime minister to serve them, and somehow it went wrong. He didn't quite have it, too much was going on in there, he was a shade from predictable, he could get out of control. As occurred perhaps when he read the free trade agreement. It's in that manic face — the fixed grin, the darting eyes — searching for something but not knowing what. He's the man who doesn't fit. The separate parts looked just fine, but they didn't go together.

He defends these candidates of his, even though their nomination fights have made him a figure of scorn yet again: he opened this multicultural door and it too hit him in the face. He looks like he can't figure out how it all happens, he's perpetually perplexed that life isn't working out as it was supposed to. Yet this is a man who abandoned, more than he was abandoned by, his class sponsors and colleagues. He had a margin of choice. He could have pleased them, gone with their deal or put up a mere token opposition and retired from politics to a wealthy, comfortable life.

At the reception for "ethnic" candidates, Dennis Mills introduces himself. He's the Liberal running in Broadview-Greenwood (against Lynn McDonald, who holds the seat for the NDP). A jock wearing a St. Michael's Buzzers jacket. Also an ex-Trudeau aide and former flack for super-entrepreneur Frank Stronach. He leans closer as he talks and says things like, "Can I tell you something?" Or, "I'm a people person." I feel like we're in a singles bar and I'm a woman he's trying to pick up. He says Lynn, who muscled a strong bill against smoking through the House, is vulnerable on the smoking issue. "We know who the smokers are," he says. I ask if this means the working class. "Lemme put it this way. If you see somebody buying granola, they're not a smoker." He leans in again. "Can I tell you something? He's gonna win. Turner is. I know it," he says. "I am so pumped up with positive feelings." In coming weeks I get messages on my answering machine from Dennis. At first I answer them, thinking something is happening. It turns out he is just checking in, calling to stay in touch. I'm on his list.

I go to Honest Ed's in the afternoon, Saturday afternoon with the incredible crowds swarming over the bargains on every floor and the long lines at the cash registers. I am pushing past the tabletops of jeans and cords, saying to this guy in front of me somewhat impatiently, "Excuse me," and he looks back, a little bewildered, at me and also at the abundance of things to buy. What does politics mean to him?

Sitting at Dooney's a little later, with a café au lait, look-ing onto Bloor Street, and a punky girl walks in and asks for a waitress application. What does it mean to her? I think of recently fired Metro Toronto Housing Authority Chairman John Sewell and the tenants of public housing who felt like human trash till Sewell came along and treated them like human beings for a while, and who have now been returned, courtesy the provincial government and the development industry, to the dungheap. What does it mean to them? People buffeted by consumerism, foreignness, race, youth, unemployment, poverty and degradation.

There are others out there on Bloor. Yuppies seeking their own kinds of bargains in antiques, high fashion or children's books among the shops around Honest Ed's.

Trendy housewives and professors wheeling their moun-
tain bikes down Albany or Howland. But I wonder less
about politics and them, I think I know. Sometimes
they're active, sometimes not; but they assume they count.
They ponder political matters, they talk with each other,
voice their opinions and cast their votes. It's the others I
wonder about — the usually voiceless, the people without
university degrees or professional credentials, who go
onto the job market as a pair of hands or with a little basic
training. They are not normally addressed by the opinion
makers; at most they overhear what others discuss.

But it's wrong to make assumptions. The day after the
deal was concluded a year ago, I wandered downtown and
walked through College Park and the Atrium on Bay as
people shopped or dawdled, thinking to myself, How
could all the members of this society possibly enter into
the same concerns, with so many different preoccupations
and the deliberateness with which they are diverted from
common themes? I went down to the Dundas subway platform, sat on a bench and waited for the train. A young
woman sat at the far end of the bench. I looked at her and
thought again. No way. She pulled out a book called *The
Free Trade Papers* and started to read.

Sunday, October 9

Dan Heap's campaign office. Heap is NDP member of
Parliament for my riding, Trinity-Spadina, formerly Spadina. It's a historic district. It elected Jewish Communist J.
B. Salsberg to provincial Parliament in the 1940s and
1950s till a Jewish Tory, Allan Grossman, defeated him in
1955 — a contest that mirrored perfectly the transformation of Canadian Jews from left-wing, working-class
immigrants to prosperous, increasingly conservative people. It's always been a feisty riding, and I'll try to keep tabs
on it. Both Heap's office and that of his Liberal rival,
Tony Ianno, are within two blocks of my home.

Heap's campaign manager is named Ashley. He says he

runs a polling and consultancy firm, but does these jobs on contract from the NDP during elections. He sounds like he just came from a course at the Harvard Business School. The NDP often looks as if it's trying to live down its earthy, earnest rep by being even more efficient and "pragmatic" than the other guys. The rest of the people around the table at this meeting look shleppier, unkempt — the basic NDP clichés.

They're discussing the Hallowe'en problem. Must they lose a night of canvassing because of it? They could hold an event, like a party, here at the office. (It's in a basement and kind of dingy.) The kids who go trick-or-treating will be off the streets by eight, says one. But even if you take your kids home by then, says another, they have to spread their candy all over the floor, categorize the haul, test taste some of it. Someone else says they've had poor turnouts for social events. The woman in charge of Chinese canvassers says she'd rather not; she tries to make it a social event every time her volunteers come in. A lot of energy goes into these details of electioneering. What might happen if it were channelled into political effort of a different kind?

There's the question of booze. Ashley is firm on this. "Booze and campaigns don't mix." Two veterans of earlier Heap campaigns don't agree. Is there some resentment of Ashley by the old messy guard? Was he sent in because the commanding heights of the party staff feared a Liberal challenge and lacked confidence in the aging corps of Heap loyalists?

Ashley seems to have a philosophy about everything. "I believe very strongly in coffee parties," he says. Coffee parties? Strongly? "The only downside," he continues, "is I believe in regimenting very tightly the amount of time the candidate spends there." He arrived only two days ago. Perhaps he's trying to establish himself in their eyes. "I know campaign meetings work up a good appetite," he concludes, "and I've ordered some Dim Sum."

The Dim Sum arrives as though on cue, and Ashley moves over to a corner of the basement to explain some innovative computer techniques he is introducing to these mediaeval campaigners. He says he's seen a copy of the cartoon booklet Terry Mosher and I worked on and, "Frankly, I have problems with it." He fears it'll go over the heads of people. Not that he doesn't like it himself; he does — but most people will find it's beyond them. He suggests we try it on a focus group, to test and improve it. It sounds like a process they call at the CBC "dumbing down" a script. That's very good, they say to the writer, now let's dumb it down for the viewers.

Monday, October 10. Thanksgiving.

Ken Traynor drops by in the morning. It's going to happen. The booklets will be in newspapers all over the country starting tomorrow. It may be of little use, it may not matter, but we have fired a shot. I am amazed. I didn't believe it till now.

Tuesday, October 11

I pad downstairs about a quarter to seven in the morning. The *Globe and Mail* is there, and the *Star*. I carry the *Star* into the kitchen and open it on the counter. There it is inside. I go upstairs and say, "It came. It's crisp and clean and full of bright colours." In her sleep, Kathleen says, "It's like Christmas morning."

Terry arrives from the airport around nine. He's brought a suit, he changes into it. As if we're going to an opening. We're holding a press conference at the press club on Wellesley Street.

Behind us is a six-foot blow-up of the booklet's cover, Mulroney's face eroding greenly under the downpour from a cloud of acid rain as he says, "And why shouldn't we trust the Americans on free trade?" The title is "What's the Big Deal?" Many of those who worked on it are there

— but it's really been a national collective effort: the demand for it, the research and analysis by organizations and individuals, the fund raising and distribution, the use about to be made of it in the ridings. Adrienne Clarkson hosts. She loves the cameras and they love her. We look, as they'd have said in the sixties, like we have our shit together. There are few questions, the best of which come from reporters for the *Washington Post* and the *Chicago Tribune*; they've done some homework, read through the booklet quickly and seem informed. The Canadian reporters are lackadaisical by comparison. Out on the election trail, the only thing that seems to inspire them at the moment is costing campaign promises, as if they're accountants, not journalists. Maybe we do need something to toughen us up, as the Business Council on National Issues says.

Evening, at a shopping plaza in the riding of Mississauga East. It's the opening of the campaign office for PC candidate Laurie Pallett. Cabinet minister Barbara McDougall is their guest.

Three spiffy old fellows are talking about free trade. I lean against a post, trying to look unobtrusive. It's not easy; I'm the only one in this big crowd with a beard. When I arrived and told a campaign official I was writing a book, he said, "I *thought* you were an artist." One of the old fellows says he doesn't know much about the deal, but you have to pay attention to who supports it. "The Consumers' Association of Canada — and they're bloody left-wing — is for it." He figures this means it's good for everyone. His friends aren't sure. One says what bothers him is the "alacrity with which the Americans have passed it. You can be sure if they want it, it's not good for us." The third says, "Well, I'm a bit of a nationalist, you know. When I go to Europe, I wear a maple leaf pin." There may be a lot of unease in this party among the rank and file, who are often conservative Canadian nationalists. The first, the pro-dealer, says, "I think what makes us different is our political system — and the monarchy." He says every country that ever abandoned the British Empire and the monarchy has "gone down the tubes." "Like Canada?" ask his friends. "No," he says, "Canada never left the monarchy." "Oh," they say, "like Ro-dee-see-ah." "Yes," he says, "or Zambia. Some of those countries are so independent, they'd rather be independent and starve."

A PC candidate from another riding is nearby. "I was canvassing this street," he tells some people, "and it was like Rotarian heaven. The first door I knocked on says, 'Are you a Rotarian?' I said 'I sure am,' and he said, 'There's three more lawn signs for you right beside me.' " Paul Rockwood, campaign manager for Laurie Pallett, says the Prime Minister's Office has targeted four thousand in this riding for personal letters from the PM, on the basis of demographic and income analysis. The sure hand of Norm Atkins in this smooth, confident, unflappable election machine.

There's nothing on the news about our booklet. A CBC producer has called in — he's doing an election feature on nationalism in Ontario. Sometimes people who claim to be experts talk as if no Canadian outside Ontario cares about the country. He says he feels the mood here has grown more confident in recent years. For example, people he meets don't seem to envy his English accent as they did when he first came. It's the psychological approach to political matters: How are we feeling about nuclear war or getting into that big American marketplace — confident? insecure? It tends to forget that there is a real world out there, with effects and consequences for people's lives, regardless of how anyone *feels* about it.

The networks, by the way, have concluded negotiations with the parties over televised debates. It looks like the Tories got their way. Since they're in the lead, they prefer minimal exposure. There will be only one debate in each language, no separate debates on women or free trade, and each will be three hours long. That ought to discourage the citizens. Even the glitziest mini-series rarely run in three-hour chunks. The networks agreed with the Con-

servatives that less is better, since they won't lose as much
ad revenue that way.

Wednesday, October 12

Today's Environics poll has the Tories at 42 percent, the
NDP at 29 and the Liberals at 25. It's the first drop for the
Tories in months. If they lost three or four more points,
there could be a minority, which would probably mean no
deal. Ed Broadbent, smelling blood, said yesterday he
thinks the Liberals may soon disappear, leaving us with a
typically European system of clear left and right alternatives, which he, for one, would welcome.

John Crispo is a sort of institution within the free trade
debate. He's a business prof at the University of Toronto
who's spoken on behalf of the deal everywhere in Canada
— before business groups, on phone-ins, at public forums. He's a proponent of the business worldview, but
he's also a kind of loose cannon, not directly controlled by
anyone. He loves to scrap in public; he's never embraced
the "benign neglect" approach to the issue. All in all he's a
plus on the democratic side of the ledger, and I don't be-
grudge him the small fortune he's made in fees for
mouthing off before business bodies all over Canada. If
the rest of them were willing to come out and fight the
way Crispo has, this would be a healthier moment in the
history of Canadian politics. This morning I debate him at
York University.
    When I arrive in the lecture hall, Crispo is already
launched. He waves the cartoon booklet and damns it in
convincing style, then piles on economic terminology and
statistics to prove the blessings of free trade.
    I say I'm not an economist, hoping this will endear me
to the student audience, and I dwell on the culture
clauses, where I feel at home. When I get to the destruction of the Canadian rock music industry, some kids start
to nod. Crispo looks a little rudderless for the first time. I

don't think he's got a position on free trade and rock. During questions, someone asks about media coverage. I get a little unhinged and say I'm ready to lead the drive to privatize the CBC. Crispo jumps up and says we can be co-chairmen. I think I've gone too far.

I drive down to Montrose Public School. When I was very small, we lived on this street in downtown Toronto. Broadbent is going to visit the "Children's Place," located in the school. I miss the event, but the media are set up in the gym with an NDP backdrop. At a press conference, Broadbent presents the party's position on family benefits, with lots of figures to prove they can pay for it. At the end I ask two women who appear to work in the children's centre what Broadbent's visit was like. "Like an invasion," they say. The kids in the hall are shouting, "Ed's the best, he's number one, he'd make the best president." "No," a teacher says to them, "not the best *president*." They try again. "The best — the best . . . government!" is the closest they get.

Later that day I go back and find the two women. Their names are Angela and Cheryl.

"We'd been told there would be a lot less people," says Angela, who's in charge of the centre. "They said it would be a pool of about four reporters and Broadbent. I understand this is what politics is about. Politicians take the opportunities they can to be seen. And we feel we should encourage our people to get involved, especially since we're servicing people — immigrants, single parents — who don't normally get involved in politics. So we said yes."

They're a drop-in, not a daycare, centre — an important distinction. They give a chance to parents who are at home with kids to come and spend time with other parents and kids. They serve a different function than daycare centres but, they say, Ed showed no interest in what they were doing. "He was with us for five minutes," says Angela. "He told me he liked my earrings. I thought it curious he would notice. I suppose I expected him to talk to me a bit about our centre. I got the impression he didn't know much about what was going on, other than that he was going to take some pictures." Lucille, Ed's wife, did ask her what they do. "There are lots of things I'd have liked to talk to him about," says Angela. "I tried but got no chance. I am recommending that we write a letter to his office complaining."

Cheryl is on a short contract with the centre. "I was angry they didn't take the children's feelings into consideration when they came in," she says. "The media. They were very arrogant. Barrelling in. Not caring there were small children, afraid, they started to cry. It was like a Martian invasion. They were going to come in, take a sample, and leave."

At the press conference, Angela says, "All I heard was something about increasing monthly benefits. Another $60 a year. That's not going to affect us much. I was unimpressed by the questions of the reporters. I thought maybe when they asked questions I'd understand what he meant. But they didn't ask anything except, How're you gonna pay? Nothing about the social implications. Just money, money, money. I'd have wanted clarification on what it means for people. All they asked was what it means for the rich. I can't believe the press. Who are they trying to serve? They could have asked, What does it mean for the single parent with three kids? Someone who makes less than $24,000."

"Like us," says Cheryl. "When I got the call from Ottawa, I was impressed and talked to the guy about our place and in the end it was all irrelevant. Broadbent wanted to know how we liked working here, not what we did." Angela says, "Parents were disappointed they couldn't exchange words with him. It was so bizarre when he said he liked my earrings."

"Diane was looking forward to talking to him," says Cheryl about one of the parents. "She was excited. She has two kids, she comes every day. A number came because they knew he would be here. Others weren't aware of the politics at all. Just that there were cameras and somebody famous. For them it's not much different from the movie being filmed up on Harbord right now." (Vans and trailers are parked just up the street near the school.)

"The only other time I saw a politician," says Angela, " I was living in a small town in the Ottawa Valley and Stanfield flew in. About two hundred people lived there. He was in a helicopter, but it was so different. He went around and spoke with everybody. There were press, but it didn't have the same feeling of invasion." Perhaps back then, in the dark ages of politics, when Robert Stanfield led the Tories, campaign events still existed in their own right as attempts to meet and sway voters. The press would come along to record them. Now we have landed on the moon: campaign events are not simply recorded *by* the press, they are fabricated *for* the press, who pass them along to the TV audience, masses of voters who never actually see or meet a candidate.

"The word, 'used,' was used a lot," says Cheryl. "By staff and by users too. Is there a connection to fast foods and all the rushing? I mean, Not taking time to smell the foods? All of us feel that this place is so important and necessary and when someone does that it feels awful. We take so much pride, and then it turned us into a circus which meant nothing."

This seems to strike deep at them, because of the devaluations they deal with each day. "We hear a lot of problems," says Cheryl, "and see a lot of things. It can be tough emotionally." "Abuse, poverty, homelessness," says Angela. "We feel we had a lot to say to him, or any political leader, and we weren't listened to."

"Or send somebody who has some time," says Cheryl. "And Dan Heap was there," says Angela of the local MP, who is widely respected. "And he didn't talk to anybody, which is a bit strange. I wanted a chance to say hello to him." They were expecting to raise their voices, be involved in the distant political process which shapes us and the institutions in which we act, but which rarely touches us directly. Instead, they felt about the same degree of involvement as if they'd been watching a TV account of the visit later tonight.

"I finally realized it was an opportunity for him," says Angela. "We're experiencing more anger than sadness, but that's politics. He has a campaign to run. Fifty days — take any opportunity. They, the NDP, are really taking advantage of a person like myself, who wouldn't vote for the other parties. I felt really abused as an NDP supporter. I think of them as a party of the people, but not today. Turner or Mulroney would not have felt any different."

Maybe this is the problem with the NDP. It's not that they're worse than the other parties. On balance they may be better, but they are judged on a different scale, and they asked for it. They say they are the party concerned with the real people of the country, the people of unprivilege, and often those like Angela and Cheryl take them at their word and give their hearts in return. When Tories and Liberals protest that they, too, are parties of the people, that they really, really care — most people respond with a degree of ironic detachment. They know how those parties are beholden, and that even if they'd like to be fair and open, their options are limited by the exigencies of fundraising and powerbroking. People aren't surprised when there's a gap between rhetoric and practice in the other parties. But the NDP should be different — they are not sewn with their guts to the pillars of wealth and power. Their claim to care has greater plausibility. When people like Cheryl and Angela discover the people's politicians are more or less like those of the other parties, the discouragement is great.

Angela says that 90 percent of the staff at the Children's Place are single parents. She does not think the work they do is divorced from politics. On the contrary. "I think what we're doing here is politics," she says. "Educating people. Bringing them together. Empowering people to help themselves through the use of information and support."

Cheryl says, "I have trouble with politics. I'm not that

involved. I've had so many troubles in my life. At times I can't turn on the radio to hear the news. It's too confusing, it's too depressing. I don't have much time for politics. I'm too tired. I deal with problems all day. I take care of a two-year-old. By 10:30 at night I'm either exhausted or — DOING" — she mimics a frantic wide-awakeness — "and when you're poorly educated like me, politics doesn't have any context. It doesn't have anything to connect to. In school I was never there. And it depends on my friends, who I'm close to. In the last couple of years, I've been on my own a lot . . . ."

These are two involved citizens, and our political system just whizzed by them. It grazed them but left them no richer nor any more aware. Or perhaps that's wrong: it sadly clarified for them the gap between the politics inherent in what they do as they live and work, and our political *system* of parties, leaders and elections.

Wednesday evening, at the Convention Centre, for the Liberal Confederation dinner. Frank Stronach, businessman and Liberal candidate, took responsibility for this bloated fundraiser, and he's filled the barn. There are about four thousand people here at three hundred a throw. They've got a stupid song called "Canada, A Celebration," sung by a huge kids' choir at one end of the hall while spotlights play and a vapid slide show slithers across the vast screens. The song is a descendant of the Expo theme: "Ca-na-da, We Love You." It is Canadian nationalism at its emptiest. We are because we are because we are: no hint of *what* we are or why it is worth preserving.

This is a party of enormous contradictions — in fact, maybe it should change its name to the Contradictory Party. For most of the forty years after World War II, Liberals presided over the economic, cultural and military incorporation of Canada into the American empire. But they gave the country a flag and whipped up a mild nationalist fervour with Expo '67. Yet when their own finance minister, Walter Gordon, tried to recapture some of the country's wealth for its people, they savaged him for it. They created the Canada Council, and Petro-Canada, and the Foreign Investment Review Agency, but continental integration never really faltered under their rule. They sold Trudeau as a nationalist when his only consuming political passion was the destruction of *Quebec* nationalism. They have always been a business-based party, with a populist program when it suits them, which it does mostly when they are out of office. The Tories have simply taken Liberal policies to their logical conclusion, purged them of contradictions and finalized the transaction in the trade deal. The people here sit on their hands, heir to an ambiguous tradition.

So there are four thousand copies of *What's the Big Deal?* strewn about this room, one at each place setting, purchased by Elvio Del Zotto, provincial party president and one of the highest rollers in the development industry. He gives the impression of not caring much about free trade either way; this is party politics for him.

Then Turner rises, to minimal applause. He tosses his prepared speech, foregoing all subjects except the trade deal. He looks out at this gathering, who have barely acknowledged his presence, and says he knows they disagree with him. After a year of mighty effort he has not budged them. Yet he argues with them still. He runs through the various elements of the deal, which he knows as well as his children's names. At the very end, he says, "I do not believe this country will throw away its . . ." and he can't get the word out; he says "birthrate." He tries again, and again it comes out "birthrate." Desperate for the word, he grits his whole face, raises his right hand and as it were plunges his fist straight into his heart — it's like a special effect from a horror or fantasy movie — and plucks from his heart the word he needs. "Birthright!" he grunts with relief, flourishing the term he sought, held in that fist before his face, then finishes with a phrase and sits without waiting for reaction. It is as though a confrontation with himself has left everyone else as spectators. He will continue to be crucified by his own in the days to come.

In the lobby, Dennis Mills, the evening's host, is talking
to Marty Goldfarb, the Liberal pollster. Goldfarb says
sternly that Turner should never have embraced the
Meech Lake accord. Next day, the papers reveal that he
and former Trudeau aide Tom Axworthy have written a
book criticizing Turner, mainly over Meech Lake, just in
time for the election. It will join Greg Weston's book
about Turner, *Reign of Error*, on the shelves: one more
gooey pie in the face for the leader of the Liberal party.

Turner's leadership rating is down to 10 percent, with
the other two at about 30 each. On the basis of their own
polls, the people running the Liberal campaign (I am told
after the election) are looking at twenty-seven seats max
— *nationally* — and the "fastest toilet shoot they've ever
seen in their lives." Someone I know says next day, "Hell,
he's just a Bay Street lawyer getting what he deserves."
Maybe. In fact, if Turner hadn't come back to take over
the Liberal party, the Tories would probably not have
won in 1984 and there would be no trade deal. Unless the
Liberals had put it through themselves, which is not hard
to imagine. On the other hand, without Turner there
wouldn't be an election on free trade either, or at least the
possibility of one. Because it still isn't clear what this election will be about. Mulroney and Atkins are hoping to run
on everything but the trade deal, and so, it seems, are the
NDP.

Thursday, October 13

There's been some reaction to the booklet, mostly from
Ontario so far, since it only came out two days ago, and in
some parts of the country it hasn't appeared yet. It con-
tains a clipout coupon for donations and comments.
Yesterday, the first day after, about $3,000 came in to the
coalition office by mail, today $7,000 more. Most of the
envelopes contain small amounts: fives, tens, twenties,
many ones and twos and the odd loonie taped in. The
phone has been ringing nonstop, and people come by as

well. In fact the traffic is creating problems for the regular
operations of the Ontario Teachers' Federation, who live
there. About half the letters also include written messages. Few of them are typed.

> Dear Sir/Madam:
> Yesterday I received your publication, Whats the Big Deal,
> together with the local newspaper the *Windsor Star*. I sat
> down at once and read all of it. . . .

Some simply scribble something on the coupon, which
reads, "It's Up To Us!" They add things like, "It sure is.
Keep up the Good Work!"

Joe Maloney in Bath, Ontario, says, "I'm a worried
Dairy Farmer there is only a few days remaining till the
election Keep on Working!"

Mark D. Nell from Brantford, Ontario, writes on the
"memo" line of his cheque, "Preventing Canada from Becoming U.S.A. 51st State."

A small handwritten note: "Stop him please! I'm a fashion design student in Toronto. If you have any spare
copies of the "What's The Big Deal" booklet I'd love to
leave them in the student lounge." Another envelope has
a home-made stamp that reads, "Don't elect a liar again."

People are going into the office for days or half-days to
clear the overflow and, by the way, recharge themselves.
Today when Laurell was there, her grade 6 teacher called.
He's retired now and wants to help. It's like writing: you
don't know what you've done till people you don't know
see it and respond. A handwritten letter from Rose Marie
Kelly in Milton, Ontario, came with a ten-dollar bill. "Dear
Sir," it says, "Thank God at last someone has explained
the Free Trade Deal! I hope and pray this message
reaches the whole country. It is terrifying to realize what
this deal would mean to our country. We are an older
couple — months to 'senior citizenship' and its frightening to think what this deal could do to us. Thank you for
making the effort to save our country." Laurell is moved

as she recalls that letter. "Somebody said thank you!" she says.

In coming weeks, over $75,000 will come in, in similar small amounts, and there are other signs. Ross Laver of *Maclean's*, for instance, is in Winnipeg tonight at a Turner rally. He says he went across the street to a variety store to buy cigarettes. The owner noticed his media badge, called his wife from the back of the store, took out a wellthumbed copy of *What's the Big Deal?* and demanded to know why people like Laver had not informed them more thoroughly.

These are new voices, rarely heard from. They represent another level of possible involvement in public life. The coalition movement has had a far greater reach than the business groups who support the deal — the organizations in the coalitions represent millions of people — but the actual numbers involved in coalition work are still relatively few. The grass roots activities against free trade reach deeper into communities and ordinary life but are also small in comparison to the mass of the population, citizens reduced for the most part to mere voters. From the response to the booklet, you start to sense what it would be like for isolated individuals, who don't belong to coalitions, movements or anything else, to become part of decisions in their society. It's a sort of hint, no more; the connection is minimal. They read a booklet, tape on a loonie and scribble a note. Then what?

Friday, October 14

Tonight the NDP is holding a dinner in honour of provincial party leader Bob Rae's first ten years in politics. It's at an Italian restaurant and banquet hall on Lawrence Avenue near Dufferin.

Here's Abby Pollonetsky, who has worked with the Coalition against Free Trade for the past three years. Now she's an NDP candidate in Parkdale, and she's had a makeover. She complains that people in the Coalition haven't supported her, and some are even helping her Liberal opponent, Jessie Flis. She says Flis's campaign has been distributing literature on the free trade deal that comes from the Auto Workers' union. She's going to ask the Auto Workers to make them stop. Not give her the same material to hand out, but make the Liberals *stop*.

When they go in to dinner, I remain in the foyer, where a bar is set up. Broadbent is coming, along with two bus-loads of press and the paraphernalia of the triumphal entry. This time I am well positioned for it. They remove the coat racks from an office by the front door, to turn it into a "holding room" for Ed. Everyone is asking, When? and, Now? Now? Someone says they could have delayed dinner if they'd known he'd be late. People with cellular phones and walkie-talkies are everywhere. One of them says, "The sign will be a lot of media people setting up, and then Ed will be five minutes behind."

The media people straggle in, like a sagging herd of buffalo with no idea where they've been or where they are, and set up their equipment: cameras, tape recorders, laptops, as though the party around them is invisible. This is supposed to be a tribute to Bob Rae, but Bob doesn't seem to mind. Suddenly Ed is right here, being led through the foyer by three or four handlers, cops and advance men. They take him to the bathroom. Then they take him back to the holding room. Lucille, Ed's wife, goes to the bathroom alone, then she returns to the holding room. Bob Rae introduces Ed, saying that he is no Dan Quayle, "programmed and pre-conditioned," surrounded by "advisers and handlers." As Rae speaks, Ed emerges from the holding room, surrounded by advisers and handlers. He stands and fidgets. He looks strange and human, not being handled for the moment, like the king loitering outside the throne room, right before the royal fanfare. Then the music bursts — "This time we have a choice . . . This time someone who cares . . ."; "This time Ed," as their signs say — the lights are up, the wave of clearers before him that he moves along behind, the people at their tables standing and clapping. Then he is at the podium, the music stops blaring, and again that effect: when the music dies, everything dies. There are a few desultory handclaps. It is like Maple Leaf Gardens, where the organ took over from the crowd years ago, and when it's not playing, the silence echoes. I leave at this point to be elsewhere, and anyway, after the triumphal entry, each time I see it, there seems to be nothing left. It is all about entrances, this kind of politics.

Mulroney brought the regal style here, copied from Reagan's imperial presidency, right down to his own version of the travelling presidential podium. With Reagan that style reached mythic heights a Canadian prime minister could only dream of. Once, at an airport in Topeka, U.S. secret service agents killed two dogs copulating on a runway near the one the president's plane was using. No one knows why they did it. You just extinguish any signs of normal life and reality in the vicinity of The Leader. It's highly staged, the regal style. It comes with a retinue and courtiers; the only missing element is petitioners, and even they appear on occasion.

There are so many obstacles in the way of accomplishing anything in politics. I don't mean winning elections, I mean acting to affect this society. Everything and everyone seems to come into conflict. "It has always been a great temptation," wrote Hannah Arendt in *The Human Condition*, "to find a substitute for action in the hope that the realm of human affairs may escape the haphazardness and moral irresponsibility inherent in a plurality of agents. The remarkable monotony of the proposed solutions throughout our recorded history testifies to the elemental simplicity of the matter. Generally speaking, they always amount to seeking shelter from action's calamities in an activity where one man, isolated from all others, remains master of his doings from beginning to end." Like writing a book, for instance. "This attempt to replace acting with making . . ." she continued, "is manifest in the whole body of argument against 'democracy,' which, the more consistently and better reasoned it is, will turn into an argument against the essentials of politics."

Next morning, Saturday, I leave for the west and north. From there I will work my way east. That night I am in Vancouver again, where I was a week ago. I am going in circles.

Week Three

Sunday, October 16

Vancouver in the early morning. I paid an extra ten bucks at this hotel to get a spectacular view. For another twenty you get a view that must be insupportable. I have been up for hours staring out the window. No matter how many horrible buildings they throw up in this city, it doesn't spoil. It is unlike other places — St. John's, for instance, — whose harbours or vistas are tarnished and eventually destroyed. Vancouver seems to have an unlimited capacity to absorb ugliness and overcome it. It may be the only place in the world to which most of its inhabitants came for the view. Like my Uncle Eddie, who dared to abandon Toronto in the 1930s and venture west. Or Larry — lawyer, potter, contractor, restaurateur — who had a dream twenty-five years ago during his final term at law school in Ontario and left for Vancouver the next day. Generations on generations drawn to the place so they could look at it.

Larry and I stroll around the seawalk at Stanley Park. He points to mountains of sulphur across the harbour. He says they don't bother him, not like the sculpted mountain/sails on the Pan Pacific Hotel. "They're real," Larry says about the sulphur mounds, "they're used for something, they don't smell or make people sick. And they're not cheap architectural copies of an Opera House in Australia." He says that his dad back in Guelph — Frank the

Pirate, from whom I used to buy a hundred-dollar used car every year — thinks about politics very little, even less than Larry does. "My father, like so many other people, doesn't have anything to do with any of these things except they affect him every day of his life," says Larry. We pass under a huge guana-stained cliff and he says that smell is caused by cormorants. It isn't pollution, it's real, therefore it's okay.

Larry wants to know what it all means. Are there explanations for any of these things — the politics, the people? What about the deficit? All the offshore money buying up downtown Vancouver. The internationalization of the world economy. "What's the take on that?" he asks. We cut back through the cedars. Joggers pass us two middle-aged guys like they're gazelles. I feel forty-six.

Afternoon. P.C. campaign headquarters in Vancouver Quadra, where Bill Clarke is trying to retake the seat John Turner narrowly won from him in 1984. Campaign chair Lisa Woodward, a well-groomed mother of four and "political junkie," says they're hearing a lot of free trade at the door. She says Bill persuades voters easily once they hear water isn't really in the deal and so forth. But it's clear they're getting strong opposition; some people won't even talk to them. They have clippings on the benefits of free trade up everywhere in the office, ready ammo for their embattled troops. With the national Tory poll figures, you'd expect them to be cocky and looking forward to knocking Turner off this time. Instead it feels like they've already given up. If the Tory tide was so strong, would it not have lapped at these shores too?

John McDermid arrives. It's a Sunday afternoon and he's in town, a lesser star they've brought out to brighten their flagging cause, especially since McDermid was an assistant minister to John Crosbie on the trade deal. Now that he's a real minister — of housing, a post created specially for this election — he's looking nattier and wears a better cut of suit. He waits to be introduced.

Candidate Clarke looks like an accountant, which he is.

He spent twelve years as an MP and seems bitter at the twist of history that sent Turner his way. He'd settled into Ottawa, doing nothing to give offence or make anyone take notice, and then Turner became leader of the Liberals and decided to make a point by running in the west. "In most cases," says Clarke to McDermid as they stand before the faithful, "I'm able to explain to people that those horrible things they hear from Broadbent and Turner about the free trade agreement are not things to worry about. They're so worried I hardly get a chance to campaign on the government record. I'm sorry I'm not part of that record, but that's democracy. I'm just worried that the party is so high in the national polls that it'll generate sympathy for the Liberal candidate here in Quadra."

He says they were leading two to one before the last election day, but the Liberals sent in throngs of organizers and mobilized a sympathy vote that pushed Turner through. McDermid stands beside him on a little raised platform, holding his styrofoam coffee cup and not quite at ease as the superior being he has recently become. Clarke says to McDermid, "Did I say something wrong? You're frowning." McDermid seems far away, but is called back by this plea and tries to recoup. "No, I'm just so enthralled with what you're saying." A few of the locals laugh, maybe to cover embarrassment.

These two are not intellectually impressive. McDermid's first act as minister was to announce that the homeless like life that way. Clarke may have a right to some bitterness. He's probably no more incompetent than the man who made minister — fate just dealt him a sideswipe. It seems to me that up close many of our leaders, political and otherwise, are pretty foolish compared to ordinary citizens, though it would be hard to persuade most Canadians; the idea seems counter-intuitive, because of the assumption that success in this society is related to merit. If they weren't smart, how did they get there?

McDermid gives a pep talk to the canvassers about free trade. "They're using lies; they're using distortion. If you saw a comic book they put out recently — and comic book is exactly the right term for it — you will not see any reference to the free trade agreement. What they say are lies, half-truths, distortions . . . ." He looks at me and past me. Is this a little unethical? They don't know I'm here, that the enemy is within. It's a strong sign of the booklet's impact. His arguments for the deal are feeble: over the past forty years, he says, as tariff barriers lowered, Canadian prosperity, social programs and cultural achievement increased. But if that all happened under a multilateral approach, why not carry on as before? Why a special trade deal? Is this their best shot? To claim the deal is nothing new? He swings hard at Bob White of the Auto Workers and "his millionaire buddy Pierre Berton." Perhaps he sees me react, because he adds, "Who's a very good writer, but a socialist." He doesn't ask for questions.

After McDermid leaves, I talk with Richard Beattie, a bearded, red-faced organizer of volunteers. He wears a colourful sweater and has an English accent, along with some spirit, humour and intelligence. He says he's a Thatcherite and they're going to have trouble from the Reform party in this riding. They're being squeezed from both sides. What's the Reform appeal? A lot of people, he says, see Mulroney as a wet, to use Thatcher's term. They think our Canadian Tories haven't been up to the task, compared to their models in the U.S. and U.K. They have been slow on privatization, on slashing the deficit, on hacking the bureaucracy. Basically, on hacking and slashing. I suppose Canada is like that: it's always been hard to get anything very left-wing going here, but it's been tough to get anything too right-wing going either. Beattie says he is a private business consultant and he often advises native groups on setting up small businesses. Though he thinks Mulroney is a wet, he believes in working within the system to change it.

I'm in a Kitsilano bistro with Victor Nowicki. Victor is one of the most laidback guys I've ever met. Even for Vancouver he's laidback. He says he came here years ago because he wanted to get away from London, Ontario. He's following politics less this election because it's become "more homogenized. Everybody says the same things. I don't like the slick packaging. Everybody wears a blue suit and a red tie. The heads of all the parties seem to be advertising guys. People who know how to manipulate people as consumers. The script doesn't seem to vary from the last election, except this time free trade is what everyone is talking about." It is the strange duality of this campaign: an election happening and a sort of referendum trying to happen within it, one familiar and tiresome, the other a surprising stranger.

His friends talk about the deal. They say they don't understand it and what's going to happen because of it. Some say if Ontario is against it, they're for. Victor wonders why we can't just give it a try and if it doesn't work, get out. A laidback, B.C. approach. If it's free, he says, it ought to be all right. "Free trade, free love, freeDOM." He's very sixties, as he says.

He always votes, always has. "Even when I didn't realize the difference between parties, I always thought I should vote. To be a good citizen." He talks about the term citizenship which neither of us recall being used in school, though we both knew American kids took citizenship classes. "I remember in grade 13, I didn't even want to run for student council," he says. He was a prefect, though, a responsible position in his school. "We'd monitor the halls, make sure nobody butted into the lunch line." A good friend of Victor's was running for president of the boys' athletic association, and their science teacher asked if Victor was going to run as well — right in front of the class! "He said, 'We can't let him run unopposed. That wouldn't be right, so you should run, Victor.'"

This put Victor in a bind that he still feels uncomfortable about. As a prefect he felt a certain, as he puts it, *noblesse oblige.* "I thought, 'Yuh, maybe we shouldn't let him run unopposed. Everybody should have a choice.' And I felt flattered. I had thoughts of power and glory in the schoolyard. I haven't thought about this in years. Never, really."

Our attitudes to politics often have deep roots, frequently buried in adolescence when our sense of humanness is expanding and idealism wells up inside. I recall, as we talk, my own political obsessions in high school. I refused to pay the student activities fee in grade 12 because it was "taxation without representation." That was based on *American* history, which we'd studied the year before. Once the student council agreed to pass the fee, I happily paid.

"I said, 'Okay,' " Victor continues, "and I won by sixteen votes. It really screwed up our relationship. We were co-captains of the football team. But I bought my teacher's argument that it was my *responsibility* to run. . . ."

Just as politics goes back to childhood, so, probably, does our fascination with voting and elections. Victor says, "As a kid, I had the idea that democracy was good, and more democracy was better. I think I got that less from school than from American movies. Jimmy Stewart going to Washington, John Wayne, Davey Crockett fighting the Mexicans at the Alamo for democracy. I really had a shock when I realized Canada was not that democratic." By this he means that Americans get to vote more often, in more elections, for more positions. "For the last ten or fifteen years, I realized that here we elect a king or queen, though we haven't elected a queen yet — and then for four long years that leader has carte blanche. You vote," he goes on, "and then you shut up because you can't change anything. That's why we should have an elected Senate." This is a different, though connected, thought. "What amazes me," he says, "is that it's the right-wingers, not the NDP, who want an elected Senate. I find that shocking. But some of my friends think I'm wrong. They say things like, Do we have to take a vote every time somebody wants to go to the bathroom?" Does Victor really think democracy equals voting? On this point, he is solid. "Yes," he says firmly, "Yes . . . Yes! The more voting the more democratic."

Victor's father was a construction labourer; his mother worked in a biscuit factory. He makes a "small living building stuff out of wood. Functional objects like tables. Cupboards in the shape of a skyscraper." In the past he's done childcare counselling. He took on kids who were about to be booted from school or whom the ministry of human resources wanted to keep out of jail, at least till age nineteen when they aren't the ministry's responsibility any longer. "A reason I did that for so long — it wasn't for the money — was to be doing something for the betterment of the world, no matter how small, on an individual basis." It was his personal political arena, his attempt to help shape our society.

He belonged to the NDP a few years ago and was once a member of COPE, the Vancouver civic reform party. No more. "I'm frankly embarrassed by some of their representatives. I can't join if I'm embarrassed by the leader or one of the candidates. I've knocked on doors quite a few times. Maybe next time it'll be for Getty in Alberta, so we can have an elected Senate," he says. It's not exactly a joke; it's one of his recurring thoughts on democracy. "In B.C., the Socreds win 2 or 3 percent more than the NDP, and then the people recognize the guy is a jerk but have to wait four or five years, and then they get sucked in again every time. Maybe there's hope, but I doubt it."

This last phrase is like Merri's: Who's the least worst choice? It summarizes politics in our society much of the time. "Vander Zalm will resign like Bennett," says Victor. "Get an attractive candidate again, cry communism about the NDP and win again. Scary, ain't it?"

Yet he's not bitter and he wouldn't dream of dropping out. He'll watch, participate when he can and, of course, vote. You could call him a combination of cynicism and democratic commitment. When he voted in his first federal election, in '71 or '72, Victor says he looked hard at the ballot. "I voted for Trudeau, but I had the same feeling as when I go into a supermarket for a detergent and see the array of detergents and don't have a previous choice in mind. So you go sort of subliminally toward one in particular. And I still don't know why I pick out one or another. My first federal election was like buying soap."

Monday, October 17

A Gallup puts the Tories at 39 percent. It looks as if the bastards have peaked. I leave for an early Broadbent press conference on cultural policy at the Orpheum Theatre.

The NDP have chosen to announce their culture policy here in the lobby of the downtown Vancouver theatre where the symphony plays. Crystal chandeliers, mirrors, pillars — this is culture à la Versailles, culture as understood by symphony subscribers. They've even brought pianist Anton Kuerti, who's an NDP candidate in Ontario, all the way out here to play three minutes' worth of Mendelssohn at 8:30 in the morning. The cameramen crowd around Kuerti and the grand. Why not Bryan Adams in this cultural context? Why not Anton Keurti *and* Bryan Adams? One of the NDP campaign staff explains why not. "It's called targeting." Does this party have a secret obsession with respectability? Or is it just a cynical calculation: they assume "ordinary Canadians" have nowhere to go but the NDP, so they take them for granted and target the more privileged. The Ontario NDP once ran an election ad when Stephen Lewis was leader that said, "His mother wanted him to be a concert pianist . . ." as Lewis crossed the floor of the House carrying a folder that maybe hid a Chopin score under the day's yellows. There's a crew out here at the moment shooting the NDP's TV ads for this election. These can start airing, according to election rules, next Sunday. An NDP person involved says their ads don't contain much about free trade, because they don't want to alienate the 50 percent of voters who are in favour of the deal.

One of the TV cameras has a "No, Eh" sticker on it. I ask the CBC producer if she knows who put it there and she looks at me like I'm trying to infect her. I ask the cameraman. He says, "Me." Has he had any flack from management? "Nah," he says. "Anyway," he adds, "we'll probably be on strike in two weeks." These camera crews travel with these producers and reporters for months and even years — but they see the world with very different eyes, and tamper with it in different ways.

This morning the government announced the CBC will get their beloved all-news channel, the one the CRTC recommended a licence for last spring, but which the Cabinet, in its wisdom, denied. "Then they could attack us twenty-four hours a day," said the prime minister at the time. It's a bit blatant. In the middle of an election, the government gives a cookie to its main media outlet. That night "The National" plays it as their number one story, with communications minister Flora MacDonald and CBC president Pierre Juneau both beaming.

Kamloops.

The ride from the airport into town seems longer than it is in Toronto or Vancouver. The cabbie says he's driven one of the candidates around, but doesn't know his name. "He's running for your MP."

Nelson Riis is the sitting member of Parliament; he's also house leader for the New Democrats. Ron Hamilton, his campaign manager, is a lineman with B.C. Tel. His union "booked him off" for the campaign and covers his wages. He wears a Riis button with Riis's face on it. Looking at it, I feel strange, then I realize Ron looks a lot like Nelson. Same kind of hair, same bland good looks, same aviator-style glasses.

He talks haltingly and keeps calling me by name, as if he took a course in communicating along with one in running an election campaign. Some unions run leadership schools for their members, in which the terrifying culmination, after weeks of preparation, involves speaking publicly for five minutes.

He shows me some riding maps that prove how complicated our electoral system can be once you're outside the urban centres. It takes five or six hours to drive from end to end of this riding in the interior of British Columbia. That almost automatically creates the need for a certain technical expertise, and guys like Ron, of a technocratic quality. It's easy for political issues to get lost in the mere task of contacting farflung voters. Ron says most canvassing is done here by phone rather than "foot-canvassing," which suddenly sounds like a quaint urban rite.

Amanda, Riis's aide, used to live here in Kamloops. She says free trade is what she's hearing at the door. "And they want details." She also hears a little abortion, but she's not hearing daycare or unemployment, though the levels in this riding are very high. "I'm hearing this deal. They want to see it and know what it actually says." Their campaign literature includes a wordy pamphlet from NDP head office in Ottawa, which briefly mentions free trade twice. Riis's own brochure is about "people" — nothing else. It could be from any party.

Ben Bobrowich is a retired worker in charge of lawn signs for Riis's campaign. He used to be a railway conductor on the Kamloops to North Bend line. He seems to be a fixture in the office, but he says this may be his last campaign.

"I came here from Winnipeg in '47," he says, "for a visit, to see an aunt and uncle. I liked it. I was playing a little hockey, a Senior B team. It was a pretty good team. I didn't make it, so I went to railroading in '51. The first seven or eight years on the railroad, I had two children and we were starving to death because it was a seniority basis. I took a leave and went carpenting, just to make ends meet. I took up my dad's trade — I had some of his tools." He now has three kids and five grandchildren. He has no personal stake in the campaign; it wouldn't bring him any perks even if the NDP formed the government or the official Opposition. Why is he involved? "Trying to make a better country for my family, you know? To me now it doesn't matter that much, but I can't see any direction for my *grand*children to go. My children are pretty well situated, but I can't see any future for *their* kids. To me it looks like we're going toward the third world. We have the rich, the blue collar and the poor."

Then he talks about the issues and how he makes up his mind. "We don't know what this free trade's gonna do," he says. "But I've watched it, I've studied it, this is what I think. I been thinking about farmers since that ad in the paper last week. You tell me what Canadian farmers produce that American farmers can't." In other words, since American farmers produce more cheaply because of their climate and market, free trade would be bad for Canadian farmers. From this model, Ben concludes that free trade with the U.S. is too risky altogether.

This kind of thinking differs from the typical middle-class way of forming an opinion, which samples "informed" views and then chooses between them. Ben looks for one corner or angle he can make sense of himself, and generalizes from that. It may sound idiosyncratic, but it's simply based on original thinking, rather than authority or expertise: you figure out the answer yourself. Perhaps it's grounded in a sense that the authorities aren't as impartial as they like to let on.

He talks about his relationship to politics. "My dad was a labour man. He was a carpenter. I remember him working for twenty-five cents an hour or less in the thirties, and he raised seven children. I was the youngest. He was a good provider. But even then, the rich people still tried to take the land from the homesteader and beat them. Even in the thirties." He repeats this, it amazes him that the rich behaved so, and it formed his worldview. "I thought I gotta do something about it."

"I'm a strong New Democrat right now," he goes on. "But I could change. If they get in power, if I'm not satisfied, I'll work to get 'em out." Why does he mention this, sitting in the middle of the NDP campaign office? It marks the attitude of other working people I've met, who sometimes seem like loyalists, but who simply assess this party as their best bet, the least worst choice. The NDP may be right when they assume "ordinary" Canadians have nowhere else to go; but they're wrong if they think many of these people don't understand that.

As for the current election, "I'd like us to be the Opposition with a minority government. Cundari is the Tory here. He's a lawyer. That's all we need. Another lawyer in Ottawa. Nelson is a teacher, a perfesser, I think he teached in college."

The Liberals are a pathetic rump here in B.C., so it's worth dropping in at their campaign office. It's an article of faith among the major parties — in fact, it's one proof you are a major party — that you run in every riding, no matter how hopeless. But what induces a particular candidate to stand in a place like Kamloops? "Free trade," says Gus Halliday, and I'm hers — she pushed my button. "I know that's your button," she says. "I read that book, *If You Love This Country*. I'm vitally concerned about the future of Canada after this deal. I probably wouldn't have run otherwise."

She is handsome and well spoken — as you might say in a novel — a woman toward sixty, who runs a small business. She was chair of the local hospital committee during a right-wing takeover of the board. She fought them for the right to abortion, and won. She's a real liberal. She believes things should be better than they are and that people should behave well toward each other, and she has no idea why they often aren't and don't. She's also a Liberal. Canada's the only country that's had a "lasting Liberal party," she says proudly. She'd hate to see a two-party system of the sort Broadbent recently yearned for, because our three-party system "works like a bugger for the people of Canada." She came from Scotland originally, via Winnipeg, and has raised her family here.

She spends most of her time talking to businesspeople, especially those in small business, about the deal. She is flabbergasted at their thickness. She's like Turner — obsessed with converting these former colleagues. "People say, 'What do you know, Gus? You're just a smalltown businessperson.'" She goes to forums sponsored by the

Chamber of Commerce where, she says, "They just lie. They remind me of lemmings rushing to the cliff." So why does she bother with them? "Because I'm a business-person too. They're who I know." I guess that's also Turner's problem. We are prisoners of who we know, even if we aspire to a larger reach.

She believes they're acting out of character. After all, they're in business, they're used to thinking their own decisions through. "I've known these people as pure Canadians for such a long time. Yet they can't see this threat. They say, Nobody can say what's going to happen, my guess is as good as yours. They don't believe it when you show them." She says hopefully that small business-people who "play with their own money" are starting to ask what's in it for them. Others, like the Chamber of Commerce, "who aren't playing with their own chips," are pumped up with an abstract enthusiasm. She thinks they're taken in by the word "trade" — anything with trade in it has got to be good. Like Victor Nowicki, who supports anything with "free" in it. Between "free" and "trade," the government product has real market appeal.

I ask if her business acquaintances couldn't do well by selling out to U.S. companies after the deal. "Bullshit," she says, in her well-spoken way. "When the Americans come in with their marketing techniques they'll just wipe our Canadians out. Like babes to the slaughter. Anyway, when the jobs disappear from the plants, the money disappears from the communities." She says this as confidently as she'd say the sky is blue — she knows about doing business in a resource-based community. Yet it would be a strange thought to many Canadians: that industrial production remains the basis of economic prosperity. Try and tell it to the shoppers in Yorkville in Toronto some Saturday afternoon.

Evening. Garry Worth's home in the Westsyde section of town. This is a Canadian worker's house. From the front, it appears modest and suburban. In the backyard he keeps three riding horses.

"I never realized," he says, "how naïve I was till I talked to Donny Ryan of the Gitskan tribe at the Festival of the Stein." Garry is the president of a major union local in the forest industry, but he was at the gathering to speak for the preservation of one of B.C.'s wilderness treasures, the watershed of the Stein River Valley. "I could see we probably don't understand the native land claims issue," he says. "Some of the questions he asked made me feel naïve. When I spoke, I referred to the environmental movement and the labour movement, but I left out the native Indian movement, and I realized I hadn't thought about it enough. I'd heard speakers before from the tribes, but then I could really see it fitting together with what I've come to realize: the key is to get the resources out of the hands of the multinationals and into the hands of community-based forest industries. And work with the environmentalists and the Indians to do that."

He says the woods are moving in exactly the other direction, "basically toward private ownership of public land." He favours control by small native groups or operators with a few hundred employees — "stump to dump" operations. He's dismayed by ads placed by COFI (Council of Forest Industries) in papers and media using the catch phrase "Forests Forever," which he feels is a cover for massive destruction.

Garry is sensitive to catch phrases, he's like a trip alarm for them. There's Quality of Work Life, in fashion among corporations everywhere. He has a small library on QWL, a management technique which provides employees with various improvements meant to suggest, eventually, that unions are unnecessary. "How can you be against the quality of work life, or forests forever, or free trade?" Garry asks.

He is a softspoken, confident worker. After finishing grade 12, he trained as a millwright in trade school and did a four-year apprenticeship. He pulls out briefs on the environment he's written to various commissions on behalf of his union. I ask if there's opposition among workers to policies that could harm their own job interests. He says two union locals might be affected by the Stein situation, but "my position is that there's enough land still in B.C. to accommodate all these concerns, and a lot of environmentalists have really helped me."

He finds environmentalists are "pleasantly surprised" to receive support from his union and several others. "They say, beside the last stand of virgin timber in B.C. is going to be an environmentalist, a native Indian, and now, of all things, a pulpworker. The IWA slogan on the other hand is Log it, Burn it, Pave it."

The IWA is the International Woodworkers of America. All the locals in Garry's union, the Pulp, Paper and Woodworkers of Canada, broke away from American unions like the IWA. They wanted to create a different kind of union, which they most often describe as independent and democratic. "It's a reflection of our type of union," he says about the policies he's helped to develop. "I grew up in the bush so I knew what was going on as far as the wastage and that. Nobody in the PPWC was doing anything on this, and when the propaganda started from the companies, it was kind of natural for me and our union to get involved. You can get this going at the local level, and then at the national. It's a sign of a democratic rank-and-file union instead of a business union."

Politics enters his life through this union connection. He grew up in Port Alberni on Vancouver Island and moved to Kamloops when the Weyerhaeuser mill expanded here. He wasn't involved till the local workers left the IWA. "I supported the breakaway," he says, "but I wasn't active in it." He found a hearing for his views in the new union, along with organizational support and a demand for leadership. He became a shop steward in '77 and in '79 was elected to the National Executive Board of the PPWC. Now he's local president and is breaking ground in relations between labour, the environment and the native movement. In this society, vast amounts of leadership ability are squandered because we tend to confine the political impulse to parties and elections. Then an opportunity arises through a union or something similar, and people display to others — and often discover in themselves — qualities of leadership no one knew were there. "But if we'd been in the IWA," says Garry, "I'd have just got beaten up."

That night on CBC's "The Journal," Bob White of the Canadian Auto Workers union and Maude Barlow of the Council of Canadians debate free trade with former Alberta premier Peter Lougheed, and Tom d'Aquino of the Business Council on National Issues. White, like Garry Worth, is a labour leader whose union was once an American branch but is now independent. In White's case, he led the change, a momentous one for Canadian workers. Like Garry, White has extraordinary leadership abilities that would probably have gone unnoticed without the labour movement — even though you could say he genuinely has charisma, one of the most misapplied terms in politics. I'm told later that as he and Barlow prepare to go on for their national televised kick at the can, they shake hands and wish each other luck. White looks around at the setting and the role he is playing. "Not bad, eh," he says, "for a guy with grade 10."

Tuesday, October 18

Morning. Russ Cundari's PC campaign office in a Kamloops mall. I talk to Richard Blair, campaign manager. Suddenly candidate Cundari dashes through. He's rushing off to try and calm a party contributor worried to death about the free trade deal. Blair says, "I thought it would be a big issue, but not this big. They want to know how it's going to affect our culture. They use the words 'culture' and 'sovereignty.' Is it going to make us a bunch of Americans?" Blair is a Socred, though he works for the PCs in federal politics. He says big government is not the answer. "You see what happens in the nations of Africa. Zimbabwe is one. Zambia is another." I've heard this theory lately, and I keep wondering where it comes from. Zimbabwe is sometimes in the news. But Zambia?

I meet Garry at the A&W. He's got the day off, but agrees to take me over to the mill. As Gus Halliday noted, it's what this resource-based community is about. We tour the plant, which is getting ready for one of its periodic maintenance shutdowns, and talk to people about politics. There's politics too — in that vaguer, larger sense — just in the way Garry shows me around. He has a sense for it.

We start in maintenance, where Garry's a shift millwright. There's his locker, with his tools. He points at shiny red mobile toolboxes parked all around. Quality of work life, he says. Before QWL came in, workers were always demanding some decent toolboxes. Then, with QWL, they got them.

Ron Pauwels, a maintenance worker like Garry, says, "It's a good place to work, I figure, because you're relatively on your own, and you can hear yourself think." Ron is a slim, self-effacing man with a moustache. Garry tells him why I'm here and he says, "I know I should do more to inform myself. I'm ignorant, and I shouldn't be."

"This free trade," he goes on, "isn't it like when we play the American high school teams in football?" He's the coach of a high school team that won the provincial championship in '85 and '86. "When we play American teams," he says, "it's so different, the attitude. And we play American rules, eh?" In B.C. high school football, he explains, they use U.S. rules. "We go down there and our kids are awed," says Ron. "They got the national turf field with the lights, they got weight rooms. They're huge. We played one team in Bellingham, in Washington state. Their quarterback was 6' 3" and 205 lbs. Their running back. They'd just go click-click click. They'd have a wide receiver who was down the field throwing blocks. We'd be lucky if our wide receiver could just catch the ball. And they'd do anything to win. Winning was the only thing for them. Our guys would just want to be respectable. If they lost by only three touchdowns, they'd feel pretty good."

Mel Stearns is a chunky worker wearing safety glasses. "I feel like I'm being brainwashed," he says. For instance, "There's toxic wastes all around us. But they're building bigger cars again, because the price of gas went down." It makes no sense, he says, yet the press report the return of big cars and omit the insanity of it. Or there's "that Micmac Indian down in Nova Scotia" — Donald Marshall, who was tucked away for life for a murder he didn't commit. Mel figures we're not getting the full story there either. He's a man who makes his way through the news by indirection. What they don't tell you is the most important part. He's also fascinated with Colin Thatcher, the Saskatchewan politician who was convicted of murdering his wife. Mel says he read Thatcher's book and was impressed with how everything went first class when you got elected: the scotch, the cars, the hotels. It explained to him what happens to politicians, even the ones you thought were trustworthy.

The mill is vast, indoor and out. Garry borrows a pickup to drive us around. We go to the new chip dumper. It tilts a double trailer truck, cab and all, straight up vertically so that the wood chips in it slide straight down into a pit. There's even a sort of shaker that shakes the truck to make sure all the chips dribble out — even the ones frozen inside during the winter. It's like a ride on the midway: you can't believe it's going to go all the way up. On the highway, you couldn't picture it on its end, with yellow metal "straps" to keep it from flipping over on its back. "We lost a couple of trucks," says Garry. Out here he suddenly says "we," identifying with the work, not the management.

The dumper is designed so trucks don't have to back up; they drive off and the next truck moves onto the lifts. The old dumpers took thirty minutes per truck, he says, now it's five. He points to a truck. One trucker used to have a contract for hauling all the chips from the sawmills, but Weyerhaeuser put out a tender and a different firm got part of the chips contract. They agreed to work for $5.00 an hour less, so the original trucker had to start taking less. Now Garry's getting calls from some of the drivers in the new firm who have complaints about their union. They're asking if the PPWC will take over. It would be difficult, says Garry, because the two unions share a building in Vancouver. "This is more of the virtues of competition," he adds. He doesn't knock it, he just points out it's not always good for the workers, even if it's inevitable for the companies. The barrier starts to lower behind another double trailer while the loudspeaker blares a tune in warning. The hydraulic rams begin to lift.

A lot of chips used to come by rail, he says. That stopped about a year ago. We drive by the rail unloading spot, which already looks like an ancient technology site waiting for the archaeologists, like Nabatea and its irrigation system in the Negev. We pass under a huge elevated pipe that runs from the mill up the mountainside. It's the smokestack and it spews from higher up so the stuff doesn't get caught in the frequent inversions here in the valley and suffocate the people of Kamloops. We go by mountains of hog fuel — sawdust and bark — from the same mills as the chips. This fuel is burned in the first of two boilers, the power boiler, to make steam. A chemical compound called the "liquor," which is full of acid, is used to cook the chips; then a residue from it called black liquor — a by-product of the original pulp-cooking process — is used to fuel the second, or recovery, boiler. "Very cost-effective," says Garry. "You can see how it's easy to make money here." We pass dozens of black tank cars full of chemicals and drive toward a series of effluent ponds that are steaming like hell, and I mean hell. They stink like hell too. These ponds process the millions of gallons of water used in the plant, which comes from the Thompson River over there and is eventually flushed back out into it. They're meant to clarify and purify the water, but by the time that water goes back, says Garry, "it's still pretty black," though you don't see it because the pipes that carry it go out to the middle of the river. We continue past mountains of sludge, then a huge warehouse for storing pulp bales when the market is down, and back to where we started. We park and re-enter the mill.

There's steam and smell in here too. Garry says, "No you don't get used to it, or if you do, that's bad too." The steam rises from the floor and from the pipes snaking up many storeys. Black ooze streams across the floor and down grates and sewers. We ride the elevator with men in monkey suits. They look determined and smile a lot, like heroes of the industrial age.

There's an electronic hum in the spacious, computerized control room for the bleaching machines. Steve, who works in here, says this election is "kind of weird. Mulroney isn't doing anything. It's a non-run for office." Why does he think people accept it? "They're afraid of the socialist hordes. They've been brainwashed."

We move on to the drying machines, another huge complex. There was too much steam here yesterday, so Garry replaced a couple of belts on the roof fans that draw it out, but it's still bad. The guys on the catwalks are complaining — they can only stay a few minutes at a time. We go into the control room for this section, really just a booth, with no hum, and talk to Ed, who's kind of conservative and very Christian, according to Garry. On the election, Ed says, "I'm not really into it that much, eh? Obviously there's the free trade thing, but I can't say I understand it 100 percent."

At the end of the process, the pulp is cut and wired in bales. "That's worth about $800 a ton," says Garry, patting a bale. "They make about 1200 tons a day. It doesn't take long to figure out how much money they're making." Like most production workers, he knows about exploitation and extraction of surplus value, simply by calculating how much he and his co-workers receive and subtracting that from what the company charges, figuring in other costs as well. You don't have to read the first volume of Marx's *Capital*.

We return to maintenance and meet Ervin Case, an older worker. He grew up in Kamloops, lived on the Gulf islands for nine years, had a business or two, worked in a sawmill, in construction and logging, as a fish packer, as an engineer on a boat, and has been back here fifteen years in the mill. Why does he vote? He shrugs. "The lesser of the evils," he says. "To try and keep it from getting completely out of control." It — a pretty broad reference, though maybe he just means the political system. He mentions some ads placed by the National Citizens' Coalition attacking Broadbent. Ron Pauwels said the kids on the football team talk about them too. The NCC's funding is somewhat murky, but it's run by a board of right-wing businessmen. Ervin thinks it's unfair. Just because these guys have money, they get to crap over anyone who challenges them. "If Ed's scary," says Ervin, "what about the rest?" Like others here, he's often bothered by the press and media, but he's not at their mercy. He reads and watches actively. People like him keep using the term "brainwashed," but when you sense you're being brainwashed, you're already on the way to beating it off.

"Oh, I pay attention," he says. "See that debate last night?" He means the one on "The Journal." "I didn't miss a word. What makes it so hard is one says one thing and one says the complete opposite. You pick the one that has the most intensity." Intensity? Others would say credibility, but Ervin puts it in terms of the gut commitment he senses.

Why did he watch? "I was looking for information. I've read quite a lot. I know the trade deal is a complex agreement. But surely to Christ, a spade is a spade. I'm definitely leaning one way, but I'd still like to know the true facts. And where do you get them? Who's nonpolitical enough to tell you? Like that woman judge who analysed it. Right away they say she's out to lunch because she doesn't agree with their side."

He already has an opinion, but he feels he has the right to know as much as possible regardless of his position. It's as though he feels cheated by having to make up his mind without a full and exhaustive discussion. He wants to participate *more* — he's a citizen, isn't he?

"I feel the whole thing is big business and we're being

manoeuvred just like every other part of our life. The whole thing is orchestrated." He *feels* this, but feelings are unreliable. They don't give you firm conviction. He wants to *know* more. Did he always think this way? He nods and says, "For a long time." Is it frustrating? He nods again. There is some pain in this subject for him. "Right. What else can you do? You pick your leading citizens to be candidates and then you find out they're thieves." So why not stop watching, hoping, participating and voting? We have arrived at the point at which cynicism lurks and beckons. Why don't people like Ervin withdraw, step out back and work on the car or the boat or feed the horses? He shrugs. His answers come slower. He becomes *zoon politikon*. "It's part of life," he says. "It's all part of the picture while you're here, I guess."

In the evening, I sit in Riis's office and watch the World Series game with Ben Bobrowich, the guy in charge of lawn signs. Another campaign worker, a cheery woman, says, "In the old days we used to work to midnight, then drink beer and eat pizza, then we came back at eight in the morning to work. Now it's all ruined. Everyone goes home to bed at eight-thirty. It's those bloody computers." She points upstairs. "They ruined us."

Riis comes in. He looks out of place with his blow-dried hair and his suit. Seeing him with his campaign workers — there's something ridiculous about the whole election process, making people like Ben centre their politics on one person and on getting others to vote for him. It turns the realm of politics into star making, and in a country like Canada, where we lack celebrities, politicians easily become the biggest stars. They are often the best-known faces in their communities. Nelson Riis is on national television each day the House is in session.

Everyone goes to a bar. I ask Riis how he feels about his party avoiding the main issue of the election. He scowls and says it's really dumb, it's like Broadbent's press conference after the election call, when he didn't even mention the deal. Riis says that made the NDP look like they were never serious about their opposition. "Hold on," I say, "You're the party House leader, you have a say in these things." "Are you kidding?" he says. "I hear about it an hour before it happens, then I say, 'This doesn't make sense.' As far as I can see, our campaign is being run by five or six hacks in Ottawa." He sounds mildly furious, which is the way a controlled person like him would get mad. "I made speeches in the House. Day after day I proposed amendments to stall the bill. You wouldn't believe all the shenanigans I went through. Then the election is called and he doesn't even mention it?"

A stout fellow comes over. He looks like a worker, as most people in Kamloops do, and are. He starts off very diffident. "Are you Nelson? I work on the railroad. I'm management, eh?" He runs a work crew. "Can you explain to me if this free trade means the CN is going to be privatized like Air Canada, the same as Air Canada or more than Air Canada?" Riis takes a pause, not a wily pause to figure out what the guy wants to hear, but to connect what he knows to the question.

Over comes someone else. He works on a highway repair crew. They're being privatized to death by the Vander Zalm government. He just came out of a union meeting here in the hotel, where the leader of the provincial government employees' union gave them more bad news. He calls himself "an ordinary working joe," and wonders if Nelson can explain to him about "this free trade." Nelson says it means American companies can come up here and bid on all government contracts like highway maintenance, and bring their own employees to do the work, and it seems to him that any Canadian working person who votes for this deal has got to be crazy. The working joe's buddy joins us. Amanda from the office has also arrived. Everybody is buying rounds for everybody else. Riis doesn't talk much. He listens, as smart politicians do. The railroad guy is getting loaded and has lost his diffidence.

The working joe, who seemed very self-deprecating,

starts talking about highway privatization as he sees it. The contract the provincial government recently signed with a private company is nine feet high and covers every possible thing. If there's so many centimetres of snow, you plough now, no matter what time of night it is, but if there's so much less, you wait for the morning. You go over the road a specified number of times. "It always seemed pretty simple to me," he says. "If it's covered, you clear it." But not anymore. They aren't going to call out people for overtime pay at three in the morning unless they absolutely have to, not when they're trying to make as much profit as they can. "And for sure," he says, concluding his discourse with a flourish, "you'll get packed snow on those roads." He's suddenly articulate, fluent, funny and informative. Riis takes the odd note. By now another seven or eight people from the next table join us. They've come from the union meeting. Riis stands there listening and asking, and saying how he sees it — behaving, you could say, as if he really is their elected representative.

Wednesday, October 19

Whitehorse. I don't know much about politics in the Yukon. Leslie McCullough, whose name someone gave me, turns out to be executive assistant (EA) to leader of the Yukon Territorial Government Tony Penikett. She's small and lively and has what looks like a diamond in her nose. She's pregnant with her first child and when I called her from Kamloops yesterday with no warning, she was at home resting and reading a book about Spadina Avenue in Toronto, to which I had written the introduction. This sort of thing happens to her. Serendipity.

She understands the problems of politics as star making from her own experience. "People aren't interested in you," she says. "They want to hear the star. It's very similar to the situation of women in marriages often, who get their status from the proximity of their man." Last night

Broadbent was in Whitehorse, the only leader to appear here during the campaign. He made the grand entry and Leslie says people loved it. "It means so much to them," she says. "They shake his hand and are thrilled."

We talk about the way elections can exclude people from politics more than they include them. She says the Yukon is "a situation that excludes participation by Indians, for example. Politics here tends to be the epitome of the middle class and the redneck working class. There have been conscious efforts by women to move into the political process, but Indian people have their own agenda." I learn later that they have developed what amounts to a parallel political system.

Jessica Carr, on the other hand, a goofy young easterner who is EA for a minister, does participate. That's one reason she came here. "Just because we're far away doesn't mean we don't have influence," she says. "Sometimes that's how we get influence. When Audrey [McLaughlin, the MP for the Yukon] had a meeting last year about defence policy, only seven people came, but what we said ended up in the NDP policy on defence." In a couple of years, Jessica says, she intends to run for city council. She's already on the transit commission. Every year they advertise for volunteers. She applied, and was chosen. There are only 30,000 people up here, about 15,000 in Whitehorse. The Indians and the poor tend to exclude themselves, as Leslie says. But if you want to get involved, this huge little place could be like Periclean Athens.

Tonight "The National" has anchorman Peter Mansbridge outdoors in a trench coat looking like Joel McCrea in *Foreign Correspondent*. It's a shocking sight. What has blasted him from behind his newsdesk into the Ottawa night? They've uncovered a Liberal plot to dump John Turner right in the middle of the campaign! The story goes on a long time, but it's pretty vaguely worded. There's a quick shot of the smoking memo from Liberal party brass, which in the aftermath turns out to be a prop they mocked up — maybe they got it from *Streetlegal,* CBC's drama series. The finale to the story is that the plot was scotched and the attempt to ditch Turner never actually happened.

Thursday, October 20

On "Canada AM"'s political panel this morning, Gerry Caplan, Michael Kirby and Hugh Segal pass judgement on the Turner story. They're jocular, as always. It's such a game, this politics.

Gord Duncan is president of the Whitehorse Chamber of Commerce and runs a small business, Total North Communications. I walk past a huge dish antenna into his place and suddenly feel at home: I am surrounded by Macintosh computers and by-products. Duncan is in his early thirties, with rugged good looks and a hesitant aw-shucks way. He grew up here, went to the University of British Columbia, graduated in commerce in '79, sent some letters out and got an interview with a big company. The recruiter asked if his name, Gordon Andrew Duncan, was Scottish. "No," said Gord, with the laconic humour of the North, "it's Polish." "He didn't get it," says Gord. "It went from bad to worse. I knew I didn't belong down there." He came home. He figured he could always work on road survey crews. "I had a chip on my shoulder from being from the North. I didn't need these guys."

He worked for the tourist association in Dawson City, which ran the only legalized gambling operation in Canada, then joined and eventually purchased Total North. It's "a bit of a skunkworks" — a term from a business bestseller, he explains. It means an operation a little off to the side. In Vancouver or Toronto, he'd be in either computers or telephone systems, but here he can do it all.

How does he describe his politics? "Changing, I guess. Since you called, I been thinking about it. I was in the PCs, I did my time, got a look at it, worked toward certain objectives. I could have kept on, but I wasn't a political junkie." He's no longer a party member.

"I thought," says Duncan, "the Canadian people have lost the stature and respect of politics. It's polls and Mulroney running a machine, Turner trying to keep the wheels on and Broadbent in a position of strength. But the average guy on the street has been removed from politics. Joe Canada doesn't talk there." How does he describe Joe Canada? "Up here it's a matter of individualism," he says, precise as a dictionary, "tempered to a degree by a necessary sense of community that comes from living in a more hostile environment than the U.S."

In the end, he chose business over politics for, you might say, existential reasons. "In business you're faced with some pretty real decisions. The political junkie isn't really up against the wall." I think of the "Canada AM" panel. "In business, you can't just shove off and say you're going to join the Rhinos. You gotta work your way out of the situation in business. You gotta dig pretty deep. It's not so true in the big companies, but I talked to an independent Apple dealer in Vancouver. It was after we tried expanding to Fort St. John and got beat up in the marketplace there and had to get out. After, I was at one of those Apple deals and this guy said, 'I felt for you. We tried to expand into Burnaby and couldn't make it happen thirty miles away. But I knew you had to try it.' He didn't say: Too bad you can't drive a Mercedes now. It was: You went through this thing. It's not for money. It's, Who creates wealth? Not banks. There's not a lot of passion there. You don't feel warm and comfortable going into a bank. They're the ultimate numbers game."

How does he feel about politics now? "Any young person has ideals and vision," he says. "But political stripe doesn't mean much to me anymore. We can't abdicate problems to government. Business has to take responsibility." He talks about business as if it's an alternate form of public service. "The Canadian Chamber of Commerce really surprised me when I went to their convention. Those guys were dealing from the heart in a lot of things. It

wasn't just cold and hard. They spoke el-o-quently." I ask
if there's a conflict between the self-interest of a businessman and the altruism of public service. "Whew," he says,
"that's tough. That's politics in itself. But you don't buy
anything when you give third prize for the C-event at the
Burwash bonspiel. You're not going to sell many Macin-
toshes. You just plug into what the community wants and
needs. Can you think of an interest group that puts more
back into the country than business?"

Is business enough for him then? Not quite. "Take the
last four years. As a businessman, I'm pretty happy. The
federal government did a good job of managing the economy." The rub is, he's more than a businessman, he's a
citizen too. "In the absence of any other vision, I'd vote
for them again. But there's no real vision that says, I'm
gonna combine good management with some vision."
That's what he's looking for, a larger vision of society. He
thinks that maybe with free trade, the government is
reaching toward one, even if they themselves claim it's
merely an economic agreement. "As the Chamber of
Commerce, we're pretty interested and we've been trying
for a long time to find out about it. The Alaskans could
give a shit! We brought three of them over to talk about
free trade and we got the Gettysburg Address. They
weren't plugged in." So he keeps searching, and the more
he searches, the more he arrives at surprising conclusions.
"Take Tony Penikett," he says, about the man who heads
the NDP government of the Yukon. "The biggest thing I
have trouble with is Tony Penikett isn't a bad guy . . . I
sometimes think I'm in the wrong racket," Duncan muses,
"because I'm fairly philosophical."

Charlie and Betty Taylor have been married fifty-two
years. They met in Mayo and have been up here all their
lives. Charlie's family owned Whitehorse's major department store, they are old Yukoners, members of the white
ruling class that used to be. They live in a modest house
behind a picket fence, a literal stone's throw from the
wide rushing Yukon River. Outside is a sign for Charlie

Friday, PC, who's running against sitting MP Audrey McLaughlin of the NDP. On their piano are music books containing 100 Irish Ballads and Favourite Hymns. This is one of those couples who don't interrupt each other, they pick up on each other's thoughts and finish them. It's like a long conversation with a single person. They talk about politics as it's always supposed to have been.

"Unfortunately, we've been in politics for fifty-five years," says Charlie playfully.

"I wouldn't say that," says Betty. "It's been fun. I left Dawson when I was five and I was always involved with George Black."

"Our MP for years," says Charlie, "and Speaker of the House sometime in the 1920s."

"1930s, I'd say," says Betty.

"George got sick and Martha moved in for him," says Charlie.

"And she didn't have to say, Vote for me because I'm a woman," adds Betty.

"She ran against two men," Charlie says, "and there was none of this business of, I'm a woman, pity me. Then George got well again and ran. We were Erik Nielsen's first delegates." (Tory Erik Nielsen was the Yukon's MP from 1957 to 1987.)

"We were there the night he was nominated," says Betty.

For these people there is no alienation from our political system of elections and no substitutes for politics either — like business, or work with the disadvantaged. For them politics is politics. I ask what they did all those years and George makes a doorknocking gesture.

"Stuffed envelopes," says Betty.

"Our parents were Black people," says Charlie, and it takes a moment to get his meaning. "I was born in Whitehorse. I was the manager of our store in Mayo. My father served the North for seventy-five years" — a lovely and sincere phrase. The North probably served Charlie's father well too. "They came up, him and his partner, during the Gold Rush. We pioneers, we got the resources out." I

ask if his father was also active in politics. He brushes at
me with his hand. "Don't ask silly questions. He was a true
supporter of Black. We've got some socialists here now.
But our economy is based on what Erik left on our behalf."

I ask about the differences between the two parties, the
Liberals and the Tories, in the days before there was an
NDP, and why the Taylors were Tories instead of Liberals. "I asked my father around 1918," says Charlie. "He
thought for awhile. 'Well,' he says, 'Reciprocity. The Liberals want to open up the markets between the two
countries. And the Conservatives feel people building the
industries here should be protected. We Tories are a pro-
tectionist group.' So I believed this all my life, and now it's
reversed."

"I guess I'm just a conservative person," says Betty.
"Pretty old-fashioned. We just had the Reform party fellow at the door. He was pushing. I said 'We're
committed.' "

"The Conservatives are builders," says Charlie. "The
others reap."

"You can't say that," says Betty. "The people we sit beside in church are Liberals."

"Through the years the Conservatives have turned very
socialistic," says Charlie. "All these social endeavours. By
the way, I spent three years — '58 to '61 — in the legislative assembly. It was nonpartisan. Parties didn't come into
it till ten years later." I ask whether he thought of running
after the party system came in. "I was a businessman in
the North for forty-five years," he says, proving he can
handle a hard time, "but I'd be scared to go into party politics, because they crucify people." I ask how they feel
about the recent NDP victories. "It was a surprise," he
says. "You get a little cocky."

"They were just so nonchalant," adds Betty, about their
own party.

They've seen enormous changes from the stable world
of privilege into which they were born and which survived

intact until recently. I wonder how they feel about the rise
of native voices in politics.

"I was instrumental in getting them the vote
territorially," says Charlie. They talk about the past social
role of halfbreeds, about whites who "lived out in the
boondocks and married Indian princesses," who were the
"best of the stock," says Betty. It wasn't just a matter of
"picking up a squaw," she explains. Current sensitivities
and taboos about racism must be a little hard for them to
adjust to.

"We should start a group called Non-Status White Natives," says Charlie.

"My grandfather was Scottish and his wife was Irish,"
says Betty, "but I'm all Canadian. I think everyone should
be Canadian. I've always worked on election day. We used
to know everybody. I used to enumerate, but it got nerve
wracking. I was scared stiff that somebody would turn up
at the polls without a vote."

"But the devil may care now," says Charlie.

"I think the fun of politics is being committed," says
Betty. "Knowing who you want and why." They recall
things as being deeply democratic back in the age of Erik.
They battled about issues, fought things out, came to solutions, and Erik never took a position or manoeuvred
behind the scenes. Those were the days. I ask how they
feel about the free trade deal.

"We're Conservatives," says Charlie, "let's put it that
way."

"In England," says Betty, "they don't care about us anymore. I love the Queen, but we can't count on them
anymore." They've even accepted the Meech Lake accord,
unpopular here because it means the Yukon may never
become a province. The grip of these party loyalties is
powerful; sometimes it's barely within the realm of reason.

I walk a few blocks — you can't go much farther in Whitehorse — and suddenly I am looking at the cabin of Sam
McGee (from Tennessee, where the cotton blooms and

blows). I never knew there was a real McGee, the model for Robert Service's "The Cremation of Sam McGee." I recall Eric Peterson's version for anti-free trade rallies, explaining that you make deals with Americans and you end up carrying them on your back for a frozen eternity.

I cross the street and find Gerald Isaac in a building that houses the Land Claims Secretariat of the Yukon government. Gerald is a consultant and a former activist in native politics himself. He says the land claims issue has affected "the degree to which people see themselves getting involved in decisions affecting their very lives and communities." I haven't heard a better definition of politics. He says a form of political activity has emerged in native communities that is almost wholly outside the standard frame of electoral politics.

"There is an outcry from the native communities that governments don't represent their own demands from a community perspective," he says. He is hellishly articulate, in an unrhetorical way. "The communities are bombarded by expertise and consultants working for governments federal and territorial, and often government doesn't know who to deal with in the twelve communities in the territory because there's overlapping jurisdictions. Some of which come from the federal Indian Act." That's the starting point: a problem created by existing ways of doing politics and making decisions.

"Many Indians see the bands as a way of getting some things for themselves and establishing municipal negotiations affecting their communities through structures and tax base, etc. But you also see villages and communities that are unorganized that have election procedures and a parallel local governing authority that protects Indians. There are two worlds really, the community level and the Yukon Territorial Government, the YTG. So there are two big players up here with jurisdictions affecting each other: the native communities and the YTG."

"I'm non-partesian myself," he says, deconstructing a word that deserves it. "I've been involved for thirteen years in Yukon Indians' claims. There's been a political growing up by people wanting to have more influence on their lives because they've been silent." I ask if he's talking just about native communities and he says, actually he's talking about Indian *and* non-native communities. There's a strong desire to work as a whole community in places like Mayo, where the land claims process has unleashed a new political dynamic in both populations.

"In our dealings with all the groups in the Territories, we have to justify to the citizens what we do, to both aboriginal and non-aboriginal interests — for example, fish and game associations, outfitters, chamber of commerce, chamber of mines." Does the white population resent all the effort on behalf of natives? "Many people in the street don't know there's a legal obligation on the government of Canada to negotiate these claims, coming from the 1763 Royal Proclamation, etc.," he explains. But they don't really seem to mind. "People like to feel part of something, they want to feel they have a right to express themselves, be heard and represented at whatever levels. I'm talking about everybody up here. They want to belong, they need to be needed, they want to have a voice in things that affect them and their communities. This is recent, this sense of involvement," he says. "It's due to the claims process. It's opened a lot of eyes. It's an educating process."

"People see the buildings over there," he goes on, nodding toward the new government complex, "but they see that as inadequate. They have their MLA, but they're out of touch." I ask how he knows that. "They say, We're out of touch," he says, "and every time you come here with your briefcases and your line of penguins behind you and you go away and we never see you. They want more direct involvement. In some communities they see a whole barge of people bombard them seeking information and they get sick and tired and run away into the woods. They want involvement but in the people whirl, they're 'meetinged to death.' The process of so much meeting doesn't satisfy the need. The need is expressed by government by formation of endless committees and boards connected to

the parent governments. Sometimes it works and sometimes it doesn't." So other forms of political involvement
are created, to fill the need.

"The communities up here are so small, the population
base is around 30,000 in an area of 186,000 square miles.
Whitehorse is 15,000. Outlying communities are from 250
to 500. About a third of the population is native. Demographics are different. Old Crow is predominantly native,
along with two others. The balance are fifty-fifty, except
Whitehorse, which is about one-third native. More and
more you hear an outcry from the communities that
they're bombarded so much by arms of government and
legs of government. Not another government agency.
Open your goddamn ears to us — we have things to say."

As a result, he says, "you could have a series of twelve or
thirteen self-governments. The Indian bands could see
self-government very differently from how the non-native
communities would. A different approach, for example,
to jurisdictions or to structural or institutional matters, or
to questions of membership and citizenship." This is a
complicated and rich mix he is describing and annotating,
a sort of laboratory of political and democratic possibili-
ties well outside the standard version.

"It sure is complicated," says Gerald. "People in the
North are very very very very strongminded about government decisions affecting their lives. They want to see
more responsible government here in the Territories," he
adds, using one of the murkiest terms in Canadian constitutional history. I think it's the first time I've ever heard
anyone say "responsible government" in a way that made
sense to me. "People want to become more involved in decision making," he says, "and to some extent, it's
happening. It varies from level to level, but this government —" he means the current NDP administration — "is
trying to make it happen."

It feels a little like ancient Greece, with its city states.
There are twelve communities in the Yukon. "Every community is different in terms of layout, make-up,
demographics, philosophical views and approaches to life

and politics," says Gerald. So the situation is complex. But it is graspable and therefore manageable. You can know all the specifics, and you can take them into account in planning.

What has been his own role in the development of the extraordinary politics he's describing? "I've been involved for some time," he says. He was born and raised in Dawson City as a traditional hereditary chief for the Han people; his grandfather was chief. "I went to school at Vancouver City College. I'd gone down to Vancouver in '70 and stayed down six years." His first taste of the power of the claims issue happened there in Vancouver, in 1973. He ran into some Indians from Fort McPherson in the Northwest Territories, who had come for the Berger inquiry on the Mackenzie Valley pipeline. "I had some discussions in my own dialect with them and we did a song and dance right on the street. Granville Street. The elder with them was Jim Edwards. He was eighty-seven years old, a translator for the Berger inquiry. There's some history between Fort McPherson and Dawson City: transportation by dog team, traditionally they used to trade and trap during the Christmas and Easter periods, feasting and potlatching, exchanging gifts. There was no drinking. I remember it when I was three or four years old. They became known as the Dawson Boys, a group of seven who frequented those exchanges. He knew some of them, he'd learned and understood our language, and he knew Chief Isaac, my grandfather. He was floored. 'Where the hell did you come from in the middle of nowhere, downtown Vancouver?' I said I was trying to become educated. And they said, 'Gerry, get your ass back with your people.'

"I came back in 1976 and became directly involved in the claims. I worked in mapping and research for six months and then I became involved politically. I represented three thousand status Indians and worked on unifying the status and non-status Indians into one body: the Council for Yukon Indians. There were originally two organizations: the Yukon Native Brotherhood, including all status Indians under the Indian Act, calling for self-determination and political rights; and a non-status association representing Indians not afforded membership under the Indian Act. They unified in '79 and formed the Council for Yukon Indians, to negotiate aboriginal claims. I was involved in that, and then in the claims process from the perspective of maps and claims and dreams," he says, alluding to a fine book by Hugh Brodie called *Maps and Dreams.*

But he had to make a living. "There were periods of breakdown in the negotiating process, layoffs," so he got out temporarily. "As a matter of survival, I left the world of Indian politics and went to the mining industry, gold mining. I still have certain holdings in that industry." He's back into Indian politics now as an adviser, not a direct participant.

It's an exciting view of things, a great story. "Because of the political dynamics, the Indian communities themselves have chosen to become more involved in the formal political process," he says. "That's never happened before." I want to find out more, and whether any of this is romanticized, or if this place really is a kind of hothouse for extra-electoral politics combining in strange and luxuriant forms with the familiar electoral varieties.

I meet Leslie McCullough back at the hotel and ask about the political renewal and innovation going on up here. She describes a government program called Yukon 2000, "a real effort to bring decision making to the people." It was carried out by the NDP after they were elected and before they had formulated legislation. They went everywhere in the territory and got people talking about the future, bringing different elements of the population together to see how much they had in common. They stimulated discussion on the role of women, for instance, and especially the role of Indian women. "You could see," says Leslie, "that in Indian politics, men are interested in land, money and economic development. Women are worried about alcoholism, breakdown of the family, violence. In social and community issues — as are the elders. It's a snapshot of how interests in the society break down all the time."

What is most striking here, it turns out, is not the gorgeous landscape: the clear river flowing swiftly, the astounding night sky. It's politics. The mere scale of it: how it humanizes even our system of representative government. "People know the figures," someone said to me today in a healthy little restaurant called the Nopop, as in No Pop Served Here. "Your TV image doesn't matter as much because people know you in person. And anyway there is no local television. People relate to you as a person, not a public figure. It's very informal." That's the lesson of this place — the importance of scale, along with the historical element, as Gerry Isaac puts it.

At night I attend a nomination meeting of the NDP for the territorial district of Potter Creek. They meet in the gym of an elementary school. The Brownies finish up fifteen minutes early to accommodate. ("Will someone take down the fairies sign?") In the hall, on the "Family Meetings" board, the categories listed are: Single Mom, Single Dad, Mom and Stepdad, Dad and Stepmom, Granma, Mum and Dad, Parents and Guardians. No Grandad, though people can't explain why. Who's the round fellow wandering about before the meeting begins? He looks familiar and I reckon he's a candidate for the nomination, but it's Tony Penikett, head of the government. He describes many things here which have not been reported in the national press, and should be. That five of nine members in the government caucus are aboriginal. "Ten years ago, when we elected our first member, it would have been impossible. Now it's not even worth comment." That at thirty-six he is the oldest member of their caucus. That they have implemented a social democratic agenda and have the healthiest economic growth rate in the country. He introduces his justice minister, who's also attending. They enthuse about the Broadbent rally two

nights ago. Penikett was an assistant to Broadbent in
Ottawa eleven years ago.

Thirty or forty people are present. They listen to the
nominating speeches, then to the candidates. Both seem
pretty yuppie, as do most of the party members in atten-
dance. (Yukon yuppies, I've been told, drive a Tercel and
have a kayak on the roofrack at all times.) There are one
or two Indians. The candidate who's favoured is a small
businessman and jogger.

It feels right that this is happening in a school gym, because it recalls student council. It's also fairly vacuous.
Someone asks the candidates if they're socialists and what
they mean by socialism. "I'm a socialist, because I believe
in people," says the younger candidate, the firebrand.
"Socrates and Voltaire wrestled with the definition of socialism," says the jogging small businessman. "Socialism is
a fundamental concern with your fellow man." Max, who
manages Audrey McLaughlin's campaign and who drove
me here, has to leave. I ask about a ride back. He says he'll
ask Tony, who's chairing the meeting. A weathered Indian woman is asking a question. Max says Tony will drive
me if I'm willing to risk my life in his Volvo.

Then comes the ritual of marking and casting a ballot.
People look childlike as they do it — it's like a regression
to school days. They perform the act with such care, a
combination of stern democratic responsibility and mysti-
cal rite.

Tony Penikett wasn't kidding. This isn't some yuppie
Volvo, it's old and battered. It's not locked, we just climb
in, and skid around the slippery roads during the long,
relaxed evening that follows. We stop at his house, which
is suburban and also unlocked; he wants to check on his
kids, who might still be alone, but his wife has returned
from wherever she'd gone on business that day. She's native, which may shed some light on this government. The
kids want help with their math. As we drive off, he talks
about the political strategy they have developed: build an
alliance between Yukon natives and Yukon workers. It
worked, he says, and it should have been obvious all along

that it would. A lot of the ideas and enthusiasm for the
NDP agenda may come from forces like feminists and environmentalists, but the base on which electoral success
has been built is that worker-native coalition. He says they
decided to concentrate on economic programs during
their first term; their only social policy was a human rights
law which provoked heavy racist and anti-gay response
from the Opposition. They stuck to it, and in the end Penikett thinks even many Tory supporters were
embarrassed by their party. We stop at the spanking new
Yukon College — it opened just weeks ago — and he
shows it off like a proud parent, talking about his fights
with technocrats and architects and bureaucrats in order
to have everything about it, down to the use of local materials, true to this place.

Back at the hotel bar, the evening winds down. Penikett
was a writer once, along with his friends Michael Ondaatje
and Martin Kinch. They were at the University of Western Ontario together. He sold some scripts to the BBC
and had shitty experiences dealing with the CBC. What
else is new? We drink Scotch and Irish, and talk writing. I
tell him about the poet revolutionaries who became the
government of Mozambique after their war of liberation,
how I went to their country to ask about the dilemmas of
art and action, but they were all too busy dealing with national economic and military crises to take time to discuss
the tortuous relations between literature and politics. I
quote the words of Hannah Arendt I have been brooding
about. "Seeking shelter from action's calamities in an activity where one man, isolated from all others, remains
master of his doings from beginning to end . . . ." It's a
pleasant moment. I'd call Penikett a hail-fellow-well-met,
if I knew what that meant. Leslie tells me next day that he
had a good time too; nobody around here thinks of him
as a writer or talks to him about it, but it's how he still likes
to see himself.

Friday, October 21

It's breakfast time, and completely dark. I come down-stairs and meet Rosemary Seaman, a civil servant here. "When you work for the government," she says, "there are only two incentives. The paycheque and job satisfaction. At least in private industry you get a wee bonus at Christmas, and you're perhaps given the opportunity, because of the need to balance the balance sheet, of a real sense of promotion. There's almost no real sense of promotion in public service."

Her father was an entrepreneur in the U.K. She came to Canada when she was young, planning to stay briefly, then head on to Australia and *real* adventure. But she married seven months later and ran a convenience store in the Peace River country with her husband. She's here now, separated and with a teenaged son, largely because of the beauty of the place. "Just driving into town in the morning, the scenery can make your heart stop." She says there are heavy drug and alcohol problems among kids, and parents too. She's given some thought to politics since I called.

"Alberta was really the place I decided politics was a nasty thing. I'd been naïve before, and thought politics was a bunch of good people trying to do good things for everyone. I didn't realize the kinds of tensions that party politics can create and how destructive they can be. What shocked me was watching Lougheed in action. When the Conservatives had their first chance at winning in years. I was fascinated by the people running — they knew nothing. If asked what they'd do, they'd say, I'll wait to be told. I couldn't deal with it. The day of the nomination in our riding, Lougheed came and people said, 'Look at whose hand he shakes, that's his choice, and watch how he treats the others. From doing that, you'll know.' Body language kind of stuff.

"The other thing is I had a friend who was a member in Alberta. We went to a wedding in Taber, and the feeling I got from him about Ottawa was how much Liberals and

Conservatives hated each other. When Jim Coutts lost in some Toronto riding, people in Alberta were literally jumping up and down with glee. In Alberta! I didn't realize how much hatred could be generated. I don't know what the issues were, but the hatred was real enough. It had become really personal. I find it hard to deal with, that people are operating from such unnatural places. I could really hate someone who did my children harm, but not because they sit on the opposite side of the House."

Coutts ran that time — it was 1981 — in my own riding, Spadina. The sitting Liberal was slipped upstairs to the Senate to make room for Coutts, who'd been working the riding for years. He was already assuming a Cabinet post was his and a run for leader when Trudeau retired. That's when the people of Spadina first elected Dan Heap and let the government know they wouldn't be taken for granted. Funny to hear, up here in Whitehorse, what those defeats meant to Tories in Alberta. It's a bizarre way to run a political system. Parties seem even more pointless and counterproductive to Rosemary than they always have to me.

She mentions the Yukon Hansard and the ugliness of some of the comments recorded there. She seems to mean things said during the debate about human rights legislation. Her despair is with electoral politics, which, like most people, she simply identifies as politics. "What is the responsibility of elected members to their constituents," she wants to know, "as opposed to their responsibility to their party?" I think about Charlie and Betty Taylor, twisting themselves into pretzels to accommodate the shifts made by their party. They say, We're Conservatives, the way they say, We're Christians.

"If you're not independently wealthy, you can't afford to run," says Rosemary, as a glimmer begins in the streets of Whitehorse, "unless you're part of a party. When I was younger, I thought it was something I might do later. Now I don't think I have what it takes. And there is so much to do on the sidelines." The sidelines is where the real people and real politics often are. Gerald Isaac was talking about the development of some terrific sideline activities up here.

Maggie T.'s Contemporary Hair Salon belongs to Margaret Tai, a funny, smart person, who says she has nothing to say about politics. "I'm probably a bad person to talk to. I've always found politics very boring. Probably if I got more involved I could do something." Like what? "I don't know! Maybe the pollution. Pollution bothers me. Write letters. But I have such a busy life, I don't feel guilty enough to do something. And I'm not living in a badly polluted area. Except for the wood smoke."

She always wanted to be a hairdresser. "But my Mom wouldn't let me because I was an A student. She told me, 'Only stupid girls do that.'" So Margaret became a stockbroker. That's what she was doing in 1982, she says, when the market crashed. She had come to Whitehorse a few years before. "Just got my licence. Lost $20,000 — everything I'd saved. It made me think, I'll never depend on anyone else to make money. Two months later I was back home in Ontario learning hair. I lived in Sarnia at my mother's, she looked after my son and I travelled to London 120 miles a day for eight months. All the other people at school were there just to escape high school. Somebody would come in, and they'd say, 'I'm not doing her hair,' and they'd go and hide, but I'd relish it. I won competitions for the school and the Ontario competition."

A year later she returned here and opened Maggie T.'s. "It was the first place in Whitehorse that did contemporary. People were walking out with purple spots. People were scared. Then I put ads in the paper that said, 'We do normal,' and they started coming." It's been a success. "When I started this place, I couldn't get a loan because there were too many salons. Within a year, I had seven people working for me."

She's had one direct experience with politics. It's connected to her salon. "My husband and I were fighting to get the zoning changed so we could put in more parking. And we wrote a letter to the council. They said, Next year.

We went a year later. They said no again. It's been in the paper, how they won't do anything. But it still hasn't happened. We all wanted the zoning changed. We knew it would raise our taxes. Nobody was against it. But they said this wasn't part of the downtown core. It would get overrun with cars." She was stymied, in other words, by the parking problem in downtown Whitehorse. "We've stopped going to city council. We won't expand. I wanted to have an aesthetic salon, and tanning, but now I don't. I'll slow down."

It's soured her on politics, but she wasn't keen to start with. "Politics! What kind of people do you find involved? I never enjoyed history in school. I couldn't stand it. I never even passed it. Or I got fifty. I'm geared more to math and science. I find politics really boring. Nothing exciting about it. Doesn't interest me." And she's a lively soul, with a high energy level, not hard to interest. If something bores her so, it must be pretty dull. What is it about our political system that puts her off?

"I don't know. We don't get many politicians in here getting their hair cut," she muses. "We have only two clients that are involved in politics. We're not stable enough, maybe. The politicians probably go to Cutters. I'm not saying anything against Marlene. It's stark in there. They're all very particular, businesslike, no joking around. We do men — one of the politicians in here is a man — and Leslie is the other one. I went when she was called to the bar and she has this outrageous orange raincoat. She's so light!" She's right about that, Leslie *is* light. "I'd bet 50 percent of them go to Cutters," Margaret goes on, "just because of the atmosphere. I can see politicians there. We have a real mix. Teachers, lawyers, doctors, lots of kids . . . ."

Maybe that's the problem. Her place is social and public in a way that contrasts with the narrowness of the political sphere proper. "When I opened this place," she says, "it was great. People came in and said they felt so comfortable and at home. Not stark — glass and brass. We cut hair outside in the summer. People eat outside the

restaurant next door. We have pig roasts and a real maria-
chi band." You sense a genuine civic zeal. This is her way
of making a contribution. She has created this place for
the community, though she would never picture it as a political act. "I'm thinking of starting a kids' section, with
special chairs, or a clothing store for kids." She's creative
— one of those people who probably can't go anywhere or
look at anything without imagining how it could be transformed for better use. If you could only enlist her energy
for social purposes, even more than she does through her
business,   into   areas   like   education,   or   the
environment . . . .

"I've thought about that," she says. "I'm quite concerned about the educational system. What's going to
happen to my son? I don't want him to go to high school
here, he won't be challenged." Her zest would be invalu-
able in the public arena. She's full of sympathetic
observations about what's wrong in the schools. "The
teachers get thirty-five kids thrown at them. We need an
arts centre too, but make it half the size they're planning
on and use the money to double the number of teachers."

I mention that Tony Penikett said something similar
about an arts centre last night — and she says he's the
other one who comes here to get his hair cut. I was wondering if he went to Cutters like the other politicians.
Politics suddenly seems as connected to the choice between Cutters and Maggie T.'s as it is to land claims,
Yukon 2000, human rights legislation and the new college. That's what politics needs: broadening, so that it
includes hairdressing salons with mariachis and doesn't
just make a place for someone like Margaret Tai; it requires and conscripts her.

She's a relaxed soul, at peace with her shambling body,
her fuzzy hair, hoop earrings, cigarette, her feet not quite
reaching the floor. "Tom," she calls to one of her employees, "do you have any clients who are politicians?" Tom —
white hair, tight pants — says, with a flick of his hips, "No-
ooo!"

"Tom has a really good rep," says Maggie. "Lots of clients won't come if he's away for a month. But lots of men won't come because he's gay. I had a girl working here with natural blonde hair dyed blue-black, somebody walked in and walked out." But they have accepted her over time, and she went halfway by saying to them, We do normal. It's a story of community, and the possibility of change.

Before I leave for the airport, I talk with Audrey McLaughlin, MP, at her re-election headquarters.

She says she understands the problem I'm dealing with. "I was involved in advocacy groups for years. Now when I canvass, people, especially women, say they don't know anything about politics. But they do know about politics, they just don't know they know. The definition of politics has been circumscribed. For women especially, politics is male. I say, Do you buy groceries? Do you have kids? What do you think about education? You are interested in the tax system, the drought in Saskatchewan, you know something about raising a family. But elections are a bad time for that kind of discussion — you're supposed to move ahead. My handlers don't like the way I linger to talk.

"The formal political process alienates people instead of engaging them. Politicians have been defined as male and the perceived expertise of politics is largely male. Politics is a specialty for men, mostly lawyers. Politics supposedly requires the interpretation of politicians. Politicians are good at getting power and poor at sharing it . . . ." She pauses and apologizes for sounding rhetorical, which is understandable. She's been campaigning at a rapid clip in this vast riding.

"As a woman," she continues, "you don't think you're going to be prime minister. I thought I'd make nurse. My father worked for a co-op; my mother was a writer and artist. I ran a mink ranch, raised my kids. If I lose, I'll be disappointed, but I'll go on. If you're heavily into power and have illusions about what power is, you have a lot to lose. Men often think about the power, keen young boys think about having that power, but women say they don't know if they could handle the responsibility."

All around the campaign office are huge posters of her gaunt, striking face, and her name in enormous letters. I ask if it ever bothers her to see her name on all those signs, and so many people running about, striving to get her face liked and her name checked on the ballot. She shrugs, apparently it doesn't bother her at all. This is the answer I get from all the candidates I put it to. I don't understand how it can become so normal for them — to have large numbers of your fellow citizens dedicated to a politics which reduces to the promotion of your surname and face. Not even a little embarrassment? Or just *claim* to feel a little embarrassment?

I haven't heard much talk about free trade these last few days in the Yukon, unlike my experience everywhere else I've been until now — and everywhere I will be in weeks to come. The remarkable democratic ferment occurring up here is happening for its own reasons: a government apparently willing to allow political discussion outside the conventional frames, and above all, the galvanizing effect of the land claims issue. In coming weeks, when signs of democratic ferment occur across much of the rest of the country, it will be almost precisely to the extent that the debate over free trade grows more and more out of control.

Week Four

Saturday, October 22

Edmonton. There may be more people in this square block of hotels and office buildings than in the entire Yukon Territory. Plus a view of another wide, rolling river. I'm back to politics via the press and television. Here in mainland Canada, almost nobody "knows the figures," except through their transmitted images. On the other hand, lack of size isn't everything. The Yukon hasn't always been very democratic, and there are sometimes radical outbreaks of democracy in highly overpopulated places.

The *Edmonton Journal* this morning says the Alberta government is planning to sell the free trade deal through an eight-page brochure to all 836,000 households in the province. That'll go on top of the $30 million the federal government has spent, and the business millions. Yet a CTV poll today says more Canadians oppose the deal at the moment than favour it, after a slight reverse in the last Environics poll. Opinion has been sawing off like this for months. If public opinion can be bought in this society, at least it doesn't come cheap.

It's especially interesting that only 29 percent think the government should put the deal through if they win the election; 72 percent say there should be a referendum on it, and that includes 59 percent of Tory voters. It amounts to saying that an election is a poor way to debate and decide an issue. Unfortunately, it's the only way we have.

Hromada means community, or nation, in Ukrainian. I spend the afternoon in a kitchen at the Hromada housing co-op in the old Strathcona section of Edmonton. Several members of the co-op are gathered.

They remind me of my own political past, the leftism of the 1960s. Someone I know recently called that a pinnacle decade. "It shaped the quarter-century," he said. "My daughter and I listen to the same music." What was it about that period? I don't think it was the ideology, which was often a trite version of what had been around much longer. Nor was it the idealism; there is always idealism among the young. I think it was the belief in change: it was the last time that large numbers of people were sure that major social change was possible. That conviction, which hasn't been around since, contained the real threat of the sixties. I guess that's why those years regularly get debunked on TV, in films and in the press. It's the only period that inspires what you could call decade bashing.

The twenty or thirty young Ukrainian Canadians who began Hromada came out of that time as socialists of different varieties. They decided to blend their socialism with another potent force of this century: nationalism — in their case, Ukrainian nationalism. They came together in the late 1970s to support Ukrainian dissidents in the Soviet Union and began Hromada as a cultural society. In 1982, they formed this Ukrainian, socialist, feminist housing co-op.

They all speak Ukrainian, though some of them only learned it as adults. A gentle, swarthy young man across the kitchen table is half-Spanish, half-Ukrainian. He is studying the role of Ukrainians and Ukrainian Canadians who fought Franco in the Spanish Civil War. Chrystia and her husband, John Paul, speak only Ukrainian at home. Robin, an American who's married to a Ukrainian, says, "I don't know if you speak it at home, but you sure speak it in the bathroom." They share a common wall in the co-op. Co-op members travel to the Ukraine frequently. Over there, says Lida, you find an un-Canadian congeniality and hospitality. "My kid's teacher in Ukrainian Canadian school told him Canadians can't enjoy themselves as much as Ukrainians can," says Robin.

They dreamed of wedding their left politics to a reinvigorated Ukrainian Canadian culture, which would liberate them from the ossified traditions of Easter eggs and embroidery they grew up with. It didn't quite happen. "We couldn't find enough Ukrainian-feminist-socialists to fill the twenty-one units," says Chrystia. They figure about 90 percent of the current members are mere social democrats. The ones who aren't even that will at least vote NDP. But the core group also found their political views changing. "As time went on, the socialism got watered down," says Chrystia. "We saw multiculturalism as a social movement, but it was co-opted by government policy. One after another, we lost everything. Maoism, revolutionary Marxism."

How did it happen? Well, for example, says Lida, when they formed the co-op, "we had an influx of yuppies and academics into the group and the issue that divided us was working at bingos." Come again? "You can make thousands doing that here," explains Chrystia. "All the artistic and cultural organizations do it. You run a bingo hall for a night."

"But it was Indians and people on welfare who go to them and we would be supporting class oppression," says Myrna. They decided to go ahead anyway. "Our rationalization was, If we don't do it, somebody else will," explains Robin. "And when we finally did it we got the shittiest bingos and made almost nothing," says Myrna. The weed of crime bears bitter fruit.

There was a debate about whether they should affiliate with the official Ukrainian Canadian umbrella organization. "It tore us apart," says Myrna, "trying to keep pure and untainted by the politicking and careerism that seemed involved there." Chrystia says, "In their constitution they support God and the Ukraine, and that makes me want to puke."

I ask how they feel about electoral politics. These are people who begin with my own antipathies. When I returned to Toronto from the American New Left, I could scarcely conceal my contempt for those who bothered with things like elections. They say the practical problems of co-op experience have turned them toward the NDP; it has good positions on housing. Chrystia's sister Halyna, a co-op member, is even running for the NDP in this riding. Her signs are planted around this block. They think she may really have a chance — as workers in almost every campaign, even the most futile, usually do.

Robin says, "It makes a big difference to have a labour party like the NDP. I was in SDS" — the chaotic 1960s New Left group — "in Indiana. I never thought electoral politics was a violation of principle. Pardon, a couple of years in SDS we thought that, but even then the pressures on us were enormous to get into it."

Changes in the Soviet Union have also discomfitted them. Those who travelled to the Ukraine used to come back and say how disgusting it was. Since Gorbachev, though, the tone of "debriefings" has changed. Now they have some pleasant stories to tell. "We haven't even talked about Gorbachev among ourselves," says Myrna reproachfully.

They speak, in a way, like refugees from a political catastrophe. They remind me of a group I met nearly twenty years ago in Paris, remnants of the 1968 student uprising, who had regrouped on the Right Bank in little cultural enterprises of their own: a bookstore, a café, a sports club. *Le Mouvement Fanshen*, they called themselves, after William Hinton's book about the Chinese Revolution. They modelled all their activities after what they had read about peasants in a Chinese village in 1948. I wonder if they're still there.

But it's hard to decide about the sixties. The mood for change was never dominant, even then. In the United States, for example, Richard Nixon was elected twice during those years. Conrad Black and Dan Quayle are also products of the sixties. But the period retains a certain power. Here they are, Hromada, occupying much of a downtown Edmonton block, still trying to make their vision real. A little battered and bewildered, that's all.

They ask how I feel about my own roots and I say that being Canadian is starting to feel to me like what being Jewish used to mean: constantly urged and tempted to abandon your hardwon identity in order to "convert" to the mighty majority. I ask, in turn, how they feel about Canadian nationalism, since it seems central to the election we're in. Chrystia says, "I hate it," and Lida says, "I love it." They all agree free trade is what's being talked about. They hear people say they "don't trust the Yanks"; they "don't want the country to go down the drain"; "You never know with the U.S."; and "Will there be a country left?" Mostly though, in Edmonton, they talk about the trade of Wayne Gretzky to the L.A. Kings. It became an instant metaphor.

Treasures and Toys on Whyte Street is owned and run by Betty Taylor — my second Betty Taylor this week. She recently opened another Treasures and Toys across town. She's blonde, small and lively, a businessperson like Margaret Tai of Whitehorse, who can't help having ideas for productive things to do. It's closing time. We sit around on little chairs.

"I'm not a political animal," she says. "But that's by choice. For years I taught children you can't complain about things if you don't do anything about them. I listen to what comes my way. On the car radio, for instance. But I don't want to know about it so I don't explore it. That's part of the choosing to be naïve. I feel very foolish admitting this because I think politics does really matter. All of us know deep down we do have some say in these choices and people died to give us these. Is it not rejecting their deaths — in the wars, people who fought for freedom? I do vote, but I tend to listen the week before the election — who got caught in the scandal just at that time. We're so busy, but we know ultimately it's important."

There was a moment in her life, though, when she got right into it. During the Berger Inquiry of the 1970s, she heard a local politician on a talk show speak in favour of extending the Mackenzie Delta pipeline all the way to Edmonton. She was enraged, she says, so she called and said he didn't speak for her. "In those days I talked myself into all kinds of things, because I was concerned. I felt we all had voices to be heard. After the talk show another talk show called me and before I knew it I was talking to half a dozen people and sounding like I knew what I was talking about and I thought I better get informed. I ended up giving a brief to the Berger Commission. I'd go to the hearings and listen to consultants with big oil companies talking, and I had this little piece of paper in my hand. And the little voices can be heard." She elbowed her way into the process briefly, as others do from time to time, but it was an exceptional moment in her life. There's no regular spot for someone like her in normal politics.

So she knows what it's like to be there. "That's what I mean when I said it's by choice. Because I once did get involved." Yet now she is a peripheral participant. "It bothers me," she says. "I listen to things and I wonder what colours my political feelings." She's thinking of an incident reported recently on the radio: Geills Turner made an unseemly fuss about having to sit beside a baby on a plane. "This is either a very tired lady," says Betty, "or she's even more naïve than I am." Is it, she frets, hearing about that sort of thing that will determine her vote? How many other such impressions, which we are hardly aware of, play a role? It's what happens when you're outside the process, but unwilling to leave it alone completely. It's the dilemma of citizens whose main political act is infrequently casting a ballot.

Her husband joins the conversation. He says he'll probably vote Rhino because at least they're honest. Betty says the Rhinos may be more serious than they seem, because they get people to think about what's going on. I contribute a potted history of the Rhino party, which began in Brazil after the military coup of 1964, as a way of dramatizing through ridicule the absence of democracy. Author Jacques Ferron founded a Quebec branch in the 1960s, to symbolize the irrelevance of federal politics to Quebec nationalists like himself. The party made its way to English Canada in the current version. So Rhinos have always been dead serious about exposing the absurdity of political systems.

"I don't understand the issue of free trade," Betty says. Translate that phrase into Latin and you could put it on the crest instead of "From Sea to Sea." "For me as a small businessperson, I can go down to the States and get my fabric for $2 a yard instead of $5 for it wholesale in Vancouver. I can pick up the newest things and patterns down there. But I don't want the country to go down the drain. I don't want to be like the States. I'll buy materials there, and L.A. is fascinating to go to, but I think we jeopardize our way of life unless we do something about it." It's complex. She can see an immediate advantage for her as a businessperson, along with disadvantages as a citizen.

And what about the challenge of that vast American toy market, for someone so obviously successful in her field? "I'm not even sure I want the second store we've opened across town," she says.

Café la Gare, near the railway station, is run by a young entrepreneur named Richard. "I'm surprised at how I've got involved in politics," he says. "I read in the *New York Times* about a painter who went away to an island to get away from politics, but he ended up getting involved with all the problems of the island. So now I've got involved in this community, with local issues. To draw people to my business, to work more with other people, you have to get involved. You can't just throw up your hands."

His views tend to the right, like the majority in Alberta. "A few issues are fairly strong with me: free trade, the Senate. I like the Reform party. The idea of the west not as a separate state, but with a little more representation." He says he liked Trudeau too, though he thinks Trudeau would have been against free trade and against an elected Senate.

"Conservatives have more open, business-minded attitudes," he goes on. "They've swept the western nations: it's done a lot of good." He talks about the right-wing turn of the eighties the way the media do: as if it's a force of nature, like a weather front moving in. "I must say the NDP is *scary*," he goes on. "I'm very concerned with a socialist government. It goes against what I believe. You can get ahead as an individual, and the government intervenes — the harder it is to get what you want. I believe in user fees, toll roads . . . ."

Yet the dilemmas of citizenship for most people really don't have much to do with whether their views are left or right. "I do feel to some degree I should get involved," says Richard. But he's reluctant. It goes back to his high school years. "As a senior I visited the legislature and was not impressed. The noise. It was so confusing. The rituals, harassing other politicians while they speak. That's hard to accept. I'll vote and I'll try to be informed, but I don't have too much time to go very deep into the issues." How will he make up his mind? "I can't really see myself going to forums. I would if I were the ultimate responsible person. I'll get most from the papers. Like the *Economist*. Canada has more to gain, they say, by accessing the U.S. market."

The dilemmas of citizenship have to do with sorting out the mix between issues and personalities, making sense of the welter of information and misinformation coming from the parties and the media, and boiling it all down to the oversimplified act of casting one vote. "You should know about some of the basic issues affecting your life," says Richard. "I try to look for bias, especially when an election is coming. I try to recall which journalist is writing. I try to look a little more in depth. The person you put in office could affect your life, you can't just pass on that, you have to make a reasoned choice." He feels "almost ashamed," he says, because he doesn't speak French. So many people — left, right and other shadings too — express shame and embarrassment when you talk to them about public issues. It's as if they feel that by being largely uninvolved in public life, they are betraying a part of themselves.

Sunday, October 23

Today I feel like Jeffrey Simpson for the first time in my life. Simpson often finds out how the world works from important people he meets at dinner parties, then passes it on to the readers of the *Globe*.

This is brunch, actually, with journalist friends and their friends. A columnist says people don't care about the trade deal, but columnists are always announcing the mood of the nation, as though they receive messages from beyond the galaxy. One of the women, who's home a lot these days with a baby, says she listens to the radio phone-ins and they all seem to be about free trade. She says people are looking for information.

I walk down to the river with a fellow named Jeff Dubois. He's from St. Paul, northeast of here. He's been active in the NDP since 1971, when he was eighteen. He ran for provincial Parliament that year, and twice more, and worked closely with Grant Notley, Alberta's longtime NDP leader. Once he got 41 percent of the vote and still lost. I tell him what Fred Gudmundson said ("I spent forty fucking years in that fucking party. . ."). Jeff nods. "Most ruthless bunch of human beings I've ever seen," he says mildly. "Talk about frustrated people." He is gentle and thoughtful, almost philosophical. He studied philosophy with C.B. Macpherson and Christian Bey, gentle radicals too. He'd never run again. Why not? "It transforms you. Ego takes over. Your handlers give you your script. You cease to be equipped to act as a decent human being and do your job." After studies at the University of Alberta, he wanted to go home to St. Paul, and had to choose between being a teacher, a civil servant or a car salesman. He chose selling cars, in the hope of maintaining some integrity, he says. He sold Volvos and Renaults all the years he worked in the NDP. Burned out by his years in the party, he now lives here in Edmonton and sells used cars.

Sunday night. Taking the train from Edmonton to Saskatoon.
Travelling like this, you're struck with the brazenness of even thinking about Canada as a community that could act in a politically cohesive way. It's mind-boggling. Easy enough for Tory or Liberal or NDP cabals or the Business Council on National Issues to coordinate their goals and strategies. But the whole damn country, all these people? Even here in the observation car of the Supercontinental, with fourteen or fifteen others, none of whom I know, or ever will know, or share anything with — how could we ever collaborate or act together? It seems romantic and

quixotic, a dream really. And what if we miraculously did all start to reason together about our collective lot? As they say in the Newfoundland film *The Adventures of Faustus Bidgood*, "When they rises up, they gets confused."

Time slows down in the Supercontinental, and the landscape is humanized as it passes. The little towns clustered next to the grain elevators owned by the wheat pools — which contain the real politics of the Canadian prairies. The domed, turreted churches. Darkness coming, the sky lowering, pink around the edges and under the clouds, a fringe of light right around the bowl of the prairie, the moon rising. The train whistle almost incessant, there are so many crossings. The pick-up trucks, their lights on now, waiting patiently at the crossings as we pass, two pulled up facing each other so their drivers can talk. It takes so long to get dark out here as you travel on, laughter drifting up from the bar car. The train makes you reflective, and feels social at the same time, especially compared to flying. The train makes for community, the plane for isolation.

Supper in the dining car at a table with two working-class guys who also signed up for this meal call. They're pretty different. The one beside me is from Timmins. He's young, unkempt and a little thick. He spent a year in Edmonton and he's going home. The most he made there was $7.50 an hour, while in Timmins he once made $13.50. His best job ever, though, was tending bar opposite the GM plant in Oshawa. He's planning to take a course at Northern College that leads to being a heavy equipment operator. He's heard lots of talk about free trade; he figures there's as much good in it as not; he can't see how it would do him any harm.

The other is older, near thirty, and more together. Maybe Timmins will look like this ten years from now, but I doubt it. This guy is an electrician at a company in Saskatoon. It's unionized and he says he goes to meetings, but he's not an elected officer or even a steward. He comes from Swift Current, has been in Saskatoon about ten years and is ready to move somewhere livelier — Van-

couver maybe. He says he doesn't know much about the
trade deal. Then, like many who say this, he starts talking
about it.

He worries that our wages will be driven down, either
by movement of money out of the country or by competition from American firms underbidding our own. He has
other doubts too, mentioning culture. "I have problems,"
he says, "with the retaliation clause in that section of the
agreement." He means an elusively worded provision that
lets the U.S. government impose penalties for any Canadian cultural policies that cost American companies
money in Canada. He says he can't see how Canadian culture will survive the full onslaught of the American
entertainment industry — we barely have much now. He
gives as an example the Canadian film industry, which is
just getting started. It's a pretty specific brief for someone
who doesn't know much.

Between them, these two men contain a deep secret of
electoral politics. One is informed, experienced, mature
and thoughtful, and the other is not. Yet their votes count
the same, and both will almost certainly use them. So as
long as the ruling elites can keep large numbers of citizens
both uninformed *and* voting, they can feel secure in their
control. In a more genuinely democratic system, where
people didn't merely vote, but got together and discussed
things beforehand, it would be different, because the electrician's viewpoint would outweigh that of the future
heavy equipment operator — in the minds of everyone
present, the equipment operator included. But our voting
process — minus almost any opportunity for exchange
and discussion — levels them out. It is a sort of system of
democracy minus. (Ever since that night on the train, and
especially on the final weekend of the campaign in Montreal, when I knew the trade deal would go through, and
saw the Tories cavort — I have been haunted by the image of the young man from Timmins: thinking about
him, trying to understand him, wondering how it might
be different. His is the face that haunts me as I look back.)

Monday, October 24

Saskatoon. On "Canada AM" this morning, Joe Clark says the Liberals are using free trade to divert attention from their leadership problems. It seems to me that's the kind of devious trick our elections could use more of.

Driving from Saskatoon to Regina, CBC-FM radio playing a Vivaldi motet as I snake across the landscape. This morning at the Bessborough, my favourite Canadian hotel, I had breakfast with a friend, a CBC loyalist. Her fervour has always irked me, knowing the vile insides of the CBC as I feel I do. Yet driving across the prairie now, I understand her gratitude. I live in a part of the country in which I can afford great impatience with imperfect institutions like the CBC. I feel as if I'm gorging on the technologies available in this society for making life more comfortable: the car, the rental and credit system, a tape recorder to make notes as I drive, the car radio. The best argument for a different social system really is that things could so easily be much better than they are for many more people. We have the resources; we just don't deploy them. It's a ridiculous waste. Maybe Canadians could be embarrassed into trying socialism.

Just outside Davidson, halfway between Saskatoon and Regina, I renew acquaintance with Elmer and Gladys Laird on their farm.

"You're the first person who's come here to talk about the election," says Elmer. "I was sitting in Coffee Row Saturday and I said to my neighbour, 'What do you think of the election?' And he said, 'What election?' " Coffee Row is a cluster of restaurants in Davidson where the farmers gather on Saturday mornings for philosophy seminars and local gossip. "Our democratic procedure is not so democratic," Elmer continues. "An election is called, the leaders get on a plane, they get off and some reporter says, 'What do you think of the latest poll?' And that's it. It's all up in the air. Literally. I haven't heard of any candidate calling a meeting within fifty or sixty miles."

Elmer has been a farmer for over forty years, and the

battle for organic, non-chemical farming has become his mission, his real politics, you might say. "I hear the politicians," he says. "They talk about acid rain, and that's right, but I never hear them talk about the food supply. And they've refused to put pest control products under the new environmental act. So I could be spraying a chemical on one side of the road, and a factory owner over on the other side could be jailed for using the same chemical, but not the farmer. And the testing of agricultural chemicals is a farce. About half the chemicals used here don't have complete data for registration, including 2,4-D."

I ask if he is optimistic or not this season. "The last year was a good year environmentally and a poor year economically," he says. "We were right in the middle of the drought. All the way up to Parkside, eighty miles north of Saskatoon. I had a bushel of wheat to the acre, worst since '49, when I got a hundred bushel off 160 acres. Normally I get about 20 bushel, and crop insurance covers 70 percent of 20 bushel. The heat was unbearable. I seeded rye and it hasn't come up. But environmentally it was so hot and dry a lot of people decided not to spray."

The cream on the table is real and heavy, and the bread is made of rye and wheat flour that's milled in their plant, one he and some other farmers opened in spring 1987. It's an organic marketing co-op, with about ninety members from around the province and Manitoba, that produces grain for the organic market. They clean it and sell it to Ontario or Pennsylvania. "We got the door open and I'm amazed it stays open," says Elmer. Maybe this is why he's feeling good. His cause has expanded, others have joined him and they've created an institution.

Last time I was here, Elmer cooked lunch — organic pancakes — while Gladys and I watched. I remember thinking it was a little unusual. They say that was June 1982. They checked it in their guest book. "The fall before, we had a West German buyer looking for 50,000 bushel, so we started the co-op," says Elmer. "Half our members are people who get sick if they go near a sprayer. And some of their kids have chemical allergies and half our customers are the same thing. We hear more about allergies than the allergy foundation. And from people who want to know, How do you farm without chemicals? Last winter I got about three calls a day."

"There's one guy over there in Coffee Row. He says, that organic stuff may be okay for you, but I can't afford it, and he's got enough money, if he never seeds another bushel, he'd live well the rest of his life. It's like an alcoholic, yes it is." Gladys, the former town librarian, says it's more a compulsion than an addiction. Elmer goes on, "Farmers feel dependent on chemicals to control weeds and pests. Our closest neighbours' wives sat here and said, 'We wish you'd stop spraying, we'd be prepared to live on less.' Since then one wife died of cancer. Her husband said to me after she died, 'You've lost a good supporter. That was the only thing she asked me to do I didn't do.' But he still sprays, and his present wife wants him to quit spraying. A lot of people wouldn't talk to me, but he would and he said, 'They're all waiting for the government to stop it so they don't have to do it themselves!'"

The talk turns to free trade. "I listen to the news and they say Saskatchewan is all for it," says Elmer, "but I don't know many people who are for it, and I don't see any good in it. Eventually it'll be a disaster. So many ways it'll be a disaster. It just means more cheap chemicals coming in from the States. And polluted food."

I say people seem to know a fair amount about this agreement. "It's not easy either," says Elmer. "I've got sent information out of Ottawa, but I was never able to get a complete version. I called my MP's office and the toll-free number in Regina. And they sent me all kinds of material but even when you ask for the deal, all you get is an edited version, some propaganda and quotes from it." He says he feels intuitively that they are trying to keep it from people.

"Raymond my cousin is called the Senator on Coffee Row because he's from the U.S., and he can't see why anyone resents the Americans, because the problem as far as he's concerned is the Japanese. But that's about the extent of the discussions we've had Saturday morning on Coffee Row." I ask how he figures people will line up. "The Wheat Pool is typically on the fence," he says. Out here clichés like "on the fence" often make sense. "The cattlemen are for it," he adds, "but they've been run by the meat packers for years, and opposed everything like marketing boards."

Cousin Raymond, the Senator, drops in just then. They agree that Davidson will vote Conservative and I ask why. Gladys says, "Because they're politically backward." Raymond says the people against free trade claim the government gave the country away, and "I don't believe they'd do that."

They watched the two nights of debate on "The Journal" about the trade deal. They found it uninformative. "But Mrs. Barlow was excellent," says Gladys, "and I was *amazed* they had a woman on." I say Barbara Frum is always on, and she's a woman. Gladys responds, "Is she?" — a cryptic and zenlike statement.

They say things are difficult around here. Farmers are going broke, businessmen are going broke, tomorrow there's a bankruptcy sale of a company that made rock-pickers. There's a neighbour, forty years old with four kids, and the Credit Union foreclosed and the Land Bank took his farm and now he's working as a repairman at the school and his wife is driving the school bus. Elmer himself had a serious accident last weekend crossing the highway where I just turned in. A truck ploughed into him and he's lucky to be sitting here talking about politics. Raymond asks Elmer why he let the police report that he'd run a stop sign, and Elmer says, "Because I did."

He says governments rarely deal with real problems, so that politics have to get handled outside of politics. This states in a few words something I've been trying to formulate for weeks. He got a call from Yellowknife recently, where they found residues of chemicals used in the American South, blown there by wind currents, so it doesn't help to live in the Northwest Territories. The caller wanted to know about biological, as opposed to chemical, control of insects. "He'd called Agriculture Canada in Ottawa and they told him to phone me!" says Elmer.

We drive to town and visit Harry Crossman in the Sask Pool elevator. I've seen thousands, I suppose, but never been in one. I'm surprised by the careful judgements Harry must pass on the grades of grains brought in. It's like the Kamloops mill, another place where the country's wealth is processed. Hidden dimensions of our lives, like the lost dimension of citizenship.

We drive to the post office to pick up Elmer's mail. "This would determine my vote even if it weren't for free trade," says Elmer. He means the government's plan to close down rural mail services. "I've always believed I have a right to postal service." This past weekend in Whitehorse, Canada Post simply pulled out, leaving the mails to a private store in a mall.

We drive around Davidson. "Notice anything?" Elmer asks. No, I don't. "There are no campaign signs!" he says. "You'd never know there was an election on." It's true. Not a sign in *all* Davidson.

We drive south to the organic co-op, Elmer's pride and joy. It's in Gervin, about twelve miles from Davidson, where the population has dropped to forty-two, and they're down to two elevators from four a few years ago. But the co-op is doing well, especially with organic oats, because available herbicides kill not just wild oats but tame oats too. We talk with Glen Hanley, a member. "Very low-key," he says of the election. "People are saying, What's the use? They've lost a lot of confidence." Elmer starts complaining about all the American items on "Canada AM." I guess farmers, like other early risers, watch the show. Glen says his daughter came back from the States last week and she pointed out that the first item on CBC's "The National" was the U.S. election.

It's not hard to get discouraged with national politics out here. Ontario has ninety-five seats and Saskatchewan has fourteen. Then there are the media. Elmer and Glen say you've got to get something in the *Globe and Mail* to reach the rest of the country. Add the drought. It isn't hard.

"The CN Tower is a monument to all the services we've lost in western Canada," says Elmer. "It was built and all our services, like the telegraph, were closed down. When I grew up, the mail went by train. Now it's all by tender, in trucks that are dilapidated. Or we can use couriers, but that's expensive as hell. If the post office worked right, the couriers are unnecessary. But they're doing it so their friends who want privatization can get the job, and then they go broke! The privatization thing doesn't work. I think the post office is as important as national defence. Why don't we privatize our national defence? I talked to a guy the other day about defence and poultry. Free trade means more imported poultry. One plant in Pennsylvania has 13,000 poultry, bigger than any operation in Canada, and our boards won't be able to stand up to it. What if the border is cut off? We'd starve! Building self-sufficiency in agriculture is an important part of national defence. With oodles of small plants this size, serving particular trading areas, we could do it." It's strange hearing someone say aloud that protection is a good thing, privatization isn't, and expanded trade isn't necessarily. These have become forbidden thoughts in the arena of public discourse; they haven't been spoken for so long that it's as though they've been forgotten.

Evening, Regina. Tonight is the first TV debate. It's in French. What I find jarring is the centrality of the panel of journalists. Not the figures who are running to run the country — but the ones who pose the questions to them and therefore determine the course of these crucial encounters. How did they get there, between the people and the politicians? And between the politicians themselves? For ages uncounted, debates occurred between the candidates, with no panels of reporters to set the agenda.

They don't just intrude during the process; they try to control the outcome as well. Hugh Segal of the Tories gave that away when he said, "The importance of a debate lies in the perception left by the media after the debate." I don't know when it became custom for the media to declare a winner of these encounters. Maybe after the 1980 debate between Carter and Reagan in the U.S. Near the end I remember thinking — Reagan is awfully vacuous; at least Carter has some information. Then suddenly there was Walter Cronkite, the most formidable father-figure of our time, saying Reagan had been relaxed and in command and won a clear victory. I've sometimes wondered about the consequences for world history had Cronkite kept his counsel.

There was a similar moment after the Canadian election debate of 1984 between Turner, Mulroney and Broadbent. The CBC turned to a panel of "ordinary Canadians" they'd assembled, and asked who won. All the panelists said Ed Broadbent. Then the CBC switched back to their own experts, Peter Mansbridge and David Halton, who proclaimed Mulroney the winner, because he waggled his finger in Turner's face while denouncing Liberal patronage. It's a little like the role of theatre critics. Their power of suggestion can be immense. Even at a hit play, an audience often seems to enjoy what critics told them would be there, rather than what they see themselves.

Next day the journalists announce what people thought about the debate or what people saw or what people would have seen if they'd spoken French and tuned in. They say the event was a draw, and keep it up until contrary evidence, in the form of some polls, persuades them Turner was the clear winner.

Tuesday, October 25

A Gallup this morning on the deal has 42 percent opposed and 34 percent in favour. This is the first significant shift one way or the other after running almost even for months. All it took was an election call, and the minimal amount of discussion that the campaign has entailed so far, to break the thing open. What remains is the election, a far different kind of fight.

The campaign office of Simon de Jong, NDP member for Regina, is a cheery place, unlike most such offices. There are creative, handmade signs on the wall and a button that says, "De Jong and the Restless," incidentally telling people how to pronounce the candidate's name. The campaign manager says, "We're not hearing abortion, we're not hearing the environment. Of 300 names we have in the computer wanting more information, over 250 are on the deal."

Peter Calamai of Southam News has become a specialist in literacy and is analysing the literature of the current campaign for readability levels. He's run everything, even the brochures from Elections Canada that tell people how to vote, through computer programs. He has discovered that the cartoon booklet put out by the coalitions is practically the only item which is accessible to people below university reading levels. *What's the Big Deal?* tests at grade 7 or 8. He wants to know if that bothers me.

Qu'Appelle House, a home for seniors, is located in Regina Wascana, a bellwether riding. It has three strong candidates, including PC Larry Schneider, longtime mayor of Regina, who is campaigning in the sunny lunchroom.

"I don't want to be an American," says a woman resident.

"I'm too old to care," says another.

"I don't want to be the 51st state," the first expands. "You're going to lose your . . . your . . . ."

"Social benefits?" asks Schneider.

"No, but you'll lose your manufacturing," she says wickedly.

"Garbage," replies Schneider.

"If they vote for free trade, they'll live to regret it," she says. "I won't, but they will."

Schneider refers her to the six-month opt-out clause, which is starting to sound like the government's main reason to go into this deal. He tells her we can get out of free trade quicker than you can get out of a marriage, even with no-fault divorce. She asks if he thinks we'll know what it's worth in just six months.

Later, he says the main thing he hears from people is they don't want to be American. Then he adds, with a shrug, "What's really the difference between us? Is there one? I mean, they have blacks down there and we have natives up here. They have two parties and we have three — and I wish we had their system right now. Anyway, if the NDP's against it, I'm inclined to be for it." He may be the best-known face in this city. He says the question he hears most is why he wants to abandon Regina for Ottawa.

He's forthright and provocative on the relations between democratic process and a subject like free trade. He says he doesn't really think a topic as complex as free trade should be laid before people to decide at all. It's too complicated. They ought to elect a government they trust, and trust it. "Should we hold a national referendum about the design of a propeller on a submarine? It's just not logical to ask the public for their opinion on a technical question." Would he make this statement publicly? "With great caution," he replies. "The public elects government to make these decisions for them. Far be it from government to come into this home and tell these people what's good for them. Similarly, these people should let government decide what is a good national defence policy." Are there any issues on which he would consult the public directly? Whether there should be a day of rest? He says, "Maybe." But he rejects the free trade agreement as a matter for open debate. "People would need to know the technical data related to its application, and they can't be expected to."

This doesn't sound undemocratic to Schneider. It's based on his experience as an elected official in government. "We're now asking citizens to give us their opinion on a rail relocation program in Regina for the third time!"

Nor is he on the far right. In a Regina referendum on a tax moratorium coming up in the municipal election to-morrow, he is for the "liberal," or spending, side. He's simply saying that representation is the way our system works: you vote, then you shut up. And he's right, more or less. It isn't a system structured for lots of direct input from the people. It's true, there are exceptions, like the Yukon 2000 program of discussion and bottom-up deci-sion making. But that depended on a uniquely small population. Or did it? It would be harder on a mass scale, but maybe citizen involvement is less a matter of practical-ity than of will. How can you know until you try?

This election, more than any I've seen, is starting to raise basic political questions like these and to reveal some attitudes and assumptions normally hidden from view. The masks are coming off — as people will say during the chaos that develops later in the campaign. Business, for instance, certainly shares Schneider's attitude on public discussion of free trade; for them it's strictly business. I remember Alfred Powis, head of Noranda, at the CITY-TV debate a year ago. He slept through most of the dis-cussion, but woke briefly to say he couldn't understand why decisions on the free trade issue weren't being left to him and his associates. We make these decisions, he said in effect, we take the risks, why on earth aren't you trust-ing our judgement? Or Crosbie's straightforward statement that once businessmen had pronounced on the deal, there was no need for other views. Or the current flow of government newspaper ads with pictures of smil-ing businessmen and the caption, "We're getting ready for free trade." As if all it takes is photographs of men in suits for the rest of the country to respond, "Hey, okay. Why didn't you say so?"

Tuesday night. The English language debate.
The networks have programmed pre- and post-debate shows, in addition to the three hours of actual debate they've conspired to inflict on us. The emphasis is on

politics as performance, not on what it all might mean for people's lives.

The CBC, for instance, has a media consultant seated at a control board, treating the three candidates like case studies in a communications course. "This is John Turner doing his Phil Donahue imitation." They also have a panel of ordinary Canadians again, this time behind newsdesks, as if they're journalists. Peter Mansbridge concludes with, "So sit back and enjoy it. This is what the election's all about." Sit back and enjoy it?

I'm in my Regina hotel room and can only stay for part, because I have to do a reading that was scheduled long before the election was announced. Bad timing.

The first confrontation is between Mulroney and Turner. The CBC's David Halton has the opening question and asks about *patronage*. It is an illuminating example of the power of the press to subvert public discussion. The people of the country have made it clear that free trade is what matters to them, that they feel terribly uninformed about it, that they're waiting to hear about it — so Halton raises patronage. Mulroney lists the marvellous nonpartisan appointments he has made, Turner flails back — by the time the segment is over, the government's communications strategy remains intact. The two main antagonists have not touched the topic of free trade and are not scheduled to get another shot at each other — the hour on women's issues will intervene — for about two long hours.

Next comes an exchange between Turner and Broadbent. Since they both oppose the trade deal, this segment becomes a battle over who owns the issue. Broadbent criticizes Turner's absence in the House during two votes on the deal. Turner's jaw drops — an impressive sight — he looks like he can't believe what Broadbent said. He has put himself on the line, fought his party, alienated his closest business buddies, ordered the Senate to block the agreement and forced an election so Canadians can vote on the matter — and Broadbent attacks because he missed two votes.

The odd thing, watching this part of the debate wind down in a yawny way and edge toward the hour of women's issues, is that I feel kind of proud for living in a society with relatively serious political discussion — especially compared to the U.S. election. After a vice-presidential TV debate between Bentsen and Quayle, one network correspondent said the test had been to see whether Quayle could enter the ring, take a punch, and remain standing at the end — and he had! Because he was simply upright when it was over. When Dukakis confronted Bush, a reporter asked Dukakis to prove he was warm and human, and Dukakis actually tried.

Compare this debate. It has issues, confrontation, choices. The things being discussed matter. Even Mulroney looks plausible compared to any of the U.S. candidates. It's like living in the Golden Age of Athenian democracy — compared to down there.

At the reading, I keep thinking, What are we all doing here while our country's future is being disputed? Back in the hotel bar afterwards, I catch the late news reports. They're showing one hypertense encounter between Turner and Mulroney about the deal — over and over and over. It lasted maybe two minutes, max. It's the closest thing we will ever get to a genuine debate about the most fateful choice in Canadian history, and the amazing thing about it — I realize after I've seen it in context on tape — is that it happened only because Turner was demanding a full-scale debate with Mulroney over the deal. They weren't even debating the deal. They were debating *debating* the deal.

Wednesday, October 26

Breakfast with MP Simon de Jong. He says electoral politics "is like theatre. If you're going to be in the play, you have to wear the costume and say the lines." I guess we all have the performances in last night's TV show on our minds. But actors, at least every so often, look down at their get-up as they stand in the wings and think, What the hell am I doing here? Or, Is this any way for an adult human being to behave? But politicians — do they?

De Jong should know, he's led a varied, creative life. He has a degree in social sciences and was once an accomplished painter in oils and acrylics. His paintings are housed in many collections, they were reproduced in *Art in America* and in the mid-1960s he was named one of the ten best young North American artists. Then he went into the streets to work with youth as an organizer. From 1969 to 1975 he was coordinator of a Vancouver community organization called Cool-Aid. It included a workers' co-op, food co-op, medical clinic, school, people's garage, candle factory, craft factory, farm and communal homes throughout Vancouver. He set out to gather it all into one city block, a sort of super-commune with no back fences. "And Ron Basford said, No. He was the minister in charge then. He wasn't going to be responsible for funding the economy of the counter-culture," says de Jong.

"I realized government couldn't have done what we did," he continues. Yet from that point on, de Jong began to move toward government himself. "When the funding stopped, I came back here, drifted, worked with the provincial government, opened a restaurant and waited for the pendulum to swing again." He ran for Parliament in 1979 and has been there since. He sees it as a different way of doing the same things he'd done from the outside. "You've got to get into the mindset and find the words that would allow a person in electoral politics to start conceiving of that alternate position. As an elected person, you have a part to play in setting the social agenda."

Concretely, how does that happen? De Jong quotes a speech he made at a UN meeting — one of those perks even Opposition members occasionally receive — in which he called both Russians and Americans paranoid. And once during Question Period in the House, he asked Trudeau about a Vancouver peace march and followed it with a supplementary, in which he compared the Cold War to his twins fighting. He thinks this helped establish a "different mindset" and may have led Trudeau to think in terms that led to his failed world peace initiative of 1983–84. De Jong says sometimes you get feedback that tells you what you've achieved and sometimes you can't be sure, but you may have had an effect. This spring he distributed a "householder" in his riding on the cost of the arms race and the cost of living. He is enthusiastic about these initiatives, even if they seem limited, compared to the breadth and passion of his activities in the old days.

I ask whether it bothers him to have so many people bending their efforts to popularize his name. No, he accepts it, that's how the game is played. "The opportunities of actually touching someone in an election," says de Jong, "are few and far between. Knocking on doors is really superficial." At best, he says, you can develop "a kind of exercise in Jungian collective unconscious" based on the lines you hear people repeating. "You suddenly spot a phrase from last night's paper or news show." He sees campaigning as a process where you "step back and develop a sensitivity to the mood or to body language on the doorstep." At some point, he says, you know whether you are going to win or lose. He laments the lack of art in his life, though some aspects of his campaign — the buttons, the lively tone of his office, the initiatives he mentions with pride — seem like at least a stunted outlet for his creativity.

Thursday, October 27

Winnipeg. Susan Spratt, a lawyer and union organizer who's worked hard with the Manitoba Coalition against Free Trade here, is talking about what happened as she watched the TV debate with friends. She's amazed even as she tells it. "We're sitting there in my basement," she says. "About twenty people from the Coalition, all left of the NDP, but all active in the NDP, and we're cheering, 'Yay, Turner, Right, go get 'im.' And then we stop and look at each other and we say, 'Hey, we're cheering for John Turner!' " At what point? When Broadbent was trying to savage Turner for being insincere about the deal, and said, You used to say you were going to tear it up, and now you don't say it anymore. Turner answered, Because I found a better way. I made sure there was an election, so the people could decide. That's when people in Sue's basement started to cheer. "We look at each other. We're cheering for a Liberal. What's happening? Quick. More wine!"

A Gallup today on the English language debate says Turner won massively at 72 percent — to 17 for Mulroney and 11 for Broadbent. This election is up for grabs, and it's largely because of the coalitions, the popular movement, all the work and slogging and kvetching that's been done for three years, including the cartoon booklet. A story in the *Globe* yesterday said there's "unanimity" among the parties that "a widely circulated pamphlet against the agreement by the Pro-Canada Network has had a major impact on voter impressions of the deal." Yesterday's poll, which says the country is now 42 to 34 against the deal, was taken after *What's the Big Deal?* came out and before the debates. Here in Winnipeg, the Manitoba Coalition has received eight hundred letters from the rural part of the province in response to the booklet. Turner did not create something out of nothing with his debate performance. He took advantage of the groundwork laid over the past three years. In Tory pollster Allan Gregg's image, what Turner did last night was build a bridge between the growing concern about free trade, and the voters.

Speaking of impact, Elmer and Glen were right about the *Globe*'s power. It's as if nothing in Canada happens until the *Globe* reports it. Even someone from the *Star* called today with congratulations about the booklet's effect — after the *Globe* story. I'm also told that the *Star* has been running a free trade hotline. The first weekend, when they got over five hundred calls, the tape ran out.

Afternoon. An all-candidates debate at St. Norbert's College, a high school here in Winnipeg. The NDP candidate is speaking when I arrive. He's a young guy with hair falling over his forehead, wearing a blue suit that hangs like it's on a rack. He says he's a letter carrier and the kids might have seen him these past few years, walking up and down on the street in front of the school. The kids nudge each other and chortle, Hey, that guy's the mailman! Hell of an opening. The other candidates can't touch it. He says it's fine to have lawyers and businesspeople like Dorothy Dobbie, his Tory opponent, go to Parliament, but there ought to be a few regular working people too. He finishes by holding up the cartoon booklet and saying, "You've seen *What's the Big Deal?* Read it."

The auditorium is dimly lit, the school buzzer goes off like torture in the middle of everything, the moderator is a red-faced boy wearing an Oilers sweater with a windbreaker over it, and a NIKE scarf. He stands so far to the side he's nearly hidden by the sound system.

When it's over, Dorothy Dobbie gives me a ride as far as her campaign office. I know she is a star Tory candidate, former head of the Winnipeg Chamber of Commerce, an anti-feminist opposed to pay equity. She called our booklet "the green slime piece." She is energetic. She has the kind of vitality that is appealing in anyone, no matter how repugnant you find their views. In a coffee shop near her campaign office, I manage to reveal I am the author of the green slime thing. She's not angry — if anything she becomes even more animated and friendly. She gets right down to basics. Anyone who has what it takes in this society will succeed. The rest don't make it because they aren't capable of the effort. I say it sounds like survival of the fittest. She says, "Pretty close to that." There's not much more to say and we each have to leave, me for another meeting and her to knock on doors. It's snowing very hard.

On the CBS evening news, Dan Rather interviews presidential candidate Dukakis. Rather says, "I know you know

the American people have an innate sense of fairness."
Neither winces at this demagogy. Then Rather looks over
his shoulder at the camera and says, "Just out there, beyond that lens, are millions of them. What can you say to
give them some insight into who Mike Dukakis is and
what he wants?" Dukakis nods gratefully and launches
some clichés about sending kids to college. American elections are no longer just dominated by television; they're
hardly anything but television. Political reporting is about
little other than the manipulation of impressions by the
parties. It's like those documentaries on how special effects in movies are achieved. American voters appear to
accept this. They say things like, "I thought he came
across as sincere," rather than, "I believe him." They
know they're getting a show, so they try to make the best
of it, not as citizens but as audience. I've talked to several
American journalists today about the cartoon booklet.
They say two things. They are astounded that anything in
print can make a difference in the age of television. And
they say they are ashamed at the level of their own country's election, compared to what's happening up here.

At night, I attend an all-candidates debate in St. Boniface,
the largest French-speaking area in the country outside
Quebec. There is a sense of siege here and of a language
threatening to dry up. Everyone present is fluent in English, but the debate is conducted and televised in French.
There's something obstinate and touching about it. There
is a foot of snow outside by the time it's over. Everywhere
I have been during these two weeks, I have brought the
first snow of winter: Whitehorse, Edmonton, Saskatoon,
now this blizzard. A few flakes even fall in Toronto as I arrive home the next day, as if I have been accompanying a
weather front from west to east.

Friday, October 28

The Environics poll in the *Globe* today says Turner won

the debates and people are switching votes because of it. They watched in high numbers — 50 percent of voters say they saw at least a part and 11 percent watched all three hours. Seventy-nine percent say free trade was the most important issue debated and only 8 percent choose other issues: 2 percent each for abortion, the environment, social services and "other." A debate about the future of the country is really happening and it is happening in the context of an election. I've never seen anything like it. I don't know if anyone has.

Toronto. As the plane from Winnipeg touches down, I come across a column in the Winnipeg *Free Press* headed, "Free trade booklet is filled with lies." It's by Alan Rugman, one of John Crispo's colleagues at the faculty of management of the University of Toronto. He quotes our booklet saying "American corporations . . . get to make their own low environmental standards, or health standards, or food standards, apply here," and says, "This is total nonsense." The ellipsis he has inserted replaces the rather small word "could" and completely alters the sense of the quote. A piece in the *Financial Post* about the booklet is titled, "What's the big deal? Telling the truth is." On the "sleazometer," it says, we make Brian Mulroney look like Mahatma Gandhi.

Leaves me speechless. Mulroney said in '83 that free trade would be a disaster for Canada, and "You'll hear no more about it from me, not now nor at any time in the future." Wilson said the same. Yet none of us have accused them outright of lying — though they have, let's say, done their share for three years. Then they read a fairly detailed, twenty-eight page booklet containing information Canadians have been begging for — according to every poll and candidate — and they scream, Liar, Liar, Pants on Fire. The level of hysteria in their response is way beyond *any* language we've used — to our discredit, maybe. Why have we been so restrained and polite? What's *our* problem?

The debate that's starting to happen is blurring boundaries, crossing in and out of the arena of official politics.
The election is breaking through its predefined borders.
Unofficial, unauthorized people are getting involved, myself among them. I find it a strange and to some extent
uncomfortable experience. It's extraordinary to think you
might be able to play a role in this society's political system
without actually enlisting in it through the parties and the
formal structures. I tend to resist the thought. It seems
odd to truly affect the shape or direction of the society I
have for so long insisted I want to affect. It's a combination of personal skepticism and the sense of marginal,
oppositional identity that many of us have. That we are
doing something wrong if something goes right. That if
this society is as recalcitrant as we say, can we possibly ac-
complish anything in it without betraying ourselves?

It also means that the distinction I began with — between politics in the broadest sense, and the narrow realm
of electoral and parliamentary politics — is starting to
break down. It won't be as easy to follow my plan of talking to people about politics, using the election as
background and pretext. The two streams are beginning
to converge, instead of staying clearly separate. This election is starting to be about politics.

Week Five

Saturday, October 29

The new Reid poll has the Liberals and Tories tied at 35
percent and the NDP at 28. Opposition to the deal is running at 54 to 35. All previous bets are off.

It's interesting, in this light, to consider last week's
Maclean's, the issue that went to bed before the TV debates. It dwelt at length on the coming encounters. "Long
before the campaign began," it said, "sophisticated market

research enabled the parties to test voters' reactions to their leaders and to a wide range of issues. Using that information, each party set about trying to satisfy the public mood with a simple, easily understood message." Except now the Tories have stopped talking about managing change and the NDP aren't sputtering about fairness — despite all that sophisticated market research. A professor at the McLuhan Program in Culture and Technology said, "Mulroney does not have to do anything" but evoke "expressions of confidence, power — and money, money, money." Yet now Mulroney's trying to evoke warmth and dialogue; yesterday in Vancouver he invited some of his hecklers to sit down with him and reason together; and within days he'll be evoking panic as well, saying rejection of the deal would lead to the loss of two million jobs. The same expert said, "Turner's basic job is to cool his image. Arguments are the last thing you want on TV." However, what turned this around for Turner was ninety seconds of televised toe-to-toe argument. John Meisel, former head of the Canadian Radio-television and Telecommunications Commission (CRTC), who may never turn on his TV set, if he even owns one, said, "It is the nature of our society that we are more concerned with appearances than substance." A York University political scientist added, "I do not think it is reasonable to fault television for failing to deal in detail with the issues, because even when the information is presented, most people do not remember it." Yet the maligned medium became a "bridge," in Allan Gregg's term, between the issue and the election, because of which this election now centres on nothing except a complex and detailed issue.

One week later, it is all rubbish. They got it 100 percent wrong. They don't understand people, who are not stupid and helpless in the face of manipulation; they don't understand TV, which is not just a boob tube and which has a capacity, when given a chance, to see *through* bullshit in ways print cannot; and they don't understand politics. They can explain things as they normally are — but they seem to think that's the only way things can possibly be.

The York political scientist said, "The moment a campaign becomes solely an exercise in political marketing, debate about the future of the country drops right out of the process." The parties tried to run a campaign that was sheer marketing, and the media played along and pretended nothing else could ever be — and now we are engaged in a mass debate about the future of the country. What really astounds me, though, is that the coming week's issue of *Maclean's* will not look back humbly. It will not attempt to account for being wrong or even acknowledge error or apologize for misleading its readers. There ought to be a law.

Sunday, October 30

The weekly political panel on CBC radio's "Sunday Morning" has a Tory, Pat Carney; an NDPer, Pauline Jewett; and Liberal Don Johnston, who left his caucus because he disagreed with it on crucial matters. Johnston voted with the Tories on the trade deal, the only Liberal to do so. So the CBC get *him* to represent the Liberal point of view? Tomorrow I go to Quebec.

Monday, October 31

Montreal. A morning press conference of the NDP's women candidates in the province. Behind them is a sexy picture of Ed with his top two buttons undone and his jacket slung over his shoulder à la Parisien. But the original campaign plan, to run heavily on him as leader, has collapsed. Instead they attack Turner for his record as finance minister fifteen years ago. What's going on? Who's the enemy? They talk as if it's more important to beat the Liberals than to beat the Tories. There are tactical reasons: the NDP has more chance of attracting Liberal than Tory voters. Technically speaking, though, it seems to me this is getting close to treason. It was Broadbent himself who said Canada won't survive this agreement. What's more important — a country or a party?

There are few questions from the assembled press. Someone asks how many women candidates the NDP has and their press officer says, "Sixteen in Quebec. In Canada, I don't know." As if Canada is a different country, which in so many ways it is. The Anglo reporters cluster and talk loudly among themselves. Then someone asks snidely, "With all these great policies, why is your party in *chute libre*?" One candidate says it's because Turner is a *"bon acteur."* In fact, if Turner is anything, he's a bad actor. It's hard to imagine him being worse. They say the NDP were first in with opposition to the trade deal, which sounds whiney. The NDP and the CCF before them were first in with many admirable policies, and of course it bugs the hell out of them that Liberals and even Tories have frequently ripped off those policies and taken credit. But credit due is hardly the issue at the moment. The press conference comes alive when they say with pride that only the NDP opposed the imposition of the War Measures Act in 1970. They also look as if they feel on solid ground when they refer to the NDP's strong stand for women's rights to abortion. On the wall along with the poster are poll graphs that chart NDP support up to mid-October, when they were doing well, but this past week is missing.

Enter Lucille Broadbent, just as things break up, looking glamorous and speaking French like a francophone, which she is. She's dynamic and sounds real. Why don't they use her more? She says her husband and John Turner "share many concerns, including free trade," taking a different tack from the rest of the party.

Ruth Rose is one of the feistiest candidates. "One problem with women in politics," she says, "is they are willing to promote others. But in this game, if you don't step in front of the camera yourself, the camera misses you." She's been active in causes outside the electoral arena, so I ask about the connection between elections and politics. "I

have a great deal of frustration," she says. "I've worked
for years and we're fighting losing battles in almost every
area. I thought we had to go for an overall political climate. I thought the degree of frustration in other areas of
struggle had reached that point, but it hadn't. Part of the
resistance to the NDP is the bad experience of a generation with the Parti Québécois. They put in all that effort
and hope and were disappointed. I've been most disappointed that this campaign is more theatre than content.
The colour of my make-up has more to do with whether I
get through to the press than what I say. If you lack a
physical presence, you don't get attention." She points to
the photo of Ed with undone buttons. "A woman dressed
like that couldn't get away with it." Nor can she win. She
doesn't have enough people to carry out the standard
three canvasses. In all Quebec, she says only five or six
NDP candidates do; another ten, including her, are rea-
sonably well organized. "I'm very disappointed with the
way the Canadian public makes their decisions," she says,
"and the lack of involvement by the progressive left in
Quebec."

Nicole Lacelle is a freelance writer. She also makes videos.
You might call her a person of the independent left, the
sort who's disappointing Ruth Rose. She's been through
the rich mix of causes and campaigns that Quebec has
seen in the last twenty years: separatism, unionism, femi-
nism. She comes from Ottawa originally, and her English
is excellent. Around us is the buzz of Montreal at lunch —
meals are serious social events here.
    "My experience of electoral politics is quite limited," she
says. "I did work on the municipal level, in FRAP, the local reform movement, in 1970, and its successor, the
MCM, and it is true that real politics is outside elections,
but even if you're outside the system, when you go door to
door and work in an election, it's exciting. Even though
you wouldn't want to be elected yourself, there is an au-
thentic connection there in those campaigns, that you
have no way of making any other time. You don't have to

believe in the results to have fun, because the connection is so great. You think often, after a little while in your own work, that people are mostly dumb; then you go to them and see how smart they are.

"When you do videos with people in the street, it's the same thing. In a video I did last spring on job training — and is that dull stuff — of the thirty-six people we asked, thirty-four had brilliant things to say about it. Only two said, What is that? And in French it's even harder to understand. The process is exciting, talking to others about what is common to us is very exciting, it's always rich. There are some activists in Quebec who have dropped out of any political activity except for elections, when they come back just for the pleasure of talking to others. *On dit, Prendre le pouls.* Take the pulse. Wonderful things you hear. You say to yourself, I never thought about that. So there is this little space in elections, which is the direct contact with people.

"Debate is the substance of politics," she goes on. "The absence of debate is why people are leary of politics, because everything is so mediated." I think about the role of journalists in this election, and in politics generally. "French Canadians are very very very hot on politics," she says, "that's a love-hate relationship too. I come from a working-class family, very suspicious of politics, but they'd go to debates between candidates during election campaigns and come back having chosen their man, as they said.

"My grandparents talked a lot about those meetings. I'll get you this, I promise you that. Or if they were already committed to the party, they'd still go to the debates and be disappointed in the party or the candidate. It started in the fifties, this absence of direct physical debate between the party leaders and also the candidates in the constituencies. Now there's not much. Even in the door-to-door process you only see the candidates one at a time." Does she think the TV debates compensate for the absence of those local debates? "Yeah," she says. "And people who thought they'd be bored still get something." Then she

starts to talk about the impact Turner had last week on
TV.

"It's very rarely that people like me look at a party
leader as a human being. As a matter of fact never, except
this time, just because he'd been so vilified; it almost
brought out the mother instinct. And even though you
don't give a shit for the Liberal party, just the fact that he
could stand up and save his own face gave it the reso-
nance it had. If he hadn't been *tellement profondément
critiqué* by all the books and party rumours — although
that didn't touch me, he could go down for all I care —
but it was the sight of him standing up there and fighting
back. The feeling he gave me was it was his own dignity he
was fighting for. It was down to the basics there. It's a
kind of face saving, saving yourself, and I was quite
moved, even though I don't give a shit for him or his
party. The tragedy brought something out of this person
that was absolutely *imprévisible*. It's also because of the free
trade thing, and Meech Lake — big issues that are involved. In another kind of election we wouldn't have
given a damn, but the combination of a big issue and a
huge defeat of a man is the combination for being
touched by what's happened. You want to say, Why don't
you all fuck off — this poor guy — I never felt like that
before."

As for the NDP's stress on Broadbent, even stronger
here than in English Canada — "In principle it's wrong,"
she says, "because the issues and program are important.
But on an image basis, the one who is a personality because of the situation is not Broadbent. *On peut pas accoter
ça.* He can't measure up, because there is no tragic element in Broadbent. It's the human, the rising to the
occasion, showing dignity in a situation that's totally ill-
fated from the start." I ask if she was surprised to discover
these feelings about Turner, of all people. "Absolutely,"
she says. "I hate John Turner. He sent the army into Quebec in 1970. I'm not indifferent to him, I can't stand him!
But I can't not see this drama unfolding in front of my
eyes."

She'll vote NDP in her riding, where she says the Liberals or the NDP are sure to win. If the Tory had a chance, she would consider voting strategically, that is, voting for either of the Opposition candidates, depending on which had the better chance of defeating the Tory. Except, she says, in a case like Liberal candidate Paul Martin, Jr., in Verdun. He's the owner of Voyageur, where scabs have been undercutting striking bus drivers for a long time. "There's a limit to voting strategically," she says. "Sometimes you can't, it's too much. It would be the right thing to do, in order to beat the Tories, but you just can't." Three weeks later, it's the Tory candidate who wins Nicole's riding.

Her feelings about politics and elections are obviously in motion, but she's the kind of person who delights in finding changes in herself. "My aging has made me more interested in elections than before," she says. "There's the compassion part. When I was twenty-one I would not have been touched by Turner. There's something rough and tough about being young, even though there were strong issues when I was twenty-one. Also, a political judgement develops in you that a little better is better than a little worse. Which I did not think twenty years ago. It's not that I became a bleak reformist, but you come to see life as hard. I was twenty in 1968, so especially then, it's not only the age, but what situation there is when you are young. I don't think the young now feel like we felt then. It was a combination of our age and a lot of effervescence in society. We thought that part of growing up was taking to the streets: you demonstrate. It was viewed as quite normal in our own lives. You see, though, that it's hard to make things move, and if you can get them moving a little bit, it's good, for progress and our ego. We had a saying when the Marxist-Leninist groups were strong in Quebec that they were going from defeat to defeat, to the final victory. I never agreed with them about 'la politique de la merde' " — she means the idea that the worse things get, the sooner the revolution will come" — I thought it was bullshit, but my emotional structure was a little sympathetic. We thought for instance that paternalistic bosses were the worst you could get, and now I think they're a little better than all-out fascists.

"It's like the old left bullshit that you have to raise consciousness among the people. It's not really that their consciousness is not raised, it's just that they do not agree with the people who are trying to raise it. It may be right or wrong, what people think, but it's their stand, and you have to recognize it and argue with it. It's so insulting — raising consciousness. It shows a definite sense of superiority because you're sure your consciousness is okay and theirs is not. I learned that forever and ever when I was in a women's group in a crisis. I was a student at the university and we had a committee of students, professors and employees, and our big campaign was that the secretaries stop doing the coffee. So simple. We campaigned and campaigned and campaigned and they never did stop. And some said, Such low consciousness. And some said, Why don't we ask them why they do the fucking coffee? And we asked and the secretaries said it was the only thing that got them up and out of the office. It really had to do with about forty-five other things. They'd go to the toilet, see their friends, make their appointments with the dentist, then they'd come back and the coffee was done. It was not a problem of their consciousness, it was something to do with their working conditions. So if you don't try to address the situation in the terms they see it, you can raise consciousness till hell burns over. You just have to ask them why they do things or why they vote this or that way. They have reasons. Sometimes reasons of desperation, but reasons. The left have always been convinced of their own high consciousness; in French we say, *On le voit venir avec ses gros sabots*. You can see him coming in his big boots, would be the English. I don't know if there's a real equivalent expression."

After lunch we walk back to the headquarters of the Confédération des Syndicats Nationaux — the organization of independent Quebec unions. She's doing some contract work there. In front of the building we pause before a dreary sculpture of noble struggling workers. They look like they're hopelessly trapped in the stone and in the stereotyped concepts of the well-intentioned people who commissioned and constructed them. "What a downer," she says.

Afternoon. A radio debate at CKVL in Verdun. Five breathy men sit around mikes making notes while they wait for a cluster of ads to finish. The Liberal and the Tory, Jean-Claude Malépart and Charles Hamelin, are big and paunchy. Roch Lasalle, the scandal-tainted Tory ex-Cabinet minister is there, too, as a "neutral commentator." The NDP candidate is a wispy little man, Pierre Beaulne. *Le petit pauvre,* someone calls him sympathetically. The two windbags simply puff him away.

They talk quickly, to make their points in the limited time, with ads crammed in too, and also because this is the pushy hyped style of AM radio. *"C'est vous qui connaissez rien,"* the big boys bark back and forth. The way they lean toward each other, drawn by their mutual gravity, and ignore the NDPer, is the way the race is going to go here in Quebec. Then they lean away from the mikes and say something *sotto voce* to each other. The host breaks in like a racetrack tout. The PC delivers a strong line about Liberal dinosaurs claiming to be an alternative to the Tories. He lists Liberal achievements like the War Measures Act and the ecological ravages of Mirabel airport and ends by asking if the listeners want to be represented by someone connected to the government or to the Opposition. This becomes a more poignant query next day when an Environics poll shows Liberals leading Tories in Quebec and nationally. Afterwards, Malépart and Hamelin, like aging twins, stand while two women, their wives or their assistants, scurry up with their jackets. They bend over a slim copy of the deal, which looks like they could wolf it down in half a swallow, and examine some clause, as though neither has bothered with this much in the past, but what the hell, it's now part of the game of politics and they came to play.

Outside in the twilight waiting for a cab, I feel it's crazy enough to try and do one country so huge in seven weeks, but to try and do two! Here in Quebec, I'm a foreign correspondent.

Hallowe'en eve, Montreal. Tonight, appropriately, the Tories are trying to scare us to death about the economic effects if their deal is derailed. Michael Wilson told businessmen in Ottawa that the U.S. will cancel the Autopact if the trade agreement fails. He called Turner and Broadbent liars. The dollar fell — it's a scenario with a Third World feel. They seem uncoordinated: Mulroney said on the debate that Canada can cancel the deal and get out, while Wilson says if it's cancelled even before it's signed, catastrophe will follow. The Alliance, the pro-deal business group, says if the deal falls through, "our standard of living will start going down on Day One." They've also announced that they're preparing a four-page ad for every paper in the country. They hadn't planned on it, they say, until they saw the cartoon booklet and its effect. They made a few calls, raised $1.5 million, and think they may spend more than that. They must be doing something right. Their mere intention to put out these ads is being extensively reported, but when the Pro-Canada Network put out the booklet (which cost $700,000 and still isn't completely paid for), it couldn't get a mention. Meanwhile, retired judge Marjorie Bowker's critical analysis of the deal, which has been circulating in photocopies, has just appeared in book form. The publisher says they printed 20,000 and have already sold over 30,000. "It's been crazy," he said.

I spend the evening with a group of Anglo Montrealers. Often when I've been in Montreal during the past twenty years, people like this have taken it on themselves to show me, since I'm from Toronto, what it's like to really live. They're aging a bit, and meeting in someone's comfortable home instead of this year's bar. There are a few francophones, including Jean-Guy Moreau, the superb impersonator. He supports the deal, because as a performer he hopes it will help him find an audience in Paris or L.A. As the evening proceeds, he gives us Liberace, Paul Lynde, and Simone Signoret, among others.

They ask a lot of curious questions about the opposition to free trade over in English Canada. I feel like a visitor from another planet. Here in Quebec, they say, you just can't find anyone really against it. People in this province aren't worried about losing their culture, for example, the way many in English Canada are. They feel secure, their language is their bulwark, and anyway, they've survived in Canada, so why wouldn't they do so in relation to the U.S.? Besides, people say they don't see much difference between Canada and the States. Since they're already part of one, why not the other? The Parti Québécois could have lent legitimacy to opposition, but they support the deal because, their leader Jacques Parizeau says, it will hasten the break-up of Canada. In English Canada, although most editorial positions favour the deal, opponents write on the op-ed pages. Here, it seems, there is practically no opposition in the press, media or among the intelligentsia. Nothing. The unions are opposed and the farmers and the Consumers' Association of Quebec. But the two major provincial parties support it, along with all the opinion makers.

Next morning an Environics poll shows more people in Quebec are now against the deal than in favour. The only province left where a majority wants it, is Alberta.

Tuesday, November 1

On "Canada AM" this morning, health minister Jake Epp talked reassuringly about social programs under the trade deal. There were no opposition voices to provide balance — CTV seems to have decided to skip that detail for the duration of the campaign — so it fell to host Nancy Wilson to raise questions. They had a pretty detailed discussion about the future of negotiations on what

constitutes a subsidy, along with the threat to social programs, since there are no explicit exemptions for them in
the current text. It was another example of the extraordinary level of complexity that has very swiftly developed in
public discussion because of this issue. It's amazing, actually. This is breakfast TV. Later, in the hotel restaurant, I
hear businessmen trying to make sense of what's happening over their coffee. They can't. But they still haven't
taken their best shots.

Marie-Josée Lapointe works at Tory campaign headquarters here in Montreal. She was in community college in
1983, did some work for the PCs as part of an advertising
course, and is now press secretary to immigration minister
Benoit Bouchard when there isn't an election on. She says
her work for the party is her "own way of making a small
contribution to the country." She just helped organize a
press conference of Tory women candidates in Quebec,
just like the NDP, or NPD. "It made me feel good. *D'une
façon ou l'autre, j'ai contribué.*"
    She never pictured such a life for herself. "I could have
sworn on a Bible I would never do politics. I had no feelings about it whatever. My family was just shocked." She
says she's a true believer: "*Je crois en ce qu'on fait, dans la
cause, la philosophie.*" But she's also an enthusiast and, as
she puts it, "a people person." What's in it for her? "Just
changing something, making things better. If I know in
my head and my heart that I've done that, I feel good. I
worked very hard on the law on immigration, and though
it seemed harsh it was fair. I've always been like that,
wanting to help. I've always helped people across the
street. A few weeks ago, someone asked for money to eat.
He had bruises. I gave him $20. For me it all comes from
here, inside. A lot of days I'm tired, I'm sick, I wanted to
go home, and I stayed because of the party and because of
him." She means Bouchard, her minister, whom she also
served when he was secretary of state. What if they lose
this election, an unthinkable thought a few days ago? "I'd
find myself another cause, something where I'd have the

same sense of contributing. I don't know if it was to go to Africa and live with cockroaches for the rest of my life, *j'sais pas*. Many times I came home and said, This is ridiculous, I don't know where I'm at. I got sick a year ago. I couldn't drive, I had vertigo, and I said, Is it worth it? And I'm still here."

At the office of the secretary of state, she enjoyed the work most "whenever we gave a grant to an organization for the betterment of *les autochthones*. We went to a little community near Yellowknife and we gave money for their community centre and I saw a guy who was blind and I felt good. Like when you go to citizenship swearing-in. Just by reviewing the grants in the minister's office, you had a small role. I remember in Digby, Nova Scotia, some elderly ladies made coffee and cookies and some little sandwiches. It was just fabulous. I was so overwhelmed. If they were honoured to have us there, I was honoured to be there. They thought we were doing them a favour. *C'est très égoiste* in a way because it makes you feel so good."

This may sound a little naïve, but it's absolutely sincere. People in public life are rarely cynical, it's too hard on the system, they want to believe that what they do is for the best. But, she says thoughtfully as I start to go, there are other sources of satisfaction too. "It's exciting. A room full of people, the fast life, doing five cities in three days, and hopping on a plane. Once we went to Duluth, then Winnipeg, then Saskatoon for the night, then Edmonton, then Prince Rupert for the night, then Vancouver and Victoria. It was just crazy, but it was exciting. And the polls, the meetings, the planning, how you respond. It's a great challenge for the mind. Like putting together documents for an announcement. How are you going to play this? I love it. It's funny," she says, "this never came out when we talked for an hour. I remember once I was on a Challenger — the jets we use from the department of defence — and I thought, Do you realize you've been on a plane like this? You're seeing the country. Do you appreciate this? You tell your friends, they go, Whoa! I think there's really three things. The people. The fast life. *Le défi intellectuel.* I haven't talked about that either. In immigration, putting together policies was fascinating. What I like is when I'm sitting down and I have to write something. The challenge of *vulgarisation.* That's my job. You know, the kind of thing that I learned in advertising. Keep It Simple. You can do anything, but if you can't explain it right to the media, you're not going anywhere. I can say I'm good at that. I have good judgement, good instincts. I make a special effort not to know too much about an issue." In this rush of words and insights into herself, she sounds strong, confident, not at all naïve, as she speaks about what she knows and is good at. "Because my brain has to work," she explains. "If it doesn't, I get lazy. And I love writing, I love my job. During the boat people, I spent thirty-six hours up writing." *Vulgarisation* is a good word. In English we'd say, "popularizing," but the French gets closer to the task and also catches the slightly unrespectable aspect of it.

The Complexe Desjardins, afternoon.
Lots of people hang out in this mall among the indoor plants and the shoppers, leaning over the balconies on various levels. This is an older man. He says he has nothing to say about politics, then talks furiously and almost nonstop for thirty-five minutes. His venom is concentrated on politicians. "There's good and bad in all of them," he says, but *"c'est le mauvais qui l'emporte.* It's the bad ones that win out. Everything that comes from the election through my door, I rip it up. It goes straight in my wastebasket." So with all this cynicism and bitterness, does he ever bother voting?

"Yes!" he says with passion. How does he decide which way to cast his ballot? Well, he voted for Mulroney last time, but he's a retired pensioner and the *"mauvais coup"* in '86 when the Tory government tried to de-index old age pensions is something he doesn't plan to forget. He's worked all his life, he says, and starts talking about how much money is spent on political campaigns which could be spent instead on homes for old people — not like himself, but like his uncle, who's eighty-seven and lives in Montreal North. "All the money for the politicians to go here, go there, go everywhere, with their wives and kids too, why can't that be spent on old people? It's a disaster, a horrible waste."

He is preoccupied with this uncle. It seems to focus his sense of what's wrong with our society. "They shouldn't have to lie in shit," he says. "It's not their fault and it's not the fault of the people who work there. They used to have to care for five residents, now they have ten or twelve. They just can't keep up." It doesn't make sense to him, and he returns to it often.

He's from Abitibi, started working in the woods at ten, and continued through the thirties and forties, six days a week on the worksite. He has two examples of personal experience with politics. One concerns a Liberal, the other a Conservative. Once, thirty or forty years ago, he was president of the Abitibi school board. Government grants were available, and they submitted their application to the provincial minister of education, along with four other boards. But a different board got the grant because, they were told, its chairman was the minister's neighbour. Incensed, he took a day off work and went with members of his board to meet with the minister. The minister told their delegation, It's this guy or nothing. He — this fellow in the Complexe Desjardins — demanded that the minister put that on paper. Then he called a meeting of his executive and said they didn't have to give up, they could still appeal to the prime minister — as he puts it — of the province. In the end, they got no satisfaction.

There's a tale with a similar moral about a federal Conservative. "They're all the same," he reiterates. "Money gets wasted. It should be spent on homes for old people, things like that. Don't tell me it's that I don't like politicians, it's that they're all the same, and the nicer they are, the worse it is." He throws up his hands and returns to his uncle once more. He is loaded with experience, insight, compassion and no confidence at all that things will ever change, not the flimsiest hope.

He's fiercely angry at Mulroney, less at the attack the Tories made on pensions than at his betrayal by yet another politician whom he trusted and voted for. He actually hisses as he speaks. "I'm autonomous and self-sufficient, but there are other old people who aren't and it's not their fault," he says. What goes for politicians individually goes for the parties too. There are three of them and there should be only one: there's the Liberals, there's *les bleus* and there's Broadbent. They're all the same.

He's worked, been active in his community, got personally screwed by politicians twice, and now, he feels, once again in retirement. He has been pissed off about politics since the early 1940s, he still hasn't got that rejected application from the board of ed off his chest. He keeps saying it doesn't matter, they're all the same, but he also keeps saying money should go to old people and not to politicians. The demands of justice won't quite let someone like him walk away from the political process completely.

"So you won't vote anymore?" I say.

"Oh yes, I will."

"Why?"

"Because I don't want other people to vote in my place."

Farther along, where a cherrypicker hangs paper snowflakes from the mall roof, stands a retired upholsterer. He's in favour of *libre échange*. He says it's time for Quebec to finish with "This is my backyard and you stay away and don't play in my backyard and I can't play in yours." That's been our narrow attitude for too long, he says. He's always been a Liberal, but now he'll vote for free trade. We have to enter the wide world, he insists, and points to Europe on the edge of the 1990s, where the borders are coming down. He says he's travelled, which helped him think the problem through. Travelled where? California, Mexico, Venezuela, Hawaii. He's trying to work his way out of his upbringing, out of the xenophobia of Old Quebec. We're not in the fifteenth or sixteenth century anymore, he says, and he thinks the free trade deal fits with his hard-won conclusion that Quebec has to strive for a new openness after centuries of closing itself off. People are really thinking about this thing.

Wednesday, November 2

Toronto. The Writers' Development Trust is holding its annual set of dinners tonight. Corporations and rich people "buy" writers for meals and conversation, and the money goes to writers' causes. This kind of event could make you think, If this is the culture we're trying to save, where do I sign that trade deal? I have dinner with the *Toronto Star*. We argue most of the evening about the *Star*'s general failure to cover the coalitions and the development of the popular movement against free trade. They insist their approach has been right; the proper place for politics is in the parties, Parliament and the electoral system; these extra-Parliamentary campaigns are not the way to go. The people at the *Star* are against free trade, but some of them seem no more in favour of the new kind of politics being practised out there in the country than are the Tories or the Business Council on National Issues.

Thursday, November 3

Business's retort to the cartoon booklet is in every newspaper in the country today, sponsored by the Canadian Alliance for Trade and Job Opportunities. It will be reprinted frequently until the election is over. It covers four full pages in the form of a dialogue between two people.

One of the people running the NDP campaign calls from party headquarters in Ottawa. He wants to know who this Alliance is. They are the mightiest, wealthiest organized force in Canada, the Business Council on National Issues in election gear, the same people who originated the free trade initiative. I take an Alliance brochure from a pile and read off the elite list of member organizations, starting with Aerospace Industries Association of Canada. He takes it down over the phone. Where is their research, their campaign budget? Minutes later another NDP staffer calls asking for information about the Pro-Canada Network, the coordinating body for the anti-free trade movement. The NDP is telling Canadians at this point that only their party can be trusted to stop the trade deal, but they don't even know the players. They haven't even got a scorecard.

Friday, November 4

Flying toward Newfoundland. It looks like another mask is coming off, the class character of the free trade debate is finally starting to emerge: wealth and business on one side, with their political retainers, versus almost every other organized voice in Canadian society. The four-page ad seems to have led people to wonder about its provenance. Yesterday Michael Kirby of the Liberal campaign team said support from big business is like a kiss from the Ku Klux Klan. Mulroney called that McCarthyism, as if North America's biggest corporations were being blacklisted like "communists" in the 1950s. The Chamber of Commerce has asked its 170,000 members to hold workplace meetings with employees to pressure them on behalf of the deal. The Canadian Manufacturers' Association has done the same.

Doug Smith, a Winnipeg journalist, says the sudden role of business reminds him of the tale of a little boy raised in Toronto's wealthy Rosedale, who tragically never spoke. Then one day when he was fourteen, as the maid was serving breakfast, he barked, "The toast is burnt!" Everyone asked why he had never talked before. "Because," he replied, "there was nothing to complain about." Smith notes that both left and right seem to have lost confidence in their traditional party representatives: the left in the NDP and business in the Tories. So they're joining in directly.

He's right, everybody wants to get into the act. Yesterday retired Supreme Court justice Emmett Hall, one of the architects of health insurance, said the deal is no threat to medicare. U.S. consumer crusader Ralph Nader is warning Canadians not to go the way his country has. There's disarray on the editorial pages of the *Financial Post*. Some say the government has fucked up by refusing to talk about the deal; others say they fucked up by letting it get talked about; someone else is already speculating about the composition of a Liberal Cabinet. This election is turning into democratic chaos. Joey Slinger, in the *Star*, catches the sense of it. "What I'd like to do," he says, "is examine free trade from a purely emotional point of view."

This morning I talked to Laurell, who had much to do with starting this roller coaster when she called a meeting three years ago. "I'm so nervous about the next two weeks," she said.

Why?

"I think it's because everything depends on what the Canadian people do — and I'm not sure I know who they are!"

The coalitions against free trade have built a popular movement, but they have largely been the work of an ever-expanding core of activists, a kind of popular elite, you could say. Something else is happening now, a broader democratic ferment, unaffiliated people getting involved in unpredictable ways, asking questions, taking initiatives on their own. It's just starting, there's not much time till the election — but there's more of it than this country has seen very often on a national scale. It's a splendid sight.

Week Six

Friday, November 4

St. John's, Newfoundland. This is such a verbal society. People standing in line at a news stand make John Crosbie sound a little tongue-tied.

Christine Chipman, a "poor person" in her own words, works in a little office with a church-based organization called Ten Days for World Hunger. "Newfoundlanders are born with the gift of gab," she explains. "Just tell the truth." It's the end of the work day; it gets dark here earlier than in central Canada.

"Poor people don't think about free trade or elections," she says. "You're to the point that the only thing you're thinking about in your lives is putting food on the table or having the light bill paid at the end of the month. You might think, Maybe I'll vote for the PCs, maybe they'll raise the welfare payments, but after a while you think they're all the same." When you're alienated from the political system and just about everything else, they're all just parties, they're equally distant, they're that establishment you don't belong to.

"I come from a family in housing," says Christine, using the universal short form for public housing. "In our neighbourhood there are about 150 families and maybe 20 go out to vote and I know most of them, and when you ask the rest, they say, Jesus No, it's a waste of time. And you can argue that politics affects *our* lives more than anybody's, and still people wouldn't vote. I felt like that till I got into this kind of work.

"The only time you usually see the politicians is during an election and other than that hardly ever. They come along and promise you the moon. Then you don't even get stardust, they're like every other Happy Jack. The only time I even thought about politics was when an election was on the go. But now I think of politics from the time I put on my shoes till I go to bed.

"Picture, if you will, my life a few years before I became involved. You get up in the morning, you check the fridge. If you don't have enough, you think about where to borrow a few dollars. Then I came onto a program where I surveyed 350 people like me, talked to them and came to the opinion that I was worth something. Because people all spoke to me and said, My God, Chris, you really know what you're talking about. And *I* thought: I'm not responsible for what's become of me!" Because she'd been active in her community, she was hired by the provincial department of social services to work on a survey of welfare recipients. When she saw other people in the same desperate circumstances, she realized this was a pattern into which they had all fallen.

"The change came from talking to people about what caused my own situation and it also came from reading. People gave me books. I could read twenty-four hours a day if I was left alone. I ate books — to arm myself. Not necessarily books. Reports on the safety net of Canada, the Canada Assistance Plan, books on how Canadians are falling through what they call the neoconservative safety net. And I guess with the project, in going out and doing the report that was going to show up under the government's name and show who were the people who helped put you in that seat, it really gave me a weapon. And even if I felt I was hitting my head against a wall — at least you feel you're doing something."

"I worked the '84 election as a poll clerk," she says, "and spent the day telling scrutineers from three different parties about my own life and about what each party would do for me or the poor people, and they sort of answered back and I almost had a row with the Liberal. A very big-business sort of person. He told me not only was I speaking wrong, but there was no longer poverty in Newfoundland. He said, 'I don't know anybody who's hungry.' I almost flipped — they had to chain me down. I just spent six weeks talking to 350 people who are hungry and I'm sure if I had another six weeks I could find another 350. So when it comes down to the brass tacks of living, just putting french fries and gravy on the table, they don't know. He must have went around with a paper bag on his head all his life not to know it."

I ask about free trade. She looks at me suspiciously. "I don't know what your stand is on it," she says. "Mulroney won't tell you nothing what's going into the free trade agreement itself. Especially the part where he's left the subsidy open to future definition, and to think it won't affect our social programs, you'd have to have a lobotomy." She stretches the word out — loh-baw-toh-mee — as if it's a chant. "If it was written down, I might believe him, but it's not." Again, the surprising and detailed knowledge people have about this deal. Imagine the level of insight someone like her would have if government and media genuinely tried to inform the public.

"There was a good thing on the radio this morning," she says. "It was buddy's point on the open-line. How can you say we've got an escape clause" — the six-month getting out provision — "when they're threatening us when we don't even have it already? The PCs are losing their composure so badly, it's making you wonder what *is* in that agreement. On VOCN's "Democracy Line," they don't cut you off no matter what you're saying. It seemed like 90 to 10 anti-free trade." I'm acquiring a new respect for phone-in shows. They may be a secret democratic weapon.

"We were at a display at the mall on World Food Day," she goes on, "and you can't talk about hunger without talking about politics. And I was saying to these elderly ladies, This deal could hurt your pensions, and they said, Aw, go on wid ye. And I said, What about the pensions?" She means the Tories' failed attempt to de-index old age pensions during their first term. "And they said, Yah, but we stopped that, and I said, Yah, but this time it's between us and the Americans — it's sort of the Americans standing behind us with a whip." This woman could be dangerous to the status quo. She goes somewhere to solicit charity for the Third World and ends up talking about the election right here.

"I try to do my best to sort of politicalize a person," says Chris, "in letting them know about the power they do have. Right now, it's that little "x" — to listen and be aware of the fact, because there's no decisions a government can make that don't affect people at the bottom of the heap. It generally affects them the most. They think of politics as a rich man's game. But if every poor person across Canada voted, Canada would become a socialist country."

She says this as if it's obvious, though the thought runs against most political and journalistic wisdom, not to mention election results everywhere during the past century. Yet it has a logic; it *should* be true. Wealthier people do vote at higher rates than poor and working people: they've learned to use the vote to safeguard their interests. But even when they vote, the less privileged often support parties and candidates that appear opposed to their own interests. In the technical literature this is known as false consciousness. It's the great mystery in the history of electoral politics and the extension of the franchise. Chris is aware of these contradictions.

"The NDP seems the only party that offers some hope," she says. "It's a party," she goes on, as if that's one strike against it, "but it's trying to get the poor people removed enough from the poverty they're living every day to get them out to vote. I think any poor person who could have a written-up summary of the three parties' politics would have to vote NDP, or at least Liberal. I know they do vote PC, but I think it's lack of awareness that causes that. For instance, a lot think, If you've got a PC government in your province, you've got to have one in Ottawa." This is a cautious and thoughtful explanation of false consciousness. Things might be different *if* people were genuinely informed . . . which would require not just institutions that *want* to inform them, but literacy skills and leisure to make use of information.

So despite her optimism she sees the emergence of politics among those at the bottom of the heap as a gradual "erosion process, a chipping away." She gives an example.

"Here we are in a province where frugality is the rule of life and poverty causes people unending distress, yet now John Buck, the minister of culture, is going to send out stamped envelopes to all householders in Newfoundland about Double Daylight Standard Time, that two hours ahead stuff, something that's really relevant to the lives of poor people!" For her, this is one of those quirky issues through which the meaning of everything around us can be suddenly glimpsed. The government of Newfoundland brought in "double daylight" this year, expecting it would be popular, but it's been a mess: kids in Labrador went to school in September carrying flashlights; old people who rise early hated the dark. Then the government announced it would spend $100,000 for a mail survey on the matter — while, as Chris notes, 21.8 percent of Newfoundlanders live in poverty and 9,000 families in St. John's alone need food help. She pulls out a letter she wrote to the *Evening Telegram*. "I could write three pages on what $100,000 could do to better the lives of the poor here in our province," it says.

She shows me the words to a song by Tracy Chapman, which she's typed up. It's called "Talking 'bout a Revolution," and it means a lot to her. It makes the connection between poverty and politics that she has made.

Marie, a researcher who is Chris's colleague at Ten Days for World Hunger, says this election is demonstrating democracy because of the intense debate outside the normal campaign process. "So even if we lose . . .," says Marie, and Chris cuts her off, "Don't say we can lose, girl. Don't even think it. We can't lose."

This moment stays with me throughout the campaign, especially election night, and long after. How do you cope with defeat after you've committed yourself to the unthinkability of losing? Do you say you managed to change the nature of the loss by how you fought the fight? Or does that only work for those whose relative privilege cushions them from defeat's fiercest effects, while those like Chris, on the front line of the war between wealth and want, feel the shock first and worst?

She concludes, "You do what you can to actively affect the issue, but sometimes you think prayers are the last resort. I pray every night before I go to sleep." Marx would have understood. It's true he called religion the opiate of the masses, but he also described it as "the heart of a heartless situation, a sigh from the soul of the oppressed." Chris Chipman has not been drugged by the promises and comfort of prayer. She is doing all she can, she'll probably assault the barricades with her last breath, but she'll mutter a prayer of ultimate hope at the same moment.

Saturday, November 5

In today's *Evening Telegram*, there's a full-page summary of retired judge Marjorie Bowker's short treatise — really a pamphlet. It's as though we're seeing a revival of the tradition of political pamphleteering. Beside Bowker is an argument for the government's position. Inside is the four-page Alliance ad created to counter *What's the Big Deal?* Op-ed is a columnist's counterattack to an attack by Crosbie's chief of staff in response to an earlier column. This is the national debate that the secret government communications strategy of 1985 said must be avoided.

Today is the day set for nationwide demonstrations on women's issues by NAC, the National Action Committee on the Status of Women. Free trade and its negative impact on women is at the centre of their message. They have been tenaciously set on this issue since the moment it arose. By being there from the beginning, they made it impossible for the government to claim that only labour opposed their deal. The women's movement has been the key to creating the extraordinarily broad popular movement now threatening to wreck the well-laid plans of business and government, and to effectively democratize our political process.

I wonder how the Tories and the business "community" see what's happening. Is this a nightmare come true for them? Do they live with a permanent sense that their hold on this society is more tenuous than it usually seems to others? Do they have a recurring fantasy about it one day slipping away? Does it start like this?

Driving along the southern shore with a friend, Anne Budgell. We stop at Petty Harbour. It looks like a movie set for a fishing village, which it frequently has been. There is a fish plant here, and some of the boys are down by the wharf. I tell them what I'm doing and ask if they'd mind talking a bit. They shuffle a bit. "Got any beer?" says one. "Wanta buy a boat?" asks another. This is the place.

"We're figuring around here, it's not gonna make a whole lot of difference who gets in."

"They're not too much for a fishing man. All right for them fellows with the million-dollar boats."

"Only thing about politicians is they should get jobs for us."

"I got two kids. There's no work for the younger crowd. They don't fish."

"We pays 65 cents a pound for squid from the U.S., and getting 20 to 24 cents a pound for fish. The government won't allow us to make money." I ask which government he means. "The government that's in."

Do they vote? "Oh yes" and "It's insane not to vote" and "Give the NDP a chance." That thing about voting again, how people value it, after they express all their cynicism.

"Don't think much of that Turner."

"They never had much chance, the NDP. Give 'em a chance."

"All we're worrying about is the fishery."

"Look what they done about them whales. Saw them on TV. Spent one million on them."

"Two million or so. Freeing two whales."

"And we're starving to death."

"We're surviving, not living."

"Lots of times you're without any money in your pocket."

"No fish since September. And we still gotta wait for un-employment."

It's classic bitching and whining, but I asked for it. Richard Cashin, a former Liberal MP who heads the Newfoundland fishermen's union, said in an interview years ago that he knew Newfoundlanders who could complain to a point near orgasm.

"They're all in it for the money."

"Brian Tobin. He's up in Ottawa. What's he doing for us?"

"They go up to a hotel and spend $900 for a weekend." This is about a trip provincial premier Brian Peckford took to Boston and the actual costs, as exposed in the press, were a lot higher. The $900 ($910 to be exact) was the "entertainment" bill for one night. It is another of those things, like double daylight and stranded whales, that make infuriating sense of the distant world of power and politics. "That's good wages for us for a month. Isn't it, Bobby?"

Do they see any point to elections?

"Yes. Somebody got to run the country." A Tory Cabinet minister in Ontario once told me why he backed one leadership candidate rather than another, even though he agreed the result would make no difference. "You gotta have somebody," he said.

"Somebody got to do it. But you can never get the right fellow in." How would they describe the "right" fellow? "He'd stand for what the people want."

"A fisherman has got to have his wife working. The family haven't got a wife working, can't find no one in town." Is that new? "Oh yes. A woman never worked."

They start in about "those boat crowd coming into Canada."

What do they think about free trade? "It's gonna kill us altogether. Gonna knock out fishing. Be all right for the big businesses." Why do they think that? "They got more ways to deal. I read about it. Watch it on TV."

"I can't see why they can't create some jobs in New-foundland for the younger crowd. You can go up to

Toronto and get a job. You can't get nothing around here."

"Its getting to a point we're just scraping up our stamps. Worst fall I've seen. Only one reason: the fish aren't coming in." Are other communities doing better? "Worse. Last year and the year before they had to go pick berries to get their stamps." Saving up your stamps for unemployment insurance is a part of the economy here. The question is not whether you'll need U.I., its whether you'll get enough work in to qualify for it during the months when there's no alternative.

"A week or two before elections, they starts on the speeches."

"They might do something."

"Put a bit of pavement on the road."

"It's not gonna change my life a big lot."

Driving farther down the southern shore, Anne talks about Father Jim Hickey, a Catholic priest here who's been charged with sexually assaulting boys — mostly altar boys. People here link that case in their minds with a recent announcement by Svend Robinson, a B.C. member for the NDP, that he is gay, and with the Tory campaign of Ross Reid in St. John's East. They say the NDP will probably retain the seat (their only one in Atlantic Canada) because Reid has refused to deny rumours about his being gay — started by a fellow Tory during a nomination fight. Of course, there's no connection between the three cases — the priest has nothing to do with politics or the election — but they get connected anyway. That's life and that's politics: it's messy, unrelated things get related. Yesterday in B.C., Mulroney made a foul joke about Svend Robinson being defence minister in an NDP Cabinet. "Departing from his text . . ." went the report, indicating it was Brian Mulroney speaking from the heart. Who knows what effect *that* will have on the outcome of the election? (In the end, Reid won, and so did Robinson. A number of other Newfoundland priests, along with

Father Hickey, have since been charged with the same offence.)

Lin Jackson is a philosophy professor at Memorial University in St. John's. He wrote a piece in the paper this week explaining why he intends to vote Liberal. It surprised people because Jackson is known as a strong supporter of Premier Peckford and the Tories, and of Tory programs like the Atlantic Canada Opportunities Agency.

"I have a reputation as an ultraconservative and even a fascist," says Jackson, "because I supported Peckford's objectives during the constitutional fuss. All my socialist friends thought it was terrible. People take parties so damned seriously. They're all just three shades of liberalism. I hate the party system, because it locks you into this thing where you agree with one thing and disagree with another. I went through a period when I hated the local unions, the local CBC people. They went off into their goddamn socialist hangups about equality, the right to strike. But on the free trade thing, it's sufficiently near the bone of the 'Canadian idea.' There could be no policy more contradictory to that idea than the free trade policy. So now I'm completely alienated from all the local Conservatives who thought I was their mouthpiece. To me free trade transcends everything. I don't care which party suggested it: it amounts to the Americanization of Canadian society, resistance to which is the only thing which represents an identifiable Canadian thrust.

"It's such a constructive thing," he says of that resistance. "It generates the CBC, a kind of theatre, an art world across the country which you won't find in the U.S. I'm convinced the reason things are so *nice* in Canada is there is that reserve against going into a flat-out competitive society.

"When Trudeau was at it, I got a reputation as a Newfoundland nationalist. I couldn't understand that, how people couldn't distinguish between a concept of Canada as an articulated country of fairly distinctive communities,

like Newfoundland; that you could be all for that *and*
against Trudeau, whose centralism was very destructive.
The notion of a separate Newfoundland was quite absurd. I was appalled by some local businessmen who were
interested in starting a separatist group during the Trudeau years. I was even taken out to lunch to see if I would
serve as a mouthpiece. Probably it was the same impulse
as the free trade impulse, because forty years ago, when
Newfoundland was trying to decide on Confederation or
staying a colony, there was also an "economic union" option with the U.S.: that you could be politically
independent but economically connected. An absurd
idea, but ideas stick around."

Newfoundland is the only place in Canada where the
word Confederation means something in living memory.
In a way, it was the free trade issue of its time because it
involved integration into a larger country. Where did
Jackson stand then? "I wasn't interested," he says, "I was
just a bucko. I went to the mainland in '49, three months
before it came into effect, before the deal was signed, you
could say. Looking back, I'd say it was inevitable."

Jackson says George Grant got him into philosophy in
the 1950s. Grant may be the finest example of what is often thought to be a uniquely Canadian political category:
the red Tory. Grant died in September, just before this
election was called, and maybe his death spared him some
sadness. His book *Lament for a Nation*, published in 1965,
introduced many people to the odd idea of Canadian nationalism at the very moment, according to Grant, when it
could no longer be a political force.

Grant didn't participate much in the fight against free
trade. A lot of his energy in recent years went into opposing the right to abortion. I was always uneasy with his
surrender, more or less, of Canadian nationalism, the
cause he helped define. Maybe despair goes better with
tenure. Those Canadians who can't help relieve the gloom
by writing a book might not agree to lament so quickly.
And look around: twenty years after Grant mourned the
country, we are in the midst of probably the biggest na-

tionalist battle in Canadian history. This election is about
nationalism; in comparison, the election of 1963, on
which Grant based his famous book, was far more narrowly focused. It revolved around the right of Canada to
reject nuclear warheads for American missiles already sta-
tioned here. Even the election of 1911, the last free trade
election, was more about losing the bond with Britain
than about Canadian independence.

We move to gossip. "Brian Mulroney always reminds
me of the kind of guy you meet in campus political clubs,"
Jackson says. "I can't define exactly what that means. Certain people get involved in those clubs for their
confidence. The impression that his relationship with
world leaders has obviously overwhelmed him, he's on
cloud nine, to think little old Brian from Baie Comeau
and St. F. X. is up there. Mulroney is a small enough person to be tremendously impressed with himself for having
risen to such a height. 'Maggie told me it was a good idea;
François said so too' — even using first names in public
statements." Joining a college political party does seem
like a middle-aged thing to do. Jackson adds that Mulroney's recent jibes about Svend Robinson smacked of a
college frat mentality.

"The Canadian people are confused," he says, returning to professorial mode, "because they have shed their
real history. They hate the colonialism of their past; they
like to think of themselves as liberated. But the real history of Canada is a *colonial* one, and I don't mind it. The
monarchy had its place. There is a running away from the
realities of Canadian history which has led to the need to
create this ghost of Canadian identity. This Canada-wide
search, and no one knows what it is or where to look. I
have a fixation with the notion of Canadian identity and
how people in central Canada are obsessed by it. But no
one can say why Canadians are different."

It's odd to sit with this Newfoundlander and hear him
expatiate on the Canadian identity, though people with
their own firm sense of cultural identity often are strong
defenders of Canada too. It goes for many Americans

who have moved here. I wonder if Newfoundland is feeling more Canadian these days. When I first worked here, in 1975, Newfoundland nationalists used to harass me for coming down to show them how to write plays about their own history. I ask Jackson what he makes of resistance to free trade in this election.

"It surprises me frankly," he says. "I've been watching the drift in the last ten years and ignoring it because I really had no confidence in Canadians rising to the occasion. I don't trust them with the things that are necessary if Canada is to maintain any kind of independence." What about John Turner in that connection? Could he be the last red Tory in Canada? "It's so surprising to find the leader of the Liberal party taking on the Tories and free trade," says Jackson. "This passion with which he has taken on the anti-free trade cause is pure Diefenbaker." Diefenbaker fought and lost the election of 1963, after which Grant wrote *Lament*.

"I really am very pro-Meech," Jackson says as we wind down, "and pro-Atlantic Accord and Newfoundland's policies on the offshore, and against the attempts of previous federal governments to screw us on resources, and it was Mulroney who sold us on the Atlantic Accord, and Peckford too. I couldn't have imagined voting for anyone except the party who Peckford is most likely to get along with, but on *this* issue, it's a national emergency. Certainly it's more important than the Newfoundland offshore. . . ."

I beat my way up the hill, as you must to get almost anywhere in the old part of St. John's, to Earl McCurdy's.

Earl is secretary-treasurer of the Fishermen, Food and Allied Workers; once he was a journalist. The fishermen have been in a bitter fight with their former union, the United Food and Commercial Workers, to separate and join the Canadian Auto Workers. Earl says it was a matter of getting out of a stagnant situation. Being in the U.S.-based UFCW, he says, was about as meaningful as whatever insurance company you have your life insurance or your car insurance with. It was created in 1979 by a

merger of two other unions, the retail clerks and the
amalgamated meatcutters, to which the fishermen belonged. It was really a takeover, says Earl, not a merger;
the ex-meatcutters said the new initials meant, U Fucking
Clerks Won. Under their new constitution, any serious
change, like independence, could be blocked by a mere
seven votes out of 23,000! He describes the money U.S.
headquarters have spent to try to hold onto their Canadian members; the attacks, slanders and threats. I've
heard the same tales from unions in the Confederation of
Canadian Unions (CCU), who went through similar fights
often twenty and thirty years ago. Because the CCU has
been isolated from mainstream Canadian labour, people
like Earl aren't very aware of the tradition. Not that it
matters. It's one thing to know these things have happened. You still have to fight them through.

We're in his kitchen and Earl is cooking a bit of a gour-
met meal. He mentions Broadbent's remark that the
disappearance of the Liberals would be good for Canada.
"That may not rate quite alongside, I Had No Option,"
says Earl, referring to John Turner's major blunder about
patronage in the '84 debate, "but it's right up there." He
says his father was considering voting NDP just this once,
but that turned him back. He doesn't want to be charged
with the death of the Liberal party. Two NDP supporters
have come for dinner too. He's a labour historian; she's a
strong feminist. They're left, though not as much as
someone who went to Anne Budgell's Hallowe'en party
two weeks ago as a Sandinista. "Other people were content to be witches, goblins and vampires," said Anne as we
drove down the coast today. These two would rather not
hear anything unkind about their party, which the fishermen's union officially endorses. Earl says it would be a lot
easier on the union to back the Liberals, since that's the
natural inclination of most of their members.

The NDP ran a fisherman in one riding, he says. Party
authorities ordered the man to wear a suit and tie, but his
only white shirt was one he'd married in ages ago. He has
a neck like a bull now; he couldn't even do the collar up.

Anyway, says Earl, electoral politics is very different from union politics. Richard Cashin was maybe the brightest young Liberal MP in Ottawa during the late 1960s, but as a union leader he has adopted a different style — much more direct. Once during a strike, after being attacked regularly on a local radio show, Cashin walked over to the station, right into the studio, and took on the host, live. Union politics are substantive and confrontational; they involve people and their emotions as electoral politics rarely does.

Today's newspaper with the four-page Alliance insert in favour of free trade is on the table. It's now appeared in nearly every paper in the country and will be reprinted once and sometimes twice before the end of the campaign. Earl says people here won't read the thing; it's too heavy. He recalls advice that Joey Smallwood, a former journalist, as well as a former socialist, union organizer and premier often quoted: Tell them what you're gonna say, then say it, then tell them what you said. (After the election, it becomes clear, this didn't quite cover the situation. People may not read your ponderous pitch. But if you *keep* saying it *and* the other side says nothing in response, mere persistence will have an effect.) The Liberals have charged that U.S. corporations paid for the insert, to which the Alliance has replied, Only 20 percent. Earl stirs something and says, "Tell it to the judge."

During dinner, the labour historian says he thinks I'm going soft on the Liberals. He asks if I know the history of the Liberal party. I ask if he knows the history of social democrats. It gets feisty around the table, with the candles flickering.

Sunday, November 6

I drive to the community of Spaniard's Bay in Conception Bay, with Donna Butt to see her dad and mother. The ride is spectacular, like the ride down the southern shore yesterday. Last time I saw Bill Butt, eight years ago, he

still lived in St. John's, worked for the railroad and was
trying to save it.

"Politics is different in the outports," he says in their
neat, newly built home, a few steps from the water. "People don't seem that concerned. They'd rather talk about
what kind of a chainsaw they're going to use this winter.
I've always had an interest in politics. That happened
around the time of Confederation. My father was anti-
Confederation. We listened to all the debates on radio.
There was no TV. We were forced to listen. I voted in favour of Confederation."

He's not happy about the effect of Canadian politics on
life in Newfoundland. It's led to dependence on government. "Joey got government involved in everything," he
says. "A fellow wants a fence painted, he's got to go to the
member for a grant. Personally, I think it's a terrible
affliction. Ninety percent of an MP's time is occupied by
that sort of thing." He tried himself to work through
government to save an institution he loved — Newfoundland's railroads. "When we started with Joey as premier,
you couldn't do a damn thing. There was no one else to
go to but the government, then came the elimination of
the passenger trains, and on that we dealt mainly with the
federal government. But you can't believe anybody. Joey
denied there was anything going on behind the scenes,
but there was. I was a union rep at the time. I always
thought unions should be independent of political parties.
You vote for people who you think will do the best for you
at a particular time. I've talked to many rank-and-file
members who agree. I don't know how the backing for
the NDP gets through. It always surprised me. The rank
and file don't vote for the NDP."

He's troubled most by changes in what you could call
the work ethic. "We're supposed to have 25 percent unemployment right now. Bunk! Ninety-five percent of the
people are working the ten-week requirement. I was over
in Heart's Content the other day to get a piece for my
stove and this old guy said, You might be surprised to
hear it, this is one of the most prosperous places in

Newfoundland, but there's very few people working. But every family's got five or six cheques coming in. The permanent jobs would be one percent. Where's it all coming from? The old age assistance, the U.I. especially. The majority of families now, the wife'll work for ten weeks and get laid off, and then the daughter and the son, and the father might be a fisherman, but they'll all get eligibility for stamps. And they barter stamps. This is what politicians and government means in Newfoundland. Since I been around Conception Bay, the unemployment statistics is a farce, because people don't want anything else. They're happy to live like this."

This is not a redneck speaking; he's a lifelong trade unionist. He's travelled around Canada as a member of the Brotherhood of Railway and Airline Carmen. You can call it the work ethic he's expressing, but it's based on a workingman's sense of independence and self-respect. "I think if you went down to the wharf and talked to some fishermen, if you were a reporter, they'd say, We want jobs. But they don't mean it. They go out for a few weeks and catch the capelin and they haven't taken off the collar since. It's not very nice to go on welfare and I don't disagree with U.I., but when it becomes a way of life! Ninety-nine percent of the people in these outports are so happy and settled because of their lifestyle, they don't need for anything. We've been educated since we moved back out here. I can't understand it. There are young men out here, their wives are working in the hospitals, they've got trucks, they've got their home built, they work up in the fish plant getting their stamps. They're living comfortably and they're happy."

The local MP is Captain Morrissey Johnson, a sealing captain, and his Liberal opponent is a retired rear admiral. Pauline Butt, Bill's wife, says, "I never voted Liberal, but once maybe, for John Crosbie" — back in Joey Smallwood's era, when Crosbie was a Liberal — "but this time I'm going to vote for John Turner and against free trade. Because I'm worried, because down the road, there could be trouble for our social programs. America is so big, and if they want to encroach on our programs, we won't be able to do much. I'd like to know more about it. I'd vote for the NDP if they had a chance. I know that's not a very good statement because if people like me don't vote for them, they never will have a chance."

Donna asks if they think Turner would stick to what he's saying. Her mother says, "There isn't a politician born who'll stick to what he's saying. But this free trade thing, I might not have gone out and voted if the free trade issue hadn't come out." Donna says with disapproval, "So now you're going to go out and vote Liberal." Her mother says, "I'm going to vote against Mulroney." Donna asks, "Against Mulroney or against free trade?" Her mother answers, "Both."

On the wall is a photo of Wayne Gretzky, posing with Donna's sister at some public event. I wonder what Gretzky thinks of free trade, and how the L.A. Kings are doing, now that they have traded for one of Canada's most finished products.

"I don't think the social programs will be affected by what's written in it," says Bill. "But let's face it," he goes on, with a thought you hear frequently, "we're getting involved. Who's gonna come out on top, in everything they want? I can't see how it can be any other way. If they called a meeting today in some big hall in Harbour Grace, they'd get a big crowd who are interested now but weren't before. Turner brought it out. The social programs. What we were getting in all this from the government side was talk about the good parts, the jobs it would create. I tuned into the Parliament debates. I thought Turner's speech on free trade in Parliament was one of the best I've ever heard. But Rick, it's an interesting point to elaborate on in your book: why this change did take place right after the debate. It changed completely almost overnight. It's a hot issue now. It's on everyone's lips: people with no interest in politics, even the old lady down there." His mother lives alone in a tiny house just below theirs. We dropped in before we came up here and asked her about the election. She said, "We don't want to be American." Like the woman in the Regina home for the aged. Not, "I don't want to lose my pension."

I ask if Bill Butt thinks Newfoundlanders are feeling more Canadian these days. "No, I don't. I feel like a New-foundlander," he says. "I never felt like a Canadian."

Sunday afternoon. Flying to Ottawa, to briefly attend the annual convention of the CAW, the Canadian Auto Workers. One real test of democracy is whether it's confined to electoral politics or thrives also in intermediate institutions that occupy our lives more directly than official politics: schools, cultural bodies, community organizations, religious groups, workplaces. In fact, you could argue unions are among the most democratic institutions we have. Leaders are chosen by the votes of members, and major decisions — particularly strikes — are usually determined by secret ballot. Most important, the performance of union leaders, measured in the form of wages, working conditions and ability to enforce contracts, is subject to constant close judgement by their members. Union members are often better informed and more critical about what their leaders do, than citizens of a country are — it's all so much more visible in the workplace. It's true many labour leaders manage to avoid being called to account for what they do, but what they do is usually known. And even at their worst, unions are a hell of a lot more democratic than the gigantic international corporations that now exercise greater power over people's lives around the world than many governments do.

Ottawa. Evening.

Looking for a typewriter in the Skyline — definitely not a businessman's hotel — I run into Bob White, CAW president. He suggests I go and watch a new film they've commissioned on the history of their union. It's just starting, he says, Victor and his wife Sophie are watching it.

Victor turns out to be Victor Reuther, brother of the legendary Walter, one of the heroes of U.S. labour history, late president of the United Automobile Workers, from which the Canadian union split in 1985. Victor is something of a legend himself, an elderly shit-disturber now, who supported the Canadian breakaway.

The film is brisk and thoughtful and it all leads up to independence for the Canadian workers. It's called "No Looking Back." People always seem to get interested in their past when they've decided who they are in the present and what they want for the future. You turn to history not to find out who you are, but to learn how you got that way. It's interesting that Canadian labour seems to be going in exactly the opposite direction from Canadian business. After years of branch plant unions, there's now no sector in Canadian society that shows a stronger national sense. Victor says he wants to take the film back to the U.S. to show American autoworkers the kind of independent spirit they should have too.

I wander to the next room, where food is laid out — and look down twenty-four floors on Ottawa and think about Kent Rowley, who said the fight for Canadian independence would have to be led by Canadian workers through their movement, since the Canadian business class couldn't be trusted to defend the country. The one thing I missed in the film was a sense of pioneers like Kent and Madeleine Parent, who put independence for Canadian workers on the agenda long ago and were pilloried for it by most of the rest of labour. I wonder if Bob White knows who they are.

Monday, November 7

There's a Gallup this morning, with the Liberals wiping the Tories and the NDP almost disappearing: Liberals 43, Tories 31, NDP 22. There's no way it can be accurate.

I drop into a breakfast meeting of the union's local newsletter editors. They're grim about the poll, because

of the low NDP standing and the Liberal rise. They recall
how the Liberals reversed themselves on wage and price
controls after the 1974 election. Yet Ed Broadbent rejected an invitation to speak to this convention, probably
because he doesn't want to be associated in voters' minds
with unionized workers. A pretty strong insult after what
these people have done for him, but their loyalty seems
unshakable.

They discuss a dues restructuring that's on the convention agenda. Here's where you sense their feeling that it
really is their union: two hours' worth of straight wages
every month from each of them. The editor of a plant paper from St. Catharines says rumours are wild about a
proposed increase — to pay the $30 million cost of their
rebuilt educational facility at Port Elgin on the shores of
Lake Huron. Peggy Nash, CAW communications director, says, No, there'll be more money for both national
and local bodies without any increase. They ask how that's
possible. She says they can reduce the strike fund — there
seems to be a shudder — but she says as long as they have
$50 million in it, they can take on GM for a two-month
strike, and that's the rule of thumb. They nod in agreement but they seem a bit stunned to have spent so much
on an educational centre, as if they knew their union
stood for more than just wages and benefits, but hadn't
quite believed it.

White's speech opens the convention. His is a worker's
English. He says, So's and Fillum. He refers to an honorary doctorate he got recently. Not bad, he might be
thinking, for a guy with grade 10. He refers to threats the
CAW heard three years ago when they split from their
U.S. parent: how they'd never be able to go it alone. It
connects seamlessly with the free trade issue. His whole
speech is that way. He is smart, the kind of guy the establishment often recruits for themselves or else keeps far
from influence. He lists many things they've been able to
do since they became independent. A lot of it flows from
just having more money. Kent Rowley used to issue a

press release each year when the government published
its figures on the *millions* in profits taken by U.S. unions
from their Canadian members; but he never sketched the
kind of movement you could build if you kept that money
here and didn't have to apply to American headquarters
every time you wanted to spend on something. Like Port
Elgin, for instance. Or their fillum. Or their role in the
free trade debate. If they'd still been a branch of an
American union, White says, "Brian Mulroney would
have looked me in the eye and said to me, 'How can *you*
talk about sovereignty? You send all that money to
Detroit.'" It's freed them to participate more fully in their
own society, not just as workers, but also as citizens.

On the plane from Ottawa to Halifax. In the wake of this
morning's Gallup, the media are getting it wrong. A
front-page *Globe* story claims Turner's rise is proof of the
amazing power of television. Yet in the same poll, Turner
still ranks third among the leaders, at a measly 22 percent,
although that's his highest rating since August '84. His
performance in the TV debates didn't hypnotize voters;
they still place him last. But he was sufficiently respectable
that people are no longer embarrassed to say they'll vote
for him. That's all people wanted. He provided a way to
turn the election into a referendum on free trade.
   For the first time I find myself speculating about what it
would actually mean if the trade deal fails to go through.
In truth, nothing much will change. The rich will still
have wealth and power, they'll still own and run almost
everything, they'll continue to dominate government, the
economy, the media. They will have missed the opportunity to shaft their country beyond all previous records,
but what else? Almost nothing. Well, one other thing. A
small dent will have appeared in their *amour propre*.

Evening. Halifax.

Mary Sparling is the cultured and elegant curator of the

art gallery at Mount Saint Vincent University. Following the first savage round of Tory cuts to culture back in late 1984, Mary mobilized almost all the artists in Nova Scotia. She'd never done anything even slightly like it. They held a protest rally that led to similar events across the country and then made an advance on Parliament itself. Now she's onto free trade.

"It's a bit like a children's crusade," she says, walking through the city in the evening. She and her friends heard Adrienne Clarkson speak about the trade agreement recently, then they compiled a chain letter of lines Clarkson had used, went down to the main post office after alerting the press and mailed the letters. I got one. It said, "Keep this chain letter going. This one counts! Give, mail, or fax copies to ten Canadian voters." It's another of the spontaneous actions happening across the country, people getting involved. In fact it's the second chain letter on the subject that I've received. I also have a couple of "flip books" produced by a baker in B.C., who says he hadn't done animation in ten years. "I wanted to voice my opposition to the FTA with humour," he said. One flip-book is called *Not a Program for Canada* and the other is *Big Map Attack*, in which Saskatchewan's boundary successfully repulses an aggressive United States border as you flip back-to-front.

Mary looks over at a statue of a nineteenth-century figure as we cross a little square and mentions Joseph Howe, a journalist, who, like Upper Canada's William Lyon Mackenzie, fought the fight for democratic government in the early years of the British North American colonies. I tell her all the places I've been, and she agrees this is probably a crazy idea for a country — but it's the only one Canadians have and it's up to us to do the best we can with it.

Broadbent is on "The Journal" tonight for a full-length interview with Barbara Frum. He looks sad when she says he must be "terribly upset" by recent polls that indicate he won't be number two after this election. There is some

Macbeth in the man, and his dreams and ambition may have overtaken him. There is no humility in how he responds to Frum's questions about his lowered expectations.

It is possible that the free trade debate and this election will expose people and forces in this country as never before — not just Broadbent, for instance, but Frum too. In this interview, she sounds all the arguments of the business side, but she seems to do it in the manner of an advocate, not just to test his responses. She starts with "the hot news of the day, and that's this dollar that analysts say has taken a dive, has plummeted, is in tailspin. Isn't the world trying to tell us something? . . . You're talking about money people, who aren't really emotional about the Canadian dollar. They just, presumably, thought that free trade was going to be good for the Canadian economy." Forty minutes later, she reiterates, "Lots of people wonder if we wouldn't have been better off if our emotions hadn't overcome our reasoning and — and — and judgement on — on debating this very central issue . . . ." She seems excited and involved, breaking in and disagreeing with him. "What government could survive ten minutes that tampered with Canadian medicare?" She contradicts him and even gets into extended arguments. I suppose it would be acceptable if she took a similarly impassioned approach to the other leaders, the ones still in contention, but in coming days, Turner declines the treatment and when Mulroney comes on, she mostly listens, raises arguments in the name of others and lobs the odd softball.

Tuesday, November 8

Early morning, about 7:00 A.M., in front of the Victoria General Hospital as shifts change. The NDP candidate for Halifax riding, Ray Larkin, is leafletting. Nancy Riche, vice-president of the Canadian Labour Congress, is there too. She's completely pissed off, in her Newfoundland manner. She's been working with the coalition movement

against the trade deal. "We did it all — for John Turner?"
She is equally furious at her own party, on whose executive she sits. "When they have their strategy meeting this
Sunday," she jokes, "we're going to have an alternate
strategy meeting."

Larkin is honest and bright, an unusually frank guy for
a candidate. He doesn't pause that telltale half-second before answering a question, to figure out what the
questioner wants to hear. He says there's been concern
about free trade on the doorstep from the very first day of
this campaign, and little else. He's tried the current NDP
line: attack Turner as a liar and point to Liberal supporters of the deal to prove they're all really free traders. But,
Larkin says, people believe Turner. "He's really against
it," they tell him. "You can't fake that on TV," says Larkin. "It would show."

People come and go at the hospital. The campaigning
consists of, "Hi, I'm Ray Larkin running for the NDP" —
if he can get it in. This is politics? Hospital staff are moving on and off twelve-hour shifts. For them to just take
time to say, I recognize you — as some do — feels like serious dialogue.

Larkin talks, on the way to a pancake house after two
hours of introducing himself with a smile. He chairs the
Nova Scotia NDP strategy committee and saw a similar
pattern in the recent provincial election. Based on vague
and general polling, the NDP campaigned on abstractions
like fairness, which, he says, just don't determine votes.

In the press today, the Tories say the PM will "return to
the high road." He'll "switch to putting emphasis on other
issues, such as the government's record and its promises
for the future, rather than continuing the attack and
counterattack with Mr. Turner and Mr. Broadbent about
the truth of particular claims concerning the FTA." Bruce
Phillips, Mulroney's press secretary, adds, "We are not
abandoning the trade agreement at all." Not very clear, to
say the least. Also today, the *Financial Post* reports businesses are pressuring their employees to vote for the

trade deal. Maybe it'll work, and maybe some will draw
the conclusion that if the boss wants it, it's bad for them.
This morning the *Globe* reprinted all its editorials in favour of the deal. They fill page seven, which till now was
known as the op-ed page, because it was for views other
than those of the editors. And yesterday the Liberals went
to court against the networks over the right to use TV debate footage in political ads — which those custodians of
the public interest have so far refused. Everything in tur-
moil . . . .

In the afternoon, I learn *Maclean's* have offered a free
two-page ad against free trade in their final issue before
the election. Apparently they called the Pro-Canada Network to try and sell some space, since the Alliance and
businesses are buying a lot. They were told the PCN is
tapped out, so *Maclean's* replied, In that case would you
like two free pages? Not business as usual at "Canada's
Weekly Newsmagazine" either.

Jan Anthony and Marie Koehler Vander-Graaf work with
Mary Sparling at the Mount Saint Vincent art gallery.
They seem like the opposite poles of political engagement. Jan says she's not involved. "Being an artist I have
another obsession. I'm a potter, in *my* spare time I go to
my basement and make pots. Some of my friends would
put time in with a political organization. I don't see there's
a whole lot of difference. It's important to them; my pots
are important to me."

She sounds like the unpolitical animal. "I think art and
culture are important to maintain in any society," she says,
"and *I* contribute too. In that way what I do is similar to
what they, my 'political' friends, do. My pots are not leisure to me, they are my alternate work."

Then she starts talking politics. "Yes, I vote, I was
brought up to believe in democracy. My father taught me.
It may have been important to his generation because of
the war, I'm not sure. They were out there fighting for
democracy and wanted to pass it on to their kids. He was

in the navy and worked for the provincial government for many years, so you're always aware of the government affecting things in your life. If people don't bother with these collective things, then you've got a problem. As in the States, where 50 percent don't vote." How does she know that figure, if she doesn't pay attention to such matters? "I saw it on the news," she explains. "We've been bombarded with elections lately: provincial, followed by municipal, then U.S., then federal . . . .

"I'm not a campaign kind of person. I would not be comfortable going door to door, saying, Please think the way I do. I've never done it. It would have to be something quite important to me as a person, that had a major effect on my life. This election, I find the controlling role of the media, the media persona of the candidates — all that has become more important than the issues. Free trade, no question, is the issue." This seems like a contradiction: either the issues aren't important and image is; or free trade is the issue and nothing else matters. But we are in an uneasy election. People are trying to sort one out from the other: a typical contentless election based on mush like "leadership," alongside a fateful decision.

"I think it's a big enough thing to demand an election. Therefore, the people deserve an election, because the effects on the country are big and can be frightening. It's hard to know the economic results. Even the economists don't seem that clear," she says — as if economists are usually clear. "Free trade scares me," she continues, "because its long-term results are so difficult to know. I'm leary of letting the U.S. have control over this country. I'm leary, even though I don't feel I know enough about it to say, This is not a good idea, guys, I don't like it. The other thing is I am not sure the government have taken a lot of efforts to help the people understand this thing. I've started looking at it and find it heavy going. Hard for people who aren't economists or politicians. I'm not sure if they've taken an effort to help people understand. And that gives me a sense of distrust, and there's just so much conflict. I'm no great fan of Mulroney, let me tell you that for sure. I mean this guy's scary."

In fact, she has views: informed and rather firm ones. She's the kind of voter that must drive professional politicians crazy. She's nice, she smiles, she says she's not involved, but she's got her own ideas and when you get down to it, she doesn't like one of the candidates. When people like her say, as they so often do, that they don't know enough, is it really code for, I'm leary, this is not a good idea, guys, I'm not willing to go along?

Marie, on the other hand, acknowledges her engagement. "I was trying to think what I really feel about politics," she says. "I never took politics seriously till I was involved personally when I lived in the country 100 kilometres from Halifax in the centre of the province, in '80 or '81. I grew up with the "Duck and Cover" nuclear films in the U.S. during the 1950s, where you go into a corner of your classroom under a desk and are saved from nuclear attack. One of my fantasies on coming to Nova Scotia was, I was going to escape the nuclear holocaust in this safe, nuclear-free farm, and I learned a lot about simple living. Then we heard the provincial government was going to allow uranium mining seventeen miles from where we lived, and that made it clear to me that I wasn't going to escape. No matter where I lived I was going to be blasted off the earth when they started, and I decided to fight.

"Before that I was a Utopian. I mean, government should exist to make a better world, but I didn't think any government ever would. But when I joined forces with other people, especially environmentalists, I began to realize the responsibility of government and what an individual human being could do. There we were, against the more powerful, rich, more *credible* opponents. More credible in the sense they had titles. For example, the minister of mines and resources was our local MLA. And the people from the mining industry. And one person was sued for libel. Sued by someone from some engineering society for an article she wrote in the local newspaper.

And she won!" She says this as if each time you win, you're up for more, and maybe even sometimes when you lose. "It was wonderful," says Marie. "I mean it was devastating for her to be sued. I think it was their strategy to make people spend a lot of money on frivolous issues, like defending suits for what they wrote, maybe we wouldn't be able to put full effort. But we won. Because of our lobbying and organization we prevented uranium mining.

"When I was doing a lot of organizing for the uranium issue," she goes on, "people would say, Are you giving your child nightmares? And my defence was that aware, active people make life easier on their kids. I read at the time how children of activist parents suffer a lot *less* anxiety than those of parents who do nothing. For my own child, I've always wanted to make 'a better world.' The world is never going to be perfect, but you can work at making it a little better. When you actually do things, work at something and throw yourself into it, it's *good* for you. I didn't make that connection before. I'd been rather contemptuous of politics."

I head back downtown, thinking about the democratic chaos. I ask the cabbie, What do you think of this deal? She says, We're damned if we do and damned if we don't. That's something I haven't heard. She says she means free trade will come now or it will come later, which may be true. Especially under Turner, who's committed to trade liberalization, Canada could easily lose at the GATT international trade negotiations a lot of what might be saved by rejecting the deal.

She thinks the Tories will get back in anyway, because these things go in waves. She'd rather have the Liberals, because they did more for people when they were in. They were especially good for the military, she says. It turns out she is in the armed forces herself; she just drives cab on the side. I ask if the Tories aren't bigger military spenders and she laughs as if that's a joke. If they were serious, they'd build up the navy, she says. I'm surprised. I'd like to ask about their promise to buy nuclear subs, but I don't want to be laughed at again. As she lets me off, she is complaining about people on welfare who poormouth all the time and end up living better than those like her with multiple jobs. It's not easy to understand, how people see politics.

Five o'clock. Mary Clancy, Liberal candidate for Halifax, is holding a meeting for people in culture. She's a lawyer and an amateur actress. She's got the kind of spunk and performance sense that will work in the public arena.

Mary Sparling is there. She says to Clancy, "I can't vote for you and I can't work for you, but I want to give you some money." She says she's been thinking hard about strategic voting — casting your ballot for whoever in your riding has the best chance to beat the Tories — and disregarding all other considerations. Mary says she can't do that, she's decided to vote NDP because they're the best party and have the best candidate, but she's going to give some money to Clancy and the Liberals as well. She's explaining all this in public. Then Mary-Ellen Herbert, an artist, says she'll be voting Liberal, because the only issue is free trade. She's agonized about it, she's seen the disintegration in culture, and she's decided with difficulty that the Liberals are the best hope of getting rid of the current government.

It's like a revival, with public testimonies. There's so much thought going into what people do with their votes in this election. It's as if politics has become an aspect of life as fraught as, say, shopping — absorbing time, full of hard, obscure, silly, weighty choices. Laurell recently told me her parents are taking their votes seriously for the first time in their lives: lifelong Tories, they finally decided to vote NDP. They found it an easier switch than moving to the Liberals. Then, Laurell says, she talked to them about voting Liberal, for strategic reasons, and they had to start thinking about *that*.

Evening. Broadbent is here. There's a rally at the Hotel Nova Scotian.

Alexa Macdonough, provincial NDP leader, introduces him. Ed enters, surrounded by more beef than ever. Strikers from the fishing industry are present, right in front with their signs, but Ed doesn't acknowledge them. It seems like more than an oversight, it's part of a pattern of slighting organized labour, a snub which subtly signals the party's respectability in conventional terms. Broadbent refused to go to a CAW protest rally in London, Ontario, when Fleck Manufacturing — a big supporter of free trade — closed its plant there and moved to Mexico on the day this election was called. Nor did he go to Sault Ste. Marie at the request of the United Steel Workers, who are in a tight election fight on behalf of the NDP. He skipped the Auto Workers' convention. And he declined to appear with the International Ladies' Garment Workers' union and all the clothing manufacturers — union and even non-union — on Spadina Avenue in Toronto. Instead, he went mainstreeting in Chinatown.

Broadbent tells this crowd they will be sending more NDP members than ever to Ottawa. This kind of predictable electioneering — you could lift it whole from any campaign in any election — seems pretty dull compared to the chaos happening outside the formal process. As he speaks, Broadbent's staff are distributing a 1981 *Toronto Star* piece in which Turner praises Reagan and Thatcher. Their campaign remains anti-Turner and anti-Liberal. They barely mention the Tories, and when they do, it's without emotion.

There's a taping tonight of a TV debate on free trade, between the three candidates for Halifax. Tory incumbent and minister Stewart McInnes seems not too swift. You wonder why he agreed to this debate, or why someone savvier didn't stop him. Mary Clancy asks why the Tories are pushing the deal and he says brightly, "It's not me, it's *business!*" — as another mask falls. Ray Larkin seems the most informed of the three, but Mary Clancy shines with her sense of the stagey line. She has probably won the election on this show — to be telecast next week — just as

McInnes has probably lost it. Ray Larkin is caught in the backwash of Ed's irrelevance.

Very late, at the Historic Properties, Halifax's tourist district down by the harbour, I enter a restaurant and run into the NDP road team. I say I'll be joining them for a few days at the beginning of next week, the last of the campaign. They say very urgently I must do so on Sunday, not Monday. They can't be specific because it's a secret, but that's when things are really going to start "moving and shaking."

One of the new batch of Tory radio commercials says, "John Turner is intentionally misleading the Canadian people. He is not worried about our country's future, he is worried about his own." This is the high road they've decided to take. The Liberals don't seem to be responding. Perhaps they're hoping for a backlash. Turner does appear to have a capacity for dignity, or his stiff version of it. To yesterday's poll, which could have had him swooning, he said, "I am prepared to accept the decision of the Canadian people in 1988, as I was in 1984." I wonder if that line was his own or if it was faxed to him from party headquarters in Ottawa, as seems to be done in all the campaigns.

Wednesday, November 9

Cape Breton, where I'm about to land, often seems to have more culture and history than the rest of the country combined. Nathan Cohen, the critic, came from here. He was a sort of prophet of Canadian culture. He believed in it when there wasn't much to believe in and criticized it when it was scarcely there. Dawn Fraser, a rhyming worker-poet of the twenties and thirties, lived and ran a bookstore here. And there's Rita Macneil, of course. Not that you can quantify these things — you can't. It's more that people here are so sure they *have* a culture and history, while many Canadians elsewhere seem far less certain.

Sydney. Jordan Bishop is an economist at the local college. "Ever since I came up here from Toronto, I've voted NDP," he says. "But I've got a Liberal sign on my lawn. It's called strategic voting. The word is out: get the Tories." We're going to see George MacEachern, a retired labour leader and lifelong communist. That brand of politics is part of local culture.

MacEachern, who's eighty-four now, says he's had many thoughts about elections over the years. He joined the communist party of Cape Breton in the thirties. "I ran in a couple of elections: once in Pictou county, and in Cape Breton here. We didn't have money to spend. A couple of leaflets, got on the radio a couple of times. I was well pleased. Something over three hundred voters in Pictou county voted for me. I know that the man in the street was a pretty backward individual; bigotry was widespread. Black people couldn't get a haircut or rent a place. I thought it was wonderful to get three hundred votes. I was exalted" — as he puts it — "to think there were three hundred thinking people in Pictou county voting for the Labour Progressive Party," the name the communist party adopted after World War II. It's a little surprising to hear this principled old communist enthuse about our political system. Like Nicole Lacelle in Montreal, burbling over how exhilarating elections can be in spite of themselves. "The electoral system can't be blamed for us getting the governments we do," he goes on, with a notable lack of cynicism. "I'm not cynical about anything I can think of," he says. I ask what ever happened to the inevitable proletarian revolution. "I still believe there will have to be one," he says, but he seems more interested in talking about elections.

They just had one in Sydney. The voters booted out the local council, who didn't back city employees during a recent strike. George says he used to think the Soviet system of elections was better than ours, but now he's not so sure. In the twenties, there was a politician here named M. A.

Mackenzie, who published a workers' paper with the masthead slogan, "An island of truth in an ocean of lies." George repeats it as if he loves the sound of it, and always has. "I think if people were given an opportunity to talk, without being bombarded from all sides with contradictory things, they might vote differently." I expected a critique of bourgeois politics; instead he offers a qualified endorsement.

Marion Matheson is an energetic Scot who's active in the Cape Breton anti-free trade coalition. She's lived here thirty-one years. When she first came, she ran a small business and sat on the Sydney Board of Trade. In 1964, though, her three-year-old son was scalded while being looked after by a babysitter and suffered brain damage. Caring for him occupied her completely for many years after, since there were no facilities that could meet his needs. Four years ago she finally got him into a home around the corner from here. She says the long wait made her start thinking about why there wasn't more money for such services. She investigated, and concluded that too much wealth is diverted into military spending. During her research, she also discovered the Business Council on National Issues and decided they were the villain in the Canadian social scenario, because they lobby for greatly increased defence spending and reallocations from social programs. She thinks Thomas d'Aquino, their director, personifies opposition to a better, weller, more sociable society. The free trade deal fits their program, she says: the BCNI helped originate it and lurks directly behind the main front organization for the deal, the Canadian Alliance for Trade and Job Opportunities. So she comes to her current activism via the peace movement and a brain-damaged child.

She's been handing out her own leaflet on the issues of this campaign, and it includes a verse by Robbie Burns. Burns was a popular nationalist, a man of the people. He suits the politics of this election. Marion says she just became a Canadian citizen and this will be her first vote federally. There's no real choice, she says. She'll vote Liberal, since they are the ones with the best chance to stop the trade deal.

The TV is on in the corner — CBC's "Midday." There's a Chiclets ad, shot with puppets from "Spitting Image," the British TV political satire. Usually they use Thatcher, Gorbachev and Reagan. This new one, though, is pure Canadian culture: Brian, John and Ed debate whether the flavour comes from the coating or the inside.

Ellen — she'd prefer I not use her real name — is a former NDP activist who has left the party, and she is bitter. She talks fluently and easily about her feelings, which she says is what she is all about. "I used to be very involved in politics. I became really disillusioned, though I couldn't bring myself to vote Tory or Liberal. I haven't even listened to the radio. I guess I think elections are a real farce. They're controlled by the media. People don't think about the past. Somebody makes a foolish promise and people don't remember the last one they heard. I don't think elections have greatly to do with people or caring about people. They're about power. So even if you start out with good intentions, you have to become corrupt."

Her political idol is Tommy Douglas, "with all his faults. He had a mission in life, was not willing to sell himself to become prime minister, and he was satisfied to be a political conscience for the country. He stood alone and fought the War Measures Act. He didn't change his mind because a poll said this is popular at the moment." She met Douglas a few times, and her father knew him. "Dad's analysis meant a lot to me," she says. "We came from the outports of Newfoundland and saw people starve. When he came here and worked on the steel plant, he knew about the struggles there. To be owned by the company. And the company store. And the militias that came to break the strikes. He'd never take the job of a man who was laid off. Dad died last December and in the ward with ten or twelve other men, as he died, he was still telling those men they should thank God for Tommy Douglas or they couldn't pay for this care. And we had a lot of sickness in our family. When I look at the threat to medicare in that deal now . . . ." For her, intense personal loyalty is practically indistinguishable from political loyalty: her father's loyalty to Douglas and his ideals; her own toward her father and Douglas and the cause they shared. This capacity for personal devotion in politics led to the disappointment that caused her to leave the NDP. "It's very personal," she says. "I worked for the party, and you come to the point where you find out that people you think are warm, loving human beings are political animals and you think, Is it people first or power first?" This is one way of using "political animal" — full of disgust.

As she recounts some of the events that occurred, they seem fairly common, even slight, but the emotions involved are volcanic. Her description of the moment of parting with the NDP echoes of Judas and the Last Supper. "When you kiss their arse," she says, "all you get is a handshake, but when you tell them to fuck off, you get a kiss."

Perhaps the intensity of these feelings has to do with their connection to class. There are differences, Ellen says, between the working-class ways of Cape Breton, with its kitchen discussions, and the middle-class, academic tenor of the NDP in Halifax. During this election the party organized a "Breakfast with Alexa" — for the party's provincial leader — in Sydney. It was a waste of time. "In our district, they're not used to wine and cheese parties. We don't even have a restaurant in our riding! If she knocked on the door, that's different. But when I call Halifax and say, This doesn't work in Nova, it's seen as spite on my part and not common sense. When I travelled to Halifax in the past and I'd say these things, they didn't want to hear it. I mean, you can't preach to ordinary Canadians if you don't understand us!"

When people from the working class move out of a state of political passivity, an enormous amount can be at stake. They have exposed themselves, given up the self-protective postures of detachment and immobility, and will only do so out of a profound sense of commitment. Then to feel betrayed . . . .

"I know that under the Tories, the working class and working poor will have it really tough. If the NDP is not going to meet the needs of the working class, where do I go? So I go back to fighting on issues, like tenants' rights, where I started my career. But it doesn't meet my needs."

The needs not met are political, the needs of her public soul. Like other working-class people, she sees the NDP as the best bet for her and people like her, she hopes for the best from it, but she does not have illusions — except when she's swept away by her emotions, through a personal identification. Then the result can be harsh and damaging. "I operate on an emotional level," she says. "What feels good to me I'll go with, and if it doesn't, I won't. And when my gut starts tightening, I know something's not right."

Bonnie Nicholson works at a halfway house for battered women in Sydney. "When I think of politics, when I was growing up at home, politics was a big issue, to the point where family and grandparents didn't discuss what party you voted for; it was a *big secret* — especially in this part of the Atlantic provinces. If I asked my father or grandfather, they'd say, I can't tell you. As if their votes weren't for sale. I grew up in The Pier" — a rough, working-class part of Sydney — "My dad was a steelworker — most dads around here were steelworkers or miners." She looks quite bourgeois: tipped hair, tinted glasses.

"Men were more involved in politics," she says. "The men sat down and discussed different parties. Diefenbaker and Pearson, I believe. There was always talk around the house, especially those two men, one or the other, in or out. And you would feel a genuine warmth for both of them. It obviously affected me as a kid.

"I went to college, graduated from the Sydney Academy in 1970. Back then it was a success story, grade 12. I didn't even consider anything but work." She's married and has two kids now. She went back to university five years ago, worked in business, managed a company, was doing well, but "I wanted to do something with my life. The transition house is a good place to work," she says, "because I've really gotten to know people. I mean really got to know them, more than my job in business. You get really close to these women, to the point where you really hurt for them sometimes." She's worked here the last few years part-time, and plans to start an M.A. in psychology. Since there are no graduate studies on Cape Breton, she'll do the M.A. through the University of Vermont. As she says, "The area dictates what we can and can't do."

I ask if she has a definition of politics. "It's not elections, not to me. I guess it's a group of people working together for common goals. We politick every day about everything. The area I live in, a few years ago, they were going to put in a landfill serving most of the Island. A group of people got together and decided they didn't want it. And we were successful — I guess that's what I look at politicking as. We always seem to end up electing the wrong party down here. So we don't have much of a say. For example, in Buchanan's victory speech after he won the last provincial election, he said, 'I won't forget you, Cape Breton.' I don't know what he meant by that. Although he grew up in Sydney. We're always poormouthing down here but we never get anything. Nova Scotia ends at the causeway. Sydney is beautiful, as is Halifax. It could be like that. Everything that affects us, affects us politically, let's face it."

Would she leave the life here? "No. Never. Never. Even advancement, better universities, better things for my children, I think they'll still have that much more from growing up in the Island because of the lifestyle. Maybe we're a little lackadaisical. We don't lead a fast life, we work hard, we want the same things for our children. Safe, I feel safe living here."

I ask how she feels about free trade. She says, "November 21 won't decide the outcome of the election, it'll decide whether we get free trade. It's a shame. I think there should have been an election on free trade, and the election should have been dealt with on its own." I've

heard people everywhere say this, though rarely so
clearly. They don't want another election; they want a
chance to deal with the country's future. They want an
election about free trade — in other words, a referendum.

"A lot of people here are scared," she says. "I, for one. I
think free trade could be good for our country but it
scares me. We do need jobs but at what expense? I remember when JFK was assassinated, it was like he was *our*
president. We closed the school, my grandparents were in
tears, a lot of people here and in Newfoundland had pictures of Kennedy. When I was growing up the textbooks
were American, and the TV programs. A lot of people
here are badmouthing the Americans now. I never heard
that before. I predict Mulroney's going to lose on the free
trade issue, which is a shame, because I believe he's a good
prime minister. He's intelligent, represents his country, is
doing this in the interest of Canada, has made a better
prime minister than Turner would, but I'll vote for
Turner in the next election."

I say with admiration that this sounds like a complex
and sophisticated political position. She says, "Yes, that's
right. It is a shame though, isn't it?" Being complex and
sophisticated isn't the important thing, as she gently
notes. The point is to try and sort out a confusing and
perilous situation. It *is* a shame. (In Medicine Hat today,
Minister of Consumer and Corporate Affairs Harvie Andre said about the trade deal, "The logic of it isn't going to
work. We have to sell" — repeating a government strategy
that goes back uninterrupted to September '85.)

Late afternoon. Bruce McKeigan has just finished work at
the CN railyards. "I never thought elections were such a
great deal," he says. "You get to vote once every four
years and then they get to do whatever they want to you
for the next four years. And this is the great process of
democracy. But every time I decide not to vote there's
some candidate asking for help who you just can't say no
to.

"You should've been at work," he goes on. "Most of the

guys're NDP, some're Tory. But even the Tories don't
think much about free trade anymore because they're
after gettin' jumped on." I ask how that happens. "Well,"
he says, "it's not the kind of arguments you hear on TV.
On TV, you hear about culture and that kind of thing. It's
more direct, like, Stanfield's son said he might move the
plant to the States." Former PC leader Robert Stanfield's
family has owned a company here in the Maritimes for
generations. "Things people heard," Bruce continues.
"Like about DEVCO" — the publicly owned development
company set up here to save the Cape Breton economy.
"We sell coal to Nova Scotia power," he explains, "but
under the deal, it'll have to be put out to tender to American companies. And we'd lose out. For years they
imported American coal because ours wasn't clean
enough, then they installed washers to wash out some of
the sulphur and stone, so they don't use American anymore. Take that 'Journal' debate, that Bob White talked
about one plant in Ontario — that Fleck Manufacturing
— shutting down. That's what workers like to hear, they
jump on it.

   "Just say Fleck. Or say: Why would anybody build a
branch plant in Canada if there weren't tariffs? It's colder
here, higher bills. Take down the tariffs and we won't
have any. Just say that to them and you don't have to say
anything else.

   "Workers are so direct. They'll say to you, You're fucking crazy. Anything goes, except there are certain rules,
like, as long as you don't drop the guys' lunchbucket. Or if
you're collecting money for a guy who's sick and you don't
give enough, they'll tell you straight out . . . .

   "A lot of workers will only vote NDP," he goes on.
"They figure it's the workers' party. That's the way I was,
but I'm after changing. I wouldn't have voted this election
if it wasn't for having to stop free trade. A guy at work,
I'm constantly having good arguments with him, he talks
just like the Tories: business, free trade, marketing. But I
find with a lot of those guys, when you bring up *hard*
things, they're not mean people, and this stuff about the

market, when you mention laying somebody off, they start to change their thinking."

He says his grandfather was J. B. McLachlan, a legendary union leader of Cape Breton's miners through the hard days of the twenties and thirties. Many of Dawn Fraser's poems were about J. B. Like, "Merry Christmas to you Jim / In your dungeon dark and dim . . ." when McLachlan was jailed during a strike. Bruce says his wife, Dawn, is named after Dawn Fraser.

Bruce and I visit Nelson Beaton, a retired miner, who lives in Glace Bay. "I remember J. B. McLachlan," he says. "I drove for him. I was always a J. B. man. He was worshipped by everybody except the clergy." We've been talking about leadership. I don't think I've ever been in a place where personal and political assessments seem so inextricable. Nelson is contrasting McLachlan with Jeremy Akerman, a former leader of the provincial NDP, who represented a Cape Breton riding.

"Jeremy Akerman was one of the most despicable men I ever talked with," says Nelson. "I said to him, You'll do what the Labour party in England did. But I said I'd take the day off and put my car on the road and I wouldn't take a cent, but I'll drive you around. It'll educate the people that you're no better than anyone else. So he was elected, and then he was bought off by Buchanan's government." After being a fierce critic of the Conservative government's patronage practices, Akerman quit as NDP leader to take a government appointment himself. Subsequently he also became a wine columnist and Halifax restaurant critic. "And the NDP in Cape Breton has never recovered," says Nelson.

Bruce adds, "He was saying all the things for the people that they couldn't say for themselves." This is often the role of middle-class people in popular political movements. "The people who were NDP were salt-of-the-earth type people," says Bruce. "Like Johnny Biscuit," says Nelson. In the 1925 strike, they explain, when workers raided the company store, someone named Johnny MacKinnon reached for a box of biscuits on the top shelf, it fell on his foot and he developed a limp, and the family ever after was called Biscuit-Foot, or just Biscuit. "Jeremy Akerman let people like that down so hard," says Nelson. "They always said he was like one of us."

"You always expected it from the Liberals and Tories," says Bruce. "People up here didn't just support him. They fell in love with him. That's what happens with the working class. They fall in love. Then when it's over, it's a terrible letdown."

What do they think is happening in this election? Nelson says, "This free trade thing, I don't know. I was over at two of the mines today. They're getting a new type of hardhat. So there'll be three or four thousand old ones for Nicaragua." One of his occupations in retirement is collecting used equipment to send to Nicaragua. "They seem more interested and informed than a month ago. They get it on TV and the phone-in. A month ago, they said they didn't know anything about it. You don't hear that now. I never heard anything people talk about so much on TV and on radio — even Conservatives saying they won't vote for free trade. I don't think there's another issue that struck as hard. I had a couple of books, and I showed my nephew the parts about medical services. And he wanted to borrow it. He works at the steel mill and he wanted to take it into the plant. Even my wife — she took one upstairs and said, By God, I'm gonna read this. And then saying, What does this mean? And that mean?" I think about weary voices on the CBC a year ago claiming Canadians had free-trade fatigue.

"It's usually just baseball and hockey," Nelson adds. "At an AHL game here," says Bruce, "a young American hockey player broke his back and they took up a collection in Sydney for him, and his parents flew up from California and they gave them a car. The community rallied round. But people were saying, if the American had been Canadian they wouldn't have had to take up a collection. The same thing happened with a young Canadian player in California. They had to take the chance to fly him back, because they couldn't afford to leave him there."

"Makes you wonder what they're gonna talk about when the election is over," says Nelson. "My daughter got back from Indonesia, says she's glad she got back for this election. My mother says she watches everything on TV."

Bruce says, "The Tory candidate came around and was arguing with Dawn. But even Lisa and David" — Bruce and Dawn's children — "were arguing with him." Bruce says he thinks maybe this debate is a good thing because Canadians never had to fight for their country when it was getting started. Nelson says, "One of the best things I've seen is the Riverview High School kids out against free trade, and they're talking and putting posters all over the area and I never saw the like of it before."

"The school had a lot of speakers," says Bruce. "Mostly pro, but the kids are against." Nelson says, "Boy, when you see the kids getting involved, it's wonderful. I'd say it's the most interesting election I ever experienced. There was never any issue just like this. On the talkback this morning, 90 percent of the people are against free trade. They had Crosbie on one morning."

"A lot of those intellectuals on TV don't go for the jugular," says Bruce. "They don't ask a direct question about a specific industry." Nelson says, "I didn't think Cape Bretoners would get worked up about something this political. I'm surprised at the interest. It's like a fire you can't put out. Each morning you wonder, What's going to happen with it today?"

This morning in the Lifestyles section of the Halifax *Chronicle-Herald*, I read a story about a bachelor auction for charity. There were pictures of the hunks available, with details about prizes like shopping trips to Toronto and weekends in Portugal. Maybe free trade has become a national obsession out of yearning to escape that kind of daily trivialization. Here's a debate which lets people involve themselves in something beyond the normal grind and their fantasies of breaking out of it.

"They talked a while that way about the CMU," says

Bruce. A few years ago there was a drive here to create an
independent Canadian Mineworkers' Union. The CCU
was involved but could only afford to send one organizer,
a young woman in her twenties. She did an amazing job,
though the campaign lost eventually, by a few votes.
Fights for independence aren't easy.

Here in Cape Breton people use "home" to mean
"here." They even talk about people from other parts of
Canada coming "home" when they're here on a visit. As
we drive back from Sydney to Glace Bay, Bruce says
everyone who leaves, wants to return. Once he drove a
friend who'd been living in Toronto, back here from Halifax. The guy kept describing great features of Toronto.
Then they started across the Canso causeway and the man
grew silent. Bruce looked over and he was crying.

Thursday, November 10

Quebec City.

I share a mini-van from the airport with nine Christian
women from all over who belong to Women's Aglow, an
evangelical organization. They're here for a convention.
They say they'll be visible throughout the city for the next
four days: praying, studying the Bible and experiencing
joy. They don't know from free trade.

Afternoon. The Chantauteuil is a little *boîte* in which I
downed many a *bière* and smoked Gauloises in 1969 when
I came to this foreign city, where I knew no one nor spoke
the language, rented a garret and tried to become a
writer. It's about the same as it was. I think I even hear
Robert Charlebois singing. How the hell do you strike a
balance between detached observation and political engagement? How did Sartre think he could wed
existentialism and Marxism? The problem is, What happens when you care about what happens?

What is the standard by which you judge the value of
action in the political realm? Is it simply a matter of

helping to achieve some measurable progress for the human race? What about Hannah Arendt's notion that politics — according to her interpretation of ancient Greece — is really about creating stories that can be told to future generations, stories that illustrate the noblest qualities of human beings? The two are so different, yet both are appealing. What is ever really accomplished? To be sure, there are certain things — abolishing slavery, defeating Hitler, installing medicare in Saskatchewan — that change people's lives for the better. But who are the real heroes of history and what is it that usually remains of their efforts? The inspiring tales of their defeats. Maybe I'm thinking about J. B. McLachlan and the warmth of response his name still commands in Cape Breton. What is the connection between the two terms of this equation? That people struggle till they succeed, which may be a long way off or never. But in the meantime what keeps them going is the tales they can tell about those who tried to do the right thing, even if they failed.

During the early evening news, you can see the Tories are going to win, they're on their way to a majority. It's clear, watching from here in Quebec, and it's because of the "liar" attacks they're directing at Turner. It's a strategy that plays on basic human generosity. People tend to think: if the government and business make all these claims about Turner lying, there must be at least something to them. Most citizens attribute their own relative guilelessness to their rulers, a mistake but an understandable and even admirable one. The Tories have managed to alter the terrain of this election to credibility, and amazingly, they have seized the high ground. A government with huge credibility problems of its own is running on the dishonesty of the *Opposition*. It's quite bold, and brilliant. You take hold of the issue on which you are most vulnerable and throw it at the other side before they can throw it at you.

Today's polls show this working. Angus Reid has the Tories up four points over the Liberals, 39 to 35, with the

NDP at 24. The CBC poll has them even at 38, with the NDP at 21. Opposition to the trade agreement is also slipping from where it was. It's now at 43 percent, opposed to 36 in favour. Here in Quebec, business has announced a huge spending campaign to push the deal between now and the election.

I call some of the people at the CAW in Toronto and propose a final newspaper ad, which would start, "Someone has lying on his mind." They say they're willing to have a meeting about it, and I say I'll try to get there tomorrow. Of course, no one knows how much money could be scrounged for this — a single full-page across the country would cost about $250,000 — or how effective it would be. But, as it says in the Talmud, "Yours is not to complete the work, only you must not desist from it altogether." It feels like a play that's just about to open, when you discover a whole new scene has to be added. Politics is much more like theatre than it is like novels.

I'm staying in the Château Frontenac, and late at night I have a little epiphany. I go for a walk in the rain on the Terrasse, the grand wooden walkway with wrought iron benches and gazebos that runs along the heights before the Château, far above the river. I'm alone, no one else is out in this mess. I turn and look back up at the hotel and see my room — a lovely corner room with many irregular little windows, almost a turret — I've left the curtains open and the lights on, and there it is, bright and welcoming. The first writing I ever published, almost twenty years ago, was a poem called "Quebec Nightwalk." It appeared in a small literary journal. It was about a midnight walk along this Terrasse, looking up at the Château, and thinking about it, and about Canada, in the light of what a ramshackle structure that hotel is. I feel now that I am back in that moment so many years past, looking up and ahead at my future, at that room, which I will occupy as the writer of a book about a moment in my country's history — so as I gaze up there, I'm inside too. I am inside, yet outside. It's a privilege, standing in both places.

Friday, November 11. Remembrance Day.

The 6:25 A.M. flight to Toronto.

I feel serene, as Turner would say. Maybe it's just the effect on your system of getting up at five and being above the clouds by 6:30. In *Le Devoir* this morning, Daniel Latouche, a veteran Quebec *indépendantiste*, attacks former Liberal health minster Monique Bégin for saying social programs are at risk under the deal. His reason? She's a Liberal and Liberals lie about social programs being at risk. His proof? They did it during the referendum of 1980 and scared the people of Quebec into voting against independence. He is stuck in past disasters. It's not hard, we all get stuck in past disasters. But learning from history does not mean ceding total authority to its analogies. I remember Latouche at an academic conference on free trade, very bitter about pleas from English Canadians to save the country. Where were you people in 1980? he said. As if he felt: We lost our dream of a country, so you can lose yours.

Yesterday, on the other hand, the Consumers' Association of Canada dropped out of the Alliance, effectively withdrawing their support for the trade deal. That leaves business virtually alone. The CAC was the figleaf covering the real identity of free trade's backers.

Afternoon at the CAW. We talk about a final ad. They think it should be in dialogue, like the booklet, using the same two characters. As for money, they're tapped out like everyone else in the coalitions, while business has started to spend, you might say, like drunken sailors. Bob White tries to call David Peterson, the premier, about some money for the Ontario portion of the cost. Getty in Alberta has already spent $600,000 for a pro-deal brochure delivered to every home in his province. Peckford has done the same in Newfoundland. Devine is sending letters to all the grain farmers in Saskatchewan on behalf of free trade. Peterson is unavailable. He's on a plane to Korea for a business trip he refused to cancel, even though this is the final phase of the fight against a deal he says he opposes zealously. His office says when he arrives in Seoul he'll return White's call, which he doesn't. We discuss how much could be done with less money. When I make some crack about the NDP, White says, "Why don't you go write your ad?"

Saturday, November 12

In the evening I drop by Royce Frith's birthday party at his daughter Val's. He has the private poll numbers for Ontario that the Liberals are working with. They're staggering in the Liberals' favour. No wonder they're complacent. "On the other hand," acknowledges Frith, "I'm one of that handful of people in Canada who will wake up the morning after the election no matter what the result is, and hear those beautiful words, 'Good Morning, Senator.'"

Week Seven

Sunday, November 13

A rainy morning. Today I join the leaders for the final week of the campaign.

I'm in the basement concourse of one of the big bank buildings on Richmond Street in the heart of downtown. It is dank. Nobody nowhere, except the press corps, assembled before the Bank of America's Toronto branch, a dreary little office in a nook. Bank of America's had a bad year, one of the reporters says. Someone explains the morning's itinerary: we're going from *Wall* Street, to *Bay Street, to Main* Street. It feels like one of those mass games we used to run at summer camp on rainy days, when the kids couldn't go canoeing or swimming. Is this rainy day programming on the campaign trail? Here comes Ed, like the camp director. He stands in front of the barred and shuttered branch office and says something about the might of Wall Street.

Then over to Commerce Court, at King and Bay. Outside now, windy and raining. Ed stands before the mikes, umbrellas whipping inside out, and explains that we've moved from Wall Street to Bay Street, from Mulroneyland to Turnertown, but there's no difference, "since, of course, the values are the same." Except if John Turner raised his head down here, it would probably get blown off. They may have wired his booth at Winston's for electrocution. Economist Mel Watkins says when he does free trade panels with people from business, they *foam* about Turner. In fact, what Broadbent is doing should suit Bay Street perfectly. He is reinforcing the government strategy: attack Turner's credibility — and he is doing it from the left, the people's party. The result is, instead of two to one against Mulroney on the deal, it's two to one against Turner on credibility. The Tories and business couldn't *buy* this kind of aid, though they can buy almost everything else.

Broadbent recites contributions made by the banks surrounding us to both Liberals and Conservatives. But his animation when he attacks the Liberals, here on deserted Bay, the wind whistling through the canyons, is notably greater than when he assailed the Tories in the basement on Richmond.

We head for Ted Reeve Arena on Main Street in Toronto's east end. Are they going to show us kids playing hockey? That would score some emotional points. "Then they probably won't do it," says Ray Aboud, sitting beside me on the bus. He's been with this tour most of the six weeks since it began. He says he's got forty-eight hours' overtime this week. "That'll pay for Christmas and maybe a vacation." He's discouraged about the way news is often covered in the compressed circumstances of broadcast journalism today. Two sentences of analysis at the end of a report about what some politician said. The Ottawa press rarely talk to real people or uncover news, though there are exceptions. He nostalgically recalls his kind of story: after Mulroney declared war on drugs, Ray went down to the National Research Council and interviewed the guys in the only section that helped cops on drug cases. They were preparing to shut down the division, victims of budget cuts and deficit desperation. He asks for the names of some children's publishers. He's thinking about writing books for kids. At Ted Reeve they announce we won't be allowed into the arena, just the lobby. Ray says wearily, "So we won't get to meet any real people again."

Not quite true. Much of the NDP crowd in the lobby is working-class. "Honest Ed for prime minister," yells a guy wearing a cap and jeans. His outburst seems slightly out of place in this highly orchestrated campaign. The NDP means so much to people like him, who could never feel at home in the other parties.

Ed speaks at length about average Canadians, ordinary Canadians, whatever word their surveys say is effective this week — while twenty steps away *they* sit, or at least the perfect image of them — sipping hot chocolate and watching their kids play hockey, and if they care about anything in connection with this election, it's free trade. They have said so. Every candidate in the country knows it. The people want to discuss the issue. But he doesn't mention it, not a word. The New Democratic Party doesn't seem so democratic.

Nor, it seems to me, are they very clear on the use of imagery. It is not a matter of photographing street signs with the names Wall, Bay and Main, and drawing a conceptual line to each party. Imagery is something that moves you. It's nuts, with that beautiful background of kids and hockey — embodying the heart of a country at stake — to turn away to the abstract symbolism of a street name.

On the bus returning, Ray says, "How could they think for a minute that free trade would NOT become the issue

in the campaign? My mother who lives in Winnipeg and
has no interest in politics asked me months before the
election, What do you think of this free trade? This sixty-
nine-year-old lady with arthritis — she asked about it. Her
and my father. They didn't understand but they had this
unease about it. And if they were concerned about it, there
were a lot of people who would be. I should have known
then that it would become the issue the election was
about . . ." One of the media stars smirks, "If the Liberals
win, Axworthy will be trade minister and we'll have free
trade with Nicaragua." It has the sound of something
heard at a posh cocktail party. And that's it for this day of
campaigning. We return to the Holiday Inn. Is there an
election a week away?

Afternoon. I drop by Tony Ianno's Liberal campaign
headquarters for my riding. He says everything changed
after the debate. People are high on Turner, though
Tony's still not talking free trade much himself. He says
people are tired of hearing about Nicaragua from Dan
Heap and of getting householders that come with Viva
Nicaragua on the front. The Russians are in Afghanistan
too, he says.

At Heap's office, Ashley denies they've suppressed the
trade deal in their campaign. We check the handouts. The
first round had practically nothing on free trade. In later
versions, it starts to appear. Kari Dehli, one of Heap's
campaign workers, has told me they were instructed not
to talk about the trade issue when they canvassed, because
that would be handled on "The Journal." She says she had
to leave the party literature in the bag and wing it on free
trade at the door, because that's what people wanted to
discuss. She's a veteran canvasser. "Until now I don't
think I've ever experienced, if you think of politics as
something that means something to people, that people at
the door really want people who come to the door to explain to them what it all means. And people aren't
explaining it, and this electoral process isn't giving them a
chance to learn what it's all about." Another campaign

worker bustles over. He says he has it straight from an
NDP insider with media connections that Turner has told
businesspeople not to fear. He won't really block the deal
if elected.

Monday, November 14

The media crews are setting up this morning outside the
Eaton Centre, where Ed will be, in the jargon, mainstreeting. He arrives in his limo and tries to greet people
getting off the Dundas streetcar. It's a bit late for rush
hour, there aren't many riders. He's looking around for
someone's hand to shake, so his handlers direct him inside
to the top of the escalator from the subway. He says hello
to bewildered people as they rise. A couple of kids from
journalism school at Ryerson stand watching. One says his
girlfriend's parents were after him all weekend because
they're in favour of free trade. He couldn't get them off
the topic.
    A friend meets me, wandered down from a nearby
office. She says that on her subway car this morning, five
people were reading a pamphlet called *Ten Lies about Free
Trade*. The Tories printed 800,000 of them, for distribution in key ridings, in reply to the cartoon booklet and
similar tracts. She says someone on the train actually had
What's the Big Deal? in one hand and *Ten Lies* in the other,
checking them back and forth like a Variorum edition of
Shakespeare. "It's what democracy is supposed to be
about, isn't it?" she says. We follow the media and Ed back
to the Holiday Inn. The bus leaves for the airport in an
hour, so we go into the restaurant for breakfast, continuing to chat about politics. "More free trade talk, eh?" says
the waitress — Lillian by her name tag. "My friends and I
haven't talked about anything else for weeks," she says,
and calls over co-workers Ellen and Martin. "This deal
scares me," says Lillian. "I don't want that line to disappear." She means the border.
    She adds that the only leader she likes is Ed Broadbent,

even though she "can't stand" the NDP. "I like Ed Broad-bent," says Lillian. "I love Ed Broadbent. He even had lunch in here. Evelyn served him. When I saw him, I wanted to go up and shake his hand and say, I like you. He seemed so real. The others seem like puppets. Broad-bent stands there and says what he thinks and feels."

Ellen says there is far more talk about politics among people she knows than is usual. "*Extremely* more than usual." She too likes the NDP and opposes free trade, but her mother, who lives in Peterborough, is for it. "My mom sat down my brothers and sisters and told them to vote PC because it's going to be better for Canada, for the large corporations, there'll be more money — and she's NDP, for years and years. She was always a blue-collar worker. My mom's point," she goes on, "— the large corporations feed the economy. It's money. Without them, we'd be nothing." This is a sobering reminder of the immense power business often wields inside people's heads. I ask how they feel about the NDP calling them "ordinary Ca-nadians." "Doesn't affect me," says Ellen. "We *are* just ordinary Canadians." Neither of them ever saw the car-toon booklet, which they doubtless would have shown around. Since it only went into home deliveries, for cost reasons, I guess none of the papers left in the restaurant that day contained it.

We get to the plane and wait for Broadbent's entourage to arrive: limos, handlers, Mounties. There is no clear-ance, no security, when you're part of these campaign tours; you drive straight to the plane and are picked up right off it. On the tarmac, Rob Mingay, campaign events director, apologizes about the great surprise — "moving and shaking" — that he and his pals promised when I stumbled on their late dinner in Halifax last week. He says they had planned to ship the press down to *le vrai* Wall Street in New York yesterday for the Big Symbolism, but it became logistically too difficult. On board the plane, as Ed's caravan appears, the journalists start yelling, "Elvis is on the tarmac."

They have a ritual when the plane lifts off. Three toy

cars hurtle down the aisle — Lyin' Brian's Limo, the crash-and-burn Chickmobile (Turner was known as "Chick" in college) and Ed's Truck — because out west early in the campaign, a man accosted Ed and said, You shouldn't be in a limo, you should be in a truck. Whichever gets farthest is declared the real leader of the polls. (Later in the week, as the Turner plane takes off, they pump out "Ride of the Valkyries" over the sound system; on Mulroney's jet, they play "Don't Worry, Be Happy." The planes get larger as the week progresses. Turner's is bigger than Ed's; there's a separate section for the campaign group at the front of the cabin. The Tory plane, bigger still, has two fully partitioned compartments up front.)

We land in Ottawa and bus to Main Street. They found one here too. They've gathered the faithful, Ed arrives, does Wall-Bay-Main, and again, no mention of the trade issue. Following this are three free hours.

They drop us at the press building so reporters can file stories on the event they just attended. Turner is in Ottawa at this very moment, doing a press conference on how he'll pay for his programs, meant to quiet the braying of recent days among the media, the Tories and Broadbent, about how a Liberal government would fund its promises. It doesn't seem like a burning issue, but it's something the press, in its wisdom, has focused on. I slouch by the South Block, where the official Opposition has its offices. Maybe visions of occupying this place have made the NDP giddy: the official Opposition gets lots of office space, extra research staff and much more prestigious treatment from the press and official Ottawa. If you spend your life in national politics, it probably gets to matter.

Back at the press building, Carol Goar of the *Toronto Star* recalls the NDP convention in Montreal in March 1987. It was their highwater point: they were leading the national polls, doing well in Quebec and starting to think seriously about winning. It's as though that moment froze them. It felt so good they wanted it to last, and ever since they've tried to pretend that nothing basic has changed. The delegates at that convention were tense, walking on eggs, fearful someone might let slip something radical — like some secret plan to nationalize the women and children — which the press could pounce on to prove the party still unworthy of exercising power.

I was there, my first time at an NDP convention. I'd been asked to write a short play in tribute to their former leader Tommy Douglas, who'd died the year before. Eric Peterson played Douglas, and near the end of the performance, he said, "Before I go, a word of warning: do not become too cautious just because things start to go well for us." The place exploded. It was like no response I've ever heard to a line in a script. It was as though Eric as Douglas had expressed a worry that was on all their minds. He went on, since Douglas had once been a preacher, "The Bible tells us, 'Woe unto you when all men shall speak well of you.'" They exploded again. Goar wrote at the time that what made the reaction possible was the darkness in the hall. The delegates could express what they felt without being seen. I say to her that they seemed so fearful, as if they were about to sell their souls. She says, "And now they have sold their souls." This is surely the NDP's tawdriest hour, just as 1970, when they stood behind Tommy Douglas to oppose the War Measures Act despite national hysteria, was their finest.

Boarding the plane for Montreal late in the afternoon. Ed is already on board. He and Lucille are in the first row, so we have to file past him. He is very friendly, asks if I've met his wife, chats. I don't want to be abrasive, just because he's dribbling away the chance to save the country. He says it looks like there'll be a good crowd at the rally in Montreal tonight, and I crack. "Do you think you might remember to mention the deal?" I say, and hurry on.

But I have seen Broadbent in meetings twice in the past year, and twice he was asked about the NDP's firmness on the question of free trade. Both times he affirmed his party's intention to strongly oppose the deal. I have been

following him for two days now and he has not mentioned
it. Maybe he is a man with a bad conscience about this
matter, and he is uneasy being reminded of it.

They bus us straight from the Montreal airport to the
Paul Sauvé Arena, site of many Quebec nationalist demos
of the seventies. This is where the Parti Québécois
marked its election victory in 1976 and its referendum defeat in 1980. More than 1,500 people are sitting and
eating and drinking. They overflow the hall, they're even
in a glassed-in balcony above, dining and listening to
loudspeakers. The NDP team are thrilled. Mind you, the
Liberal dinner in Toronto was jammed too, and that was
at their lowest point. This feels like a party Louis Laberge
of the Quebec Federation of Labour promised to throw
for the NDP, and he has delivered, as Frank Stronach did
in Toronto. On election night the NDP gets no Quebec
seats.

Laberge's speech is strong. Michel Agnaieff, Quebec
NDP leader, talks about *"un choix entre nous et eux,"* hitting
both nationalist and class notes. These are effective speakers stirring a stirrable crowd. Just as well, since Broadbent
in French is less than stirring.

The gathering is working-class, and they're here for a
good time: when you manage to get out for an evening,
what's the point in not enjoying it? They represent that
working-class, social democratic — even socialist — element of the Parti Québécois vote that no longer has a
home in the PQ and would die before it went Liberal; in
fact, it would much rather go Tory than Liberal, because
the federal Liberals of Quebec are such diehard anti-
nationalists, and the Tories have deftly made themselves
into Quebec nationalists in the mould of both Duplessis
and Lévesque.

The candidates are called to the front one by one. Some
get huge cheers; others don't. It seems arbitrary — the
fickle finger of fate. The crowd is into the fun of it, like
some kids this morning at the Eaton Centre chanting,
"NDP, NDP," or the guy yesterday blurting, "Honest Ed
for prime minister!"

Enter Ed. It's the only time his triumphal entry seems fully appropriate, because this crowd is up for it. It complements their mood, rather than replacing it. His French is abominable. He does, however, spend time on free trade, along with his standard themes. He tries a zinger. John Turner would no more say no to Bay Street than Mulroney would say no to a pair of Guccis. In French yet. People are sort of getting into it, laughing and winking at each other and cracking up every time he makes it through a phrase. It's very good-natured. They sing *"Gens du pays"* for him, which is hailed by press and party as the first time anyone not French has received this honour. He seems deeply moved, tries to sing along and at the end says his whole political life has led to this moment.

The party people are ecstatic, they're hugging and kissing each other as if the Winter Palace or the Moncada barracks just fell. George Nakitsas of the NDP high bureaucracy introduces himself and expresses some careful optimism about their prospects in the province. The buses proceed to the Ramada Inn in the shadow of the Parc Olympique.

Late at night I'm told by people in Toronto that the "Lying on His Mind" ad has been killed by the NDP. Some of the labour representatives in the coalitions who are also connected to the NDP say the party wanted it stopped. It fits their policy of downplaying the free trade issue, especially in Ontario, where they're sure it draws votes to the Liberals. In truth, the effect will not be great, since the scope of the ad has already been scaled way back for lack of funds. At this point it is scheduled only for the national edition of the *Globe and Mail* and perhaps a couple of other papers. But it's infuriating. For weeks Broadbent and his party have decried Turner's insincerity in opposing free trade. And here they are, stifling a rare chance to speak against it, while claiming to be the only ones sincerely fighting it.

I slam the receiver down, go into the hotel corridor, down to the bar, looking for some way to vent my anger,

and there's Anna Maria Tremonti of the CBC and Paul
Koring of the *Globe*. I turn and walk out. I walk along the
hall again. Some doors are open: people are filing stories
through modems or drinking and lying on the double
beds. A party staffer is kneeling on the floor of a room,
running something through a portable printer. I ask
where the bigwigs are. She points farther down the hall.
There is Nakitsas, in his shorts, kibbitzing in the afterglow
of the evening's success. I tell him I want to talk and we go
into his room.

I say he's lucky I ran into him and not a reporter because his party has been trumpeting across the land that
Turner is a liar not really out to stop the deal, and now
they killed this ad. He says he knows nothing about it,
which may well be true. He'll talk to Bill Knight, NDP
campaign director, in Ottawa. I can check with him tomorrow noon, when they're in Windsor. I say if they've
done this, they deserve to be exposed publicly as hypo-
crites. I'm not sure I'd really do such a thing. It strikes me
I may be employing the Kissinger-Nixon madman theory:
in the late sixties, as a way of pressuring other nations,
Nixon and Kissinger nurtured the idea that Nixon was
crazy enough to drop nuclear bombs. Nakitsas says very
strongly that his opposition to the deal transcends party
loyalty, although he cannot let the NDP simply succumb
to a Liberal surge.

Tuesday, November 15

Terry Mosher comes by for breakfast. He describes four
guys he saw on a street corner yesterday. They called him
over to talk about Mulroney and free trade, and an old
woman going past with shopping bags stopped — you
could tell she was listening — then she came over to them
and hissed, "He's a liar!" It's everywhere, the ferment.
Now that I am here among the press and the campaigns, I
miss the action out there in the country, where the real
election is happening. Today I leave the NDP and fly to

join the Turner campaign. I tell Terry what's happened
to the ad, but he's not perturbed or even surprised. He's
more surprised at the way we've been able to raise our
voices so far than at the setback. He says this experience
has taken him beyond the cynicism which is often a political cartoonist's lot. I say for many artists this is the first
time they've really been part of a fight, rather than just
lending their names or making a donation. He says, For
me too.

We go to his office at the *Gazette*. He sends down to the
library for the front pages of the *Montreal Star* in the final
week before the free trade — then known as Reciprocity
— election of 1911. It's not exactly objective journalism.
There are headlines every day like, "The United States —
No Wonder They Want Reciprocity!" Or, "We Don't
Want the Stars and Stripes — The Union Jack Is Good
Enough for Us." Each front page has a big cartoon. For
instance, the cigar-smoking "Yankee press" says to
Canada, "You vote for reciprocity or it will be worse for
you — see!" And confident Canada answers back, "Is that
so?" There's a letter from Rudyard Kipling on election
day: "It is her own soul that Canada risks today . . . ." And
a reference to Stephen Leacock, who used to carry
around a blank sheet of paper which he said contained
the names of Canadian companies that would be destroyed if reciprocity succeeded. The election result is
headlined, "Reciprocity Is Defeated," with a row of Canadian ensigns under it and a huge cartoon called "The
Archangel Chains the Destroyer." One difference between that free trade election and the current one is clear:
in 1911 a large segment of business, especially manufacturing, opposed the agreement.

Before going to the airport, I talk to Tony Clarke, head
of the Pro-Canada Network, in Ottawa. He's trying to get
the ad reinstated. At the airport, before boarding for Halifax and then Charlottetown, where I'll meet the Liberal
campaign, I call Nakitsas in Windsor. He puts on his co-
hort, Bill Knight, who swears he too knows nothing about
killing the ad. He agrees to call Tony Clarke to put that

straight. He does so and on that basis, apparently, the ad is revived, though it doesn't run till Friday, instead of Wednesday.

Flying to meet the Liberal campaign. It seems surreal that John Turner has become the anti-business voice in Canadian politics. Yet it was Turner, not Broadbent (nor even Hardial Bains of the Communist Party of Canada, Marxist-Leninist) who said, when the dollar fell, "It is the Canadian people, not the money markets, who will decide this election." This week in Quebec Turner said, "The Ritz club is ready to compete with the Americans, but only on one condition: that the workers pay the price." According to the press today, he announced, "There it is in black and white. Big business is saying that if [the trade deal] goes through, big business will cut medicare, auto insurance and workmen's compensation so that they can make more profits in order to buy this election for their boy Brian." Their boy Brian? Is sibling rivalry at work here? Who else was once "their boy"?

I've got *Maclean's* final issue before the election. The long Alliance ad — five full pages — is set right in the middle of the report on free trade and the election, just after an interview with Mulroney; the two-page Pro-Canada freebie is back in "The World," beside Bolivia — but it would be churlish to complain about placement considering the cost. There are interviews with the three leaders, and columns for and against the deal. The lengthy section "explaining" the agreement seems to me quite biased in its favour, but what the hell, it's discussion of the subject, lots of discussion, and it's invigorating.

You can see the free traders' problem in a *Le Devoir* report this morning. Benoit Bouchard says, "To claim, like Monique Bégin, that the Red Cross will be unable to operate, or that Americans will export their blood to Canada, with the risk of spreading AIDS — there is a limit." He has to repeat all the arguments from the anti-free trade side in order to deny them. They were right three years ago: benign neglect would have served them best.

Halifax airport. The headline in today's *Chronicle-Herald* is "Tories Dismiss Deal Charges." The subhead is "Mulroney Misled Public — GATT-Fly Spokesman." GATT-Fly is a little monkish group with a shoestring operation on the second floor of an old house in Toronto, just barely funded by Canada's churches, where they hectically analyze global economic trends from the standpoint of the world's poor. They've discovered evidence that the government tried to deal away regional development grants during free trade negotiations. Minister for International Trade John Crosbie spent the last day replying to them. In the normal exercise of his power, he never would bother. But there has been a kind of breakdown of authority, so that the meek get to challenge the mighty.

Economist Diane Francis' column in the current *Maclean's* blames the Canadian people for the breakdown. She says they must spend their time reading gardening columns because they clearly haven't absorbed her many impeccable arguments for free trade. "Interestingly, as I travelled," she writes, "mostly females and passengers in the economy class had doubts, unlike most men and those in business class." The masks are falling like autumn leaves. Michel Vastel, in yesterday's *Le Devoir*, said Mulroney's great mistake was letting the trade issue become a question of class during this final phase of the campaign. I sit here in the airport thinking of sociologist Edgar Friedenberg, who came to Halifax to teach and escape the values of America. He coined "deference to authority" to describe the Canadian character.

Could even the business class now be in danger of losing its docility? Yesterday a Truro businessman told the Rotary Club there that he's against the deal. It's so rare an event that it's worth a story in the paper. In Montreal this morning, a friend mentioned two shmatah manufacturers who say the trade deal will be a disaster for their industry. When I asked for names, she pulled back; she doesn't think they'll say in public what they express with outrage in private. That's more like it.

These events remind me of the opening for dissent that occurred briefly in the U.S. during the years of the Vietnam debate, so that critics like Noam Chomsky could write occasionally in the *New York Times*, and Abbie Hoffman could go on national TV talk shows. It hasn't happened there since. I wonder if in years to come we'll be able to explain to people how exhilarating this moment was, and that it came to pass in Canada in connection with such apparently technical and economic matters, so that ordinary people argued with each other on streets and in buses about details of subsidy and countervail.

Desperation is appearing too, on all sides. Laurell says she was leafletting outside Maple Leaf Gardens in Toronto last Saturday night before the hockey game. A fan gave her a hard time about the deal, so she said, Look, have you read it? He said yes, but she was certain he hadn't. So she did something she says never even occurred to her before. She said, Look, I'm a lawyer and I understand these things . . . .

A journalist from Alberta recently compared the cartoon booklet put out by the Pro-Canada Network and the coalitions to the *Protocols of the Elders of Zion* — the most notorious anti-Semitic forgery of all time. Because, she said, *What's the Big Deal?* creates hatred toward Americans
. . . .

Other journalists I've talked to say their professional commitments and standards have been sorely tested by the recent tactics of the government and business, and by their sense of what the outcome will mean to the country. They are tempted to make statements they would not normally make, or which they have not fully verified. They say this has never happened to them before, sometimes in decades of writing. These are times that try men's souls . . . .

Charlottetown. This makes ten provinces I've been in
during the campaign, and the Yukon.

Evening in the Prince Edward Hotel — the CP, as
everyone calls it. A "popular hearing" on free trade is being held in a small room at one end of the hotel. Wayne
Easter, president of the National Farmers' Union, is
speaking. He's appeared at anti-deal meetings and rallies
across Canada for the past three years, but home is a farm
about twelve miles from here. The provincial premiers
are going bananas, as he puts it. Devine has sent letters to
all the grain farmers in Saskatchewan and Charlie Mayer,
minister responsible for the Canadian Wheat Board, has
written to grain growers across western Canada, promising that there's absolutely no threat to the Wheat Board
under the trade deal. People like Wayne always brought
some reality to the Coalition against Free Trade in Toronto. At a meeting last spring, a farmer from the
Niagara Peninsula said he wouldn't be available for a few
weeks. "I'm out in the field all the time now," he said. "I
came straight from the field for this meeting." Everyone
sighed. Imagine — somebody who actually produces
things that others need.

They look a scraggly crew at the popular hearing.
Meanwhile, down a corridor the length of a Canadian
football field, at the other end of the hotel, a huge Turner
rally unfolds in the grand ballroom. It has slickness, glam-
our, money, a big crowd. Yet the two gatherings are on a
continuum, more or less, and this kind of meeting prepared the way for that.

The Liberal rally gets going with local talent. Fiddlers,
step dancing, the place is blocked — as they say in this
part of the country. A local singer plays her guitar and
sings "Working Man" by Rita Macneil. It's not a rich
crowd. They look like Wayne Easter. Someone in the
lobby says, "We're here to watch the hecklers." The heck-
ling and fighting have given this campaign an edge, a little
blood to the usually bloodless pursuit of politics in the
country. It's like Canadian politics was a hundred years

ago. Doug Kirkpatrick, tour director for the Liberal campaign, says, "This is going to be one of the most
interesting weeks in Canadian political history."

You can smell the slickness of the party, the years of
grease and power, and it's not pleasant. It's easier to
understand how beleaguered the NDP feel, knowing what
they're up against. Local candidates are introduced to the
sound of "In the Mood." One of them is named George
Proud. I think about Milton Acorn — another Island
name. Wonder if I'll be able to find his grave and visit it.
Writers in Europe simply will not believe a great Canadian poet could have been born with that name: Milton, as
in *Paradise Lost*, plus Acorn.

Premier Joe Ghiz introduces Turner, with some jokes
about Liberals and Tories. Ghiz is a real regional pol, he
has the pulse of this place, and speaks in genuine "periods," like classical rhetoric. You hardly hear that kind of
oratory anymore.

Turner gets into his speech slowly, but really gets into
it. It's odd for a standard "stump speech": often technical
and economic, but he's clearly gripped by the material
and seems to grip the crowd too. He says he believes in
free market forces *but*. But Canada would never have existed except for a conscious decision to resist those forces.
More thoughts Broadbent would be reluctant to utter —
maybe even to think in his closet with the door shut. As
Turner's a Liberal and a businessman, such notions seem
to come easier from him: his opponents may call him trai-
tor, but they'll never call him Bolshevik. He says he told
his daughter today, "You are walking in the cradle of
Confederation. Here, right here, this is where the country
was born." He speaks about Canadian history as if he had
been there, linking himself to the Fathers of Confederation, and as a matter of fact, he is probably the kind of
person they were: a businessman, a member of the elite,
but with a little breadth of social vision and sense of responsibility. A business mentality with a nationalist bent.

"That was what we began 121 years ago," he says, then
corrects himself, "began 124 years ago and finished 121

years ago" — because the original Confederation meeting
was here in Charlottetown in 1864, but the plan was not
finalized until 1867. It seems a rather fine historical point
to pause over, but Turner is into this and has to get it
right. "I never believed I'd have the opportunity to stand
before you and before my fellow citizens and defend what
I believe about our country," he says. A guy wearing a cap
in the third row blurts, "Thanks for doing that, John,"
and Turner says, "Thank you."

Afterward I'm in the hotel gift shop sifting through the
Anne Shirley stuff, and Turner lurches by. His pinched
nerve looks pretty bad. He and Geills step out into the
street and point to where Ragweed Press is located.
They've talked to the woman who runs it, Libby Oughton,
who says she'll be hammered by this deal. "Of course, she
probably votes NDP," he says. "Like you." I say that's not
necessarily so. Lots of people are thinking carefully about
how they're going to vote, and he says, "Well, vote for
whoever can stop the deal," and then adds as if he can't
stop himself, "and that's us."

   I go down for a late supper and talk with Lysiane Gagnon, front-page columnist for *La Presse*, the most
powerful paper in Quebec. She's all for the trade agreement. She asks if I realize there is not a single respectable
voice in Quebec opposed to this deal. I ask if that doesn't
bother her and she says, "Not at all." Herb Denton, the
Washington Post's Canadian correspondent, is with us.
Herb is black, he was in school in Little Rock in 1957
when Eisenhower sent in federal troops to enforce de-
segregation. He has a Bronze Cross from service in
Vietnam. He says, "If Canadians reject this deal, Americans will start to respect them for the first time."

Wednesday, November 16

Morning. We're shepherded over to Province House,
where the first Confederation meeting was held, and Roy

MacGregor of the *Ottawa Citizen* says he thinks this thing
— he means the deal — has become a class issue. It only
became clear to him, he says, when he saw some of the
things happening at his own paper. There has been
conflict between management and staff at many papers. I
know that at the *Citizen*, one day early in the campaign, an
editorial supported the Liberal's housing policy. Management disagreed; later the same day, the editorial had
turned negative. Turner slips up the stairs past us toward
the Confederation Chamber — a modest place really, of
which little has been made by the tourism people here; it
is that typical Canadian diffidence that practically begs
someone to come in and take over. Turner looks in great
pain. Someone says he looks better today, you should
have seen him earlier in the campaign. Last night I asked
a member of his staff why he doesn't use a line like,
"Brian Mulroney says I'm a liar, I say he's a liar. You decide." She said Turner wouldn't say that about Mulroney;
he just wouldn't speak the words. It sounds to me like the
old cricket spirit, a bit of upper class bluster, but she says
he's obstinate about it, as he was obstinate about running
the election on free trade. Doesn't make sense to me. The
Tories have made lying an issue and you shouldn't just
hover above the charge. People want to know if it's true or
not, and you have an obligation to present your viewpoint
and help them make up their minds. That's democracy.

I ask Roy if he feels a conflict between his own feelings
and his professional responsibility, and he says, Sure.
Then he adds, "It's scary, but it's exciting. I love this election. I'm trying to remember to step back and realize I'm
here, and not think too much about things like what the
result could mean to my kids. It's given me a new respect
for the people," he says un-self-consciously. He means
their willingness to overcome the media and establishment barrage, the polls, all the bullshit shovelled at them.
He says this one will go on after it's over, because of the
class character it has acquired.

Montreal, afternoon. A cup of tea with Joyce Fairbairn,

Liberal senator, at the Château Champlain. About a week ago, I started fiddling with what I think Turner should say in response to the Tory charges of lying. I've written some of it down, but I haven't shown it to anyone, and I feel extremely ambivalent. I show her the page of text — it looks withered, like something I found on a dig. I feel like I'm pitching a series idea to a TV producer. This is not my idea of politics, this politics the whole world knows as politics. I don't like parties and I don't like this party, and I make it clear to her I've never done anything like this and don't plan to make a career of it. Christ, I sound like everyone who ever sold their soul (or their body) and explained it isn't what they're really like. "It's a great game, isn't it?" she says.

While Turner is doing an interview at *Le Journal de Montréal*, and the journalists are shmoozing in the lobby, I walk up and down rue Mont Royal, just to see people living their lives, working, not obsessed with the election. A corner shop with novelties and toys, a used appliances store, a guy eating a hamburger on a stool in a window. The world of Life Goes On. It's not that, for people living normal lives, political events are unfelt — they are felt, often very directly and for their symbolic and emotional impact as well — but such people can't usually afford to dramatize their responses the way some of us, with more time on our hands, tend to do.

Back at the hotel, I learn that the ad with "Lying on His Mind" will come out Friday in the *Globe* and in papers in B.C. and Saskatchewan; the Manitoba Coalition has a full-page ad of their own, writer Michael Ondaatje has organized an artists' ad against free trade; and the man who invented the board game "Scruples" wants to pay for putting "Lying on His Mind" in the Sunday issue of the *Toronto Sun*. Business, meanwhile, has prepared an overpowering blitz for the final few days. There is so much happening, and people will be inundated as the vote approaches.

Tonight there's a Turner rally in east end Montreal, hosted by MP Marcel Prud'Homme. You feel the sleaze of the Liberal party all over this church basement. The many private cops, the anti-nationalism of Trudeau vintage — this party is a corrupt and decaying body, trying to embody a vital message. But the rot, and the hatred so many Québécois feel for it, along with their revulsion at the thought of voting for these guys — nowhere else in Canada has Liberalism been this odious.

Yet Turner's speech, in this hole, to this decrepit and somewhat spare crowd, is strong and urgent. I believe if he — or someone else — had given it to the NDP in the Paul Sauvé arena, they'd have torn the place apart: his shafts at *les boys du Ritz*, for example. When it's over, the music blares and Turner waves and they all wave back. Is it just people together, connecting in some way, that is so touching, after one of them expresses something on behalf of the rest, and it doesn't matter who the voice is or whether he is stupid, venal or devious, so long as in that moment he embodies for all of them something better? Right now it has fallen to this klutz Turner, as he stands there on the stairs, a dumb grin on his face, looking surprised he has moved them so. They beam and wave their tiny Canadian flags back.

Thursday, November 17

Today in the *Globe* Atwood takes a final swat at Mulroney. She explains the gender gap by saying he reminds women of the guy your father warned you about: "the smoothie with the slick line who'd try to talk you into the back seat and then get furious with you if you said no." All but one of the letters to the editor are anti-deal. They must be receiving little besides opposition views. The *Toronto Star* has been printing letters against in a three-to-one ratio, though they say the actual mail has been running ten-to-one opposed. According to CBC radio, the *Ottawa Citizen* has been getting cancellations because of their rather fawning endorsement of the Tories — people are even complaining to paper boys. (On election day, nine of eleven seats in the Ottawa area will go Liberal). Mulroney yesterday called the Liberals Luddites, a scholarly reference which required detailed explanations and lengthy parentheses in the press.

The latest NDP slogan, "We're on Your Side," was apparently lifted from the disastrous Dukakis presidential campaign in the U.S. — great credentials. They got it from Vic Fingerhut, their American pollster, who shopped the same phrase to both parties. So we have the Tories taking their "negative ad" strategy from the U.S. Republican campaign and the NDP swiping their slogan from the Democrats. Last night I saw the latest NDP TV spot, a passing panorama of ordinary people with thumbs up, like a Coke or McDonald's feelgood ad or the "Up with People" singers.

In the *Globe* Report on Business there's a story about a joint press release from the Business Council on National Issues, the Canadian Manufacturers' Association and the Canadian Chamber of Commerce, denying in unison that they are unpatriotic. Imagine them having to go on the record with such a thing.

A front-page photo in the *Financial Post* this morning shows Toronto taxis with signs on their roofs that say Free Trade and an arrow indicating that Canadians should go for it. More great chaos. The Coalition against Free Trade version is the No-Deal Mobile, a battered rental van that chugs around Toronto distributing literature.

The *Financial Post* also has a supplement in favour of the trade deal, a multi-page pullout written by *Post* staff. It's in dialogue form, with cartoons, and some lines taken directly from the cartoon booklet put out by the Pro-Canada Network and the coalitions. Is this how you cease to be marginal: being copied by the forces you set out to defeat?

Le Devoir has an editorial endorsing the free trade agreement. Everyone onside in Quebec, as Lysiane Gagnon said. The unanimity of Quebec elite opinion makes

English Canada look like a garden of intellectual diversity. This week, Gagnon wrote in her column that Mulroney isn't actually English, he's Irish, and "the Irish, it's well known, have never been real English." She recently dealt with English Canadian revulsion at Mulroney's lavish personal spending while he was demanding restraint from pensioners. In English Canada, wrote Gagnon, "Puritanism is bred into the bone and . . . many find it perfectly normal for their prime minister to shop at Eaton's bargain basement and live at the YMCA . . . ."

Her quasi-racial analysis is drearily similar to the racial stereotyping about Quebec which has gone on so long from the Anglo side. Is this supposed to be progress?

Today in the States Reagan will make a speech about trade, with references to the U.S.-Canada agreement. The Tories seem worried about reactions to it here.

Quebec City. Radio station CHRC. A Canadian Press reporter says he just heard Reagan's speech and it's nothing but windy praise of free trade. Turner comes on air and responds: he says Reagan is a lame duck coming to the rescue of a dead duck. The press set up for a scrum, right after the radio interview. Could this become a key event, pinning the deal on Reagan, and not on Mulroney? There are current polls that show the Liberals doing well in the Maritimes and Montreal. On the other hand, someone says the Tories have a Decima poll that puts them ahead 39 to 30.

It's very hard to tell what's happening from here in the middle of the campaigns. How much of a sense of momentum is created by being on board one particular car of the roller-coaster? It's easy to feel that the party you're with is doing well. The reporters on the NDP tour thought Broadbent was coming back from his post-debate dip, and tomorrow those with the Tories will feel the government has locked it away.

Many of these journalists say they still don't know what they think about the trade deal. Why the hell not? They're the full-time reporters paid to look into these things. Why haven't they figured it out? Is it because they're lazy or in-competent — or that it's just in their interest not to get the thing figured out? Most of them didn't realize till halfway through the campaign how important it was going to be. The rest of the populace was way out ahead of them, wor-rying about the matter, trying to come to a responsible conclusion. Sometimes you feel the main attraction of a career in journalism is the excuse to avoid decisions other citizens have to make.

At night in Quebec City, another Liberal rally. They sing "O Canada." I'd forgotten how good it sounds in French, how it *only* sounds good in French. Rémi Bujold is m.c. Another Quebec machine Liberal, like Prud'Homme. This is a very middle-class crowd compared to last night's. They won't have the same response to the same Turner pitch with its class elements. Raymond Garneau, Liberal finance critic, tells them they're going to form the next government. In his mouth it sounds like another election promise.

Enter Turner. Earsplitting music, old ladies waving their Canadian flags. "*Chez nous,*" says Turner, "*on est Libéral.*" Then he does a shtick about hockey in connec-tion with a rumoured sale of the Quebec Nordiques. "A few weeks ago . . . all of Quebec mobilized against the sale of the Quebec Nordiques, to be sold to unknown interests. For some it seemed just a business transaction," he says. "There is a seller, there is a buyer — *Il y a un vendeur, il y a un acheteur.* But for the people of Quebec," he goes on, "the Nordiques are more than some property. They are a part of their consciousness, part of their tradition and their collective pride." It's a perfect Canadian metaphor for distinguishing social from private property, and here's *Turner* doing it. It's endlessly disorienting, this election, including the transformation of this man. Even if Turner doesn't mean these things he says, at least he *says* them. Broadbent doesn't even say them. Then Turner uses the pet phrase of Quebec separatism, *maîtres chez nous*, to explain his opposition to the deal. Carole Beaulieu of *Le Devoir*, sitting beside me, gasps when he says that.

Geills is up there as Turner finishes, playing the role, at some cost, of the pol's wife. With a strong touch of *noblesse oblige*, a clear sense coming from her that occasionally ruling class folk like her and John must take on the responsibility of leading the unwashed or even the partly washed. Will the people ever lead themselves?

The guy who drives me to the airport from the Turner rally is tired. He's been working for three days, putting stuff on the ceiling for this meeting. I don't ask what it was, I don't want him to know I didn't notice. Normally he's a draughtsman for an architect who is a Liberal, and gets lots of work from the government, or did. He sighs because he has to spend all day tomorrow taking that stuff down.

A friend of mine in Toronto, a Marxist academic who knows I'm out here, keeps leaving messages on my answering machine about Turner. He's mystified by the man's behaviour. "What I want to know is," he says, "Is this guy employable?" The best thing you can say about John Turner could be that, after this election, he may not be able to get a job.

Fredericton. I arrive late at night, but the Tory campaign will not be in until a lot later. A local Tory worker sits waiting for them, and waiting and waiting. "We would have breezed through," she says, "till that debate. Then the calls started about free trade. In the last few days, we've had some calls about abortion again." She sounds wistful, even nostalgic, for those calls about abortion. In the supermarket, she says, someone saw her PC button and said, loud enough for her to hear, "If you want a load of taxes, vote for Bud Bird" — the Tory candidate. She was shocked, she says. She's never heard people talk like they are during this election. "He was just a working person," she adds.

Friday, November 18

The *Daily Gleaner*, a local paper, is full of ads for Tories and the deal, many of them placed not by the party but by business. They can't be pleased with Mulroney. His job, for heaven's sake, is to look after their interests so they need not be directly involved. He's like their designated hitter. This election, in which they've had to come forth to save *his* ass, must drive them nuts.

On the bus, I meet Linda Diebel of the *Star*. Everywhere I've gone, the *Star* reporters have been good. I don't think they're genetically superior to other journalists, but they know that their paper, unlike most of the rest in the country, has a critical view of this government and the trade deal, so they feel encouraged to dig and prod. Linda looks like Laura Secord behind enemy lines.

The Tories have got their numbers, she says, and are convinced they're back in. She's talked to her editors in Toronto, who think the Tories have it. The rumours about polls due on the weekend say so too. This news will have its effect in the election's final days. "*La vague est bleu*," as one voter told a reporter during last summer's by-election in St-Jean: the wave is blue. If issues seem abstruse or impenetrable, or just too damn complicated, some voters will gauge the way the tide is running, and join it. We bus to a nearby hotel for the first Mulroney rally of the day, and my first of the campaign.

There are protesters outside the hotel, mostly Indians with handmade signs against cutbacks and free trade.

Inside, this has the feel of power. There is a handsomely outfitted Tory youth corps with expensive sweatshirts and printed signs and flags. A great high school band plays "In the Mood." Why is this the anthem for so many campaign events? Did some consultant sell the idea to every party? There's an absolutely huge Canadian flag onstage. They protest too much — it's as big as the one in one of Terry's cartoons, except in his version it's a Stars and Stripes, and Mulroney is pledging allegiance before it. It heads the full-page ad about lying that should be in this morning's *Globe*, which I'm leafing through.

There it is, hard to miss. It makes me feel a little like one of the rebels of 1837 after they lost the Battle of Toronto and retreated to the U.S. border. They set up on Navy Island and occasionally fired their puny cannons across the Niagara River, just to let Lieutenant-Governor Francis Bond Head and his Tory troops know they hadn't gone away.

Here comes Bud Bird, local candidate. Until a month ago, as the lady said last night, he had it made in the shade. The crowd seems dubious about the confidence he now expresses. Everything in the hall says, Real Money. The decorations, the signs, the women's haircuts — especially the haircuts. They chant, "Four more years," like Nixon in 1972 before he swept the election that was followed by his humiliation.

And here comes Brian, my first sight of him live, ever. The businessman beside me, in a pinstripe and trench coat, holding a sign, starts to whistle along with the blaring music. You get the feeling he didn't want to come out here and do this any more than they wanted to come out in the papers from behind their respectable blandness, but they were forced to. He holds the sign uncomfortably, like someone just ran by and handed him a stolen TV.

Turner is interesting in this election, because he has *not* become the centre of a personality cult, and probably couldn't, due to the cool — to say the least — attitude people have toward him. Just yesterday, a friend returning from a book tour said, "People still think he's a creep, even if some of them are willing to vote for him." Instead Turner has become the voice of an issue that was chosen, at bottom, by the country. So his rallies are not built around him, as the Mulroney and Broadbent rallies are. They're about that issue.

Brian and Mila stand onstage and swing their linked hands to the music. It looks completely unspontaneous. The Tory *Jugend* in their shiny sweatshirts, backing them.

What's the theory of him coming here? The seat must be close, his visit may get a few sullen voters to say, Well, he bothered coming . . . I'll vote for him after all, even though I wasn't going to.

His rhetoric is empty, as the free trade pitch — the "selling job" — has been all along. A content analysis of the government literature on this subject would be a vain pursuit. "This free trade agreement is going to take New Brunswick out of the box and into the winds and sunshine of prosperity. That's what it's all about." He plays the anti-Ontario card heavily, then more wind: "One Canada, built on growth, fairness and prosperity, that's what this election is all about." It's perfectly normal election bilge. What's abnormal is the amount of substance that has slipped through anyway.

Suddenly I look up and there is Mulroney passing under my nose. Now that he is right here, I have no different impression than all the times on TV, in Question Period, in interviews. He's one of those rare people who seems to have no dimension that requires a personal presence to reveal it. It's like seeing Roger Rabbit — a fabricated character mixed among real humans. Nor is he an asset like Reagan, capable of selling blood and shit; he's a liability, which is why they tried to hide him when the campaign began. Looking at him, I'm not sure whether I feel more offended by his longstanding attempt to sell us a catastrophic trade deal or his current efforts to re-debase our political process, so recently born anew.

Back on the bus, reporters talk about the increasingly heavy hand exercised by their editors. At the *Globe and Mail*, for instance, polls had been played very prominently until the post-debate turnaround. That day, a decision was apparently made to place the poll on page one but below the fold — a matter of great significance in the *Globe*'s system of signals to its readers. Eventually the poll article went above the fold, but only slightly. *Globe* reporter Lorne Slotnick said he and other reporters were clearly informed that the paper was "not interested" in stories like the plant closing at Fleck, which reflected badly on free trade. Today there's a piece in the *Globe* about those rumours that Turner has offered secret reassurance to business on the deal. The article says the rumours came straight from Bruce Phillips, in the Prime Minister's Office. Apparently that story's been available for days, but was delayed until now, when it finally appears on the comic page. So the NDP insider's news I'd heard in Heap's campaign office in Toronto was disinformation direct from the PMO.

On the tarmac, as the journalists shuffle up the staircase into the anus of the campaign plane (it has one of those rear entries), I try to ask the tour director where to sit. He makes a wide detour, waving his arms and shouting over the engines, "I don't want to be seen talking to you." He's a nice guy and he's kidding, sort of. Eventually he sits me at the front, far from the other journalists, between two party functionaries in dark suits who look like the Blues Brothers. There's a partitioned compartment immediately ahead with fax, xerox, etc. And a compartment past that with the prime minister and his wife. I can see the back of his head.

Yarmouth, Nova Scotia. Hordes of school kids clamour at the airport for autographs from Brian and Mila.

The rally is at a nearby hotel. The campaign theme song says, "Together for ever and ever / Together for ever and ever with you / To be together with you." What does that mean? Robert Stanfield, former Tory leader and premier of this province, speaks. He sounds very sincere, especially about Quebec and about his hatred for the Trudeau Liberals. Then Mulroney again. "The fundamental issue is do you want John the Ripper or Brian the Builder?" And, "Monday is a time for Nova Scotians to rise up and say we want prosperity and we've had enough of protectionism." The point is not that these lines are laughable, especially in the context of the real discussion that has been going on. The point is, Who will the joke be on? As he speaks, a sense of genuine emotion

emerges only in his moments of anger, hate and partisan-
ship.

They exit with another song: "We got to stand together,
to make the dream come true." Of course, this vacuous-
ness is not uniquely Tory. The Liberals once ran an
election campaign on the slogan, "The Land Is Strong,"
and the final batch of NDP TV ads is sheer mush. The
struggle continues over whether this will be one more
election laced with vagueness and emptiness or a national
referendum on the nature of Canadian society.

Montreal. A night rally in Longeuil. You can see how the
Tories are doing it here in Quebec. The crowd is re-
hearsed beforehand to give childlike responses: "When *I*
say Brian, *you* say, Ooh, Ahh!" It has the flavour of the
Duplessis years and of the authoritarian church, the kind
of thing familiar from the twenties and thirties, based on
the compactness, unity and relative insulation of the population at that time. "The Pecs never treated people like
this," says one of the reporters, who worked here during
the PQ years in power.

Mulroney looks, in the glare of this rally, with its corps
of spiffy uniformed youth running up and down the
aisles with billowing banners and the programmed reactions of the crowd, like the main character in *The Resistible
Rise of Arturo Ui*, Brecht's parody about Hitler's political
beginnings, the theme of which is that any ass will do, so
long as he is available to serve the right interests. I hasten
to add that the Tory program, grungy as it is, is not Hitle-
rian. But that is not the point of Brecht's play: it is about
how mediocrity can rise to power if it makes the proper
bows.

You get the feeling too that here in Quebec free trade
means something utterly different from what it means
elsewhere. Motives in Quebec run so deep and are not
easily addressed. They are rooted in the history of exploi-
tation and suppression of this society and come back to
visit themselves on the rest of the country time and again.
At this moment it is as though free trade has become a

way, the only way left, of escaping the hated embrace of
Canada, after more than two hundred years. It is the re-
venge of Quebec separatism, the Return of the
Suppressed. They were so humiliated by the defeat in the
referendum of 1980 — even many who voted against independence — and by the economic and psychological
pressures applied to prevent them from asserting their
dignity and their right to separate.

Watching "The Journal's" final show on the election. The
entire program is people, all members of the elites, to be
sure, saying how they feel about free trade. Many for,
many against. It is exciting to see this debate continue
right to the end. It is now accepted that the election is a
virtual referendum on free trade, at least this edition of
"The Journal" says so, which will displease those trying to
get away from it again. No matter what the polls show, it
seems to me this last flurry of activity could bring the deal
back into focus as the centre, and the volatility could start
again. You have to hand it to "The Journal." This is a
bloody good final set of thoughts for people to chew on.

Saturday, November 19

The first two of the final four polls due today show the
Tories with large leads. In the rest of the morning's papers, the debate continues full throttle.

The ads in the *Globe* are incredible. "Anti" artists
against "pro" artists, for instance, though many of the
"pro"s seem to be journalists, architects and lawyers.
From the fine print it's apparent they didn't even pay for
the ad. It was covered by the big business lobby, the
Canadian Alliance for Trade and Job Opportunities. But
what the hell, the battle has been joined, conflicting voices
are being raised in the media, some of them pretty unexpected. Like Gordon Lightfoot — anti.

More masks are coming off. On the front page of the
Montreal Gazette, there's an editorial by publisher Clark

Davey. He says, "A careful reader of the *Gazette*'s editorial pages in the last year could be forgiven for concluding today that we believe the Free Trade Agreement to be so bad that almost any alternative, including no deal, would be preferable. However, such is not the case. As with every editorial policy decision, the final judgement on political endorsements rests with the publisher . . . ." He goes on to endorse the Tories. It's like the 1958 U.S. election when the *New York Post* endorsed Averell Harriman for governor, but Dorothy Schiff, the publisher, cancelled the endorsement sixteen hours before the vote — "much as she might have returned a dress to a department store," according to A. J. Liebling. Liebling also noted that freedom of the press is guaranteed only to those who own one.

Parizeau is in today's papers, explaining again that free trade will lead to the breakup of Canada and therefore an independent Quebec. Crosbie and Reisman have been insulting student audiences who criticized or merely questioned them. At a recent rally in Toronto, Cabinet minister Otto Jelinek actually pulled a heckler off a chair and threw him to the floor.

There's an unusually complex analysis of Canadian nationalism by Southam columnist Don MacGillivray. Literate, practically scholarly, you just don't see journalism like this. Terry Mosher's final cartoon is Turner in nineteenth-century boxing garb and stance, putting 'em up against Mulroney and big biz and Bourassa and almost everyone else, with Broadbent lost in the crowd, wearing oversized trunks that say "Everlose," not knowing which way to throw his punch.

The *Globe* has a page one story on business's role and the emergence of the class issue. They actually use the c-word. The *Globe* usually acts as if its mission is to deny or cover up the existence of class conflict in Canadian society. The headline and lead editorial are on free trade; the entertainment section examines culture and the deal, pronouncing both sides wrong. A story in the Report on Business says the government has sent out more than *ten million* pieces of literature promoting the agreement. By the time I board the campaign bus, I'm very high.

We bus-stop around Montreal with Mulroney. A francophone radio reporter says her story last night was about the warmup to Mulroney's arrival at the Longeuil rally. Her technician said, "I feel like a dummy listening to this tape over and over." She says she felt humiliated by it too. These people seem to recall, even if they weren't born yet, the climate of the Duplessis years.

At stop one, I see a black maple leaf pin with *Oui au libre échange* on it. It's hard to believe that this party, so sensitive to the manipulation of images, is unaware of the connotations. The same holds for the red, white and blue colours used on many of their logos and signs.

One of the pro-deal TV ads in French shows a young buck saying, *On va grandir*, ostensibly about the effects of the deal, but with a sexual implication. Is this the emergence of the macho factor in the trade debate? The Tory musical theme here in Quebec has a heavy disco beat and the line *"Continuons dans le bon sens . . . ."* Disco? A Québécois reporter says, "This is the party of the obvious. And it works." At every stop Mulroney predicts that Canadians will "vote yes to prosperity and yes to unity" — as if he's finally managed to beat back the tide of all those citizens committed to poverty and disunity. Good old politics is back in town.

A Saturday evening rally at Laval, probably the last big one of the campaign. Lysiane Gagnon stops me and cheerfully displays the CTV poll figures: 43-32-20. Almost exactly where this election began, though it was quite a ride getting here. I don't want her to see how the news makes me feel. I try to keep the look off my face, but it's hard to do.

On the bus coming back, the Tories have sent in bottles of champagne, people are acting convivial and one of the Mulroney staff asks whether the unions, especially the

CAW, paid for the cartoon booklet. I start to run off figures, how labour only paid about a third, the rest was widespread — and I stop and think, What if the unions *had* paid for it? What would have been wrong with that? Tories like this one don't mind when business pays the entire cost of their campaign plus launching a huge blitz of their own. Why is it that they get to set the terms for everything and make others feel defensive and apologetic?

I lie on the bed in my room at the Queen Elizabeth. People in different parts of the country who have worked at this issue for three years seem to be avoiding a sense of helplessness with thoughts of what they might have done to make it turn out differently. Laurell complains that the type size naming the anti-deal organizations in the final Pro-Canada ad should have been larger, because that was the most important part. Kathleen says she should have taken the $5,000 from her grandmother's will and gone across the country in an anti-deal van. Someone phones from the west, desperately trying to organize a press conference for tomorrow to tell people how to vote strategically. For myself, I still think it would have mattered for the Liberals to take on the lying issue. But I didn't realize that till quite late and even then wasn't certain, and anyway someone like me can't really affect what the parties do. In the end, to tell the truth, I don't think the popular forces opposing free trade could have done much more than they did. I drag up to Ste-Catherine for a bad midnight supper. Kids are promenading up and down.

Very late, I talk to Kathleen. For her, she says, it's just the start of the fight. She thinks the country needs a PCNI, a Popular Council on National Issues, to go up against the Business Council on National Issues, who have been having too easy a time dictating the national agenda on matters like free trade. They plan ahead, they have a vision of the future — why shouldn't others? She's elated at starting to do something during this campaign, maybe picking up political activity where she left off when she quit the Maoists in disgust about twenty years ago. For her and others, this could be the start of something, a new kind of politics and the end of an old kind.

Sunday, November 20

Morning. At the airport, I go into the smoke shop, look at the papers, decide the hell with it, today I don't want to read news. But I pick up the Sunday *Gazette* and *La Presse*, thinking I'll go through them a few days from now. As I pay, I glance at Lysiane Gagnon's front-page column in *La Presse*, her final word before the election. Her lead says, "At Laval, during the last Conservative rally of the campaign in the Montreal region, the result of Monday's vote could be read on two faces: the joyful face of Brian Mulroney, relieved and now certain of victory. . . and the face of Toronto writer Rick Salutin . . . ." It's a little snippy: she refers to "*le nationalisme 'Canadian'*" in that scornful Quebec way, as if they don't really believe such a thing exists, and says that I'm on my way home because Quebec has become *trop bleu*. But that's true, more or less. She says it was the cartoon booklet, on a par with Turner's debate performance, that turned this election into a fight and almost an upset. I assume this evaluation comes straight from the Tory camp. It's quite a tribute to the popular movement against free trade and to the entire collective effort that made the booklet happen. She says we had our "guts and heart" in it, and my protestations last night reminded her of the wan hopes of the *Oui* side leading up to the referendum of 1980. It's nice to see someone in Quebec get that analogy right: that the opponents of free trade are the ones with the dream — like the *indépendantistes* in Quebec in 1980 — about to be dashed by the forces of conservatism and money. I feel as if I've been at war and can go home now — defeated but with some honour.

Toronto. Laurell says she's working on a scenario that

says it's just as well for the Tories to be in charge for the recession that's coming. She says she and others made a pact last night at a rally at the Bamboo not to be discouraged.

Ken Traynor drops by, very energetic about how much has been learned, and it almost worked, and it probably will next time. There's a lot of support for the idea about the PCNI. I propose John Turner for next chair of the Pro-Canada Network — it's meant as humour. "Don't even say that to *me*," says Laurell.

Monday, November 21

Election day. Laurell is on her way to leaflet in the ethnic communities, in the driving rain: one area, she says, where more should have been done.

Seventeen million voters are out there, says Doug Small on "Global News." He adds — rightly, I think — that this is the first election in which people will really consult their consciences and be called on to make a personal decision.

There is a kind of quiet hope among people I know. I guess it's common — even necessary — in situations like this. And it has been a very unpredictable time.

After school. I speak with Wren, who's sixteen.

"Lots of people at school talk about it," she says of free trade. "Most of them are against it." She says they don't usually talk about political things, but "it's in all the newspapers, it's on everything constantly." Her father lives in Kingston and she spends summers and holidays with him and her grandparents there. "I haven't really discussed it with my dad," she says, "because he's against it. My grandmother's against it and my grandfather's for it. He was born in the States. Last summer I argued with everybody. Like with Dave, my uncle, from Mississauga. Dave works for Dupont, so he's for it. I guess they basically think there'd be more of a market and stuff. My cousins both say they're for it, but I don't think either of them know much about it."

I ask how she feels about politics. "I always liked politics," she says. "That's how I got my history award. It was all about politics. Canadian government and Canadian politics." Her mother has been active in the peace movement and related causes, and she's watched carefully. "In all those groups," she says, "they just hand stuff out to the other groups. My mother goes to meetings against free trade and hands out stuff against free trade. I mean, what's the point? She doesn't do that as much because I told her. Now she puts stuff up on lampposts.

"People at school aren't really into issues. Lots of people go to marches and stuff, but they're not in a group." She means issue-centred groups. "But I think you can do more by getting in the government. I don't think those groups are too great. There's something wrong with them, they don't seem to be able to *do* anything. They seem kind of too . . . the peace groups just want everybody to kind of get rid of everything, but it won't work that way."

How does she feel about the parties? "I used to kind of, because of my mum, I thought the NDP should be in power, but I don't know, I think now they're screwed up. Ed Broadbent never seems to say anything too intelligent. You read in the papers, Turner makes some brilliant statement and then Broadbent says — what he says isn't as good. Turner says all this stuff like about Canada, like Turner says, "This is more than an election; it's your future." And then Broadbent says, "Mulroney promised fairness and he did the opposite." And then he's always attacking Turner. He's just figuring he has to fight with Turner for the votes of people who are against free trade. He wants to get into power — doesn't really care about anything." I don't think anyone has put the historic failure of Ed Broadbent and the NDP better. Then she adds, "I think the NDP is worth putting effort into. I guess I would join, not because I think they're great now, but I think they could be better."

She cares, she's watching carefully, she's going to do something about this society when she gets her chance, and she's going to figure out her own way of doing it — no matter what the result of others' efforts, as that becomes known later tonight.

"The World at Six." Two hours till the polls close and CBC radio is still disinforming listeners. Ken McCreath, summing up the campaign, makes no mention of the popular movement. He says wrongly that Canadians were "evenly divided" on the deal before the debate and says Turner appealed to emotion rather than fact. Then they play the debate clip, which has Turner throwing facts at Mulroney, and Mulroney spitting back high emotion. I flip it off and go into Tony Ianno's headquarters.

Tony looks grim, like he's about to lose, or maybe he's just wiped. (It was the former.) Over at Heap's office, Ashley has many tales about the dirty tricks of the Liberals. For example, the security guard at an old people's home helped residents down the stairs, whispering to them how to vote.

I drive to Tory minister Barbara McDougall's campaign office at about 6:45. I walk in and there's a former student of the course I teach in Canadian culture at the U. of T. She's very Tory-looking now, with the expensive haircut. Says I gave her an A. She takes a campaign manager aside and then they start coming at me in waves, pushing me toward the door. I ask if other journalists have been booted out today. It ends impolitely.

I drive down to the Danforth, to Lynn McDonald's NDP office, for the final moments of her combat with Dennis Mills, Liberal. There's another ex-student, now at Oxford, who's been working here while on vacation. She says Mills' campaign has been dirty beyond anything she's ever seen. She'll tell me more when the result is known. After McDonald loses, I don't hear from her.

Ex-students of Canadian culture seem peppered through Canadian politics tonight. Everybody thinks everybody else plays dirty, and they probably do. I think I would if I were in this game. I go over to Mills' office, where there's a hubbub but no Dennis. I leave.

Back at my poll, during the last minutes of voting. I voted here earlier in the day. The Deputy Returning Officer is Jesse Nishihata, director of a fine documentary film on the Berger inquiry of the late seventies. He hasn't done much filmmaking since. It's what often happens to experienced Canadian artists. Jesse says the turnout in this poll is enormous — about 80 percent — and the Liberals have been dragging everybody in. People keep coming with almost no time left, and after. A young woman arrives with her dog, a husky pup. An NDP worker looks after the dog while she votes. It's homey in the polling room, with streamers and balloons, and people sitting on a couch in the centre. There's Leo Panitch, a left-wing political science prof, a scrutineer for Dan Heap. He's worried about the high turnout helping the Liberals. I say I don't think it matters much who wins between Heap and Ianno, and Leo registers dismay. Heap is good on militarization, Central America, issues like that, he says. I am derisive — still mad at the NDP, I guess — and Leo says he spends his *life* criticizing social democrats, so don't throw that at *him*. In the grocery on Bloor weeks later, I see Leo again and he says I was monomaniacal about the deal on election night. I say anyone who wasn't monomaniacal that night is an idiot. These emotions will not subside readily.

There's heavy tension inside between NDP and Liberal scrutineers. I hear Jesse's voice calming them down and urging them to work quietly and carefully. He's perfect for this job. He'd obviously be excellent in the harried situation of a film shoot. He shuts the door with a little wave and a smile. Someone predicts they'll be an hour or an hour and a half, with the size of the turnout.

In a parking lot at University and Richmond I listen to the results coming in: the Liberals winning Atlantic Canada, the Tories sweeping Quebec, then Ontario, which splits and ensures a Conservative majority. I decide to skip the

Tory party in the Hilton, which I'd hoped to hit before the outcome was clear. I go into the Four Seasons, up to the floor where some of the people from the Canadian Auto Workers are watching results. I get to the door and hear that the CBC has called a Tory majority. Inside are Bob White, Peggy Nash, a few others. They have a pool on how many seats the parties will get. Everyone has called a Tory majority. White seems energized by the defeat, positively energized and bloody-minded, revving up already for coming rounds. There's a little talk about what happens next, etc. I feel I should get along to Marjorie Cohen's, where the Toronto Coalition people are gathered.

Marjorie's not even there. Like a real martyr to the cause, she's spending the night on CKO all-news radio, commenting on the results alongside John Crispo. The people at her place are watching Barbara Frum interviewing journalist Christina McCall, who talks about the mountains of money business spent to win it. Frum challenges the notion that, as she puts it, "it's somehow illegitimate for business to have advertised." She adds, "The trade unions spent millions on that very effective comic book" — a highly uninformed statement. (The booklet cost $700,000, 40 percent raised by labour — as publicly announced five weeks ago.) A voice behind me says it's time for a group called The Enemies of Public Broadcasting. Everyone has a lot to drink. Laurell falls asleep on the floor.

When Ed comes on to concede, someone asks, Do you think he'll mention the deal *now*? He barely does. Somebody else says he looks relieved — that the Liberals didn't win. And at least that fucking deal — which may have cost him the victory that once seemed possible — is finally behind him. Mulroney does not wait for Turner to concede. When Turner finally comes on from Vancouver, he talks about the free trade agreement, the fact that a majority of votes went against it, but not the election, and that's the system.

I drive Laurell to her place. In the car, she starts to cry. I ask, What is it. "We deserved to win!" she says. "We really did." I laugh, quite a lot. It's true. We did. We really did.

An Interesting Blip

I've always had these instincts but I never had to express them. Canadians are bad at expressing things. We're probably too reticent.

John Turner, March 1989

The Longest Roller-coaster

The fight over free trade was the longest political roller-coaster I've ever ridden. Emotions soared and dipped and flipped over incessantly. The ride continued after the election. For many who had been consumed in the popular movement against the deal, it assumed some of the well-documented traits of the phases of mourning. There was, for instance, in the wake of election day, an unexpected, even bizarre, sense of elation, akin to the "denial" phase. The movement had done well; it hadn't just fired a shot, it almost won. Could this be the first step toward a new kind of politics in Canada, based on issues and popular mobilization around them? For a while we'd had an election that was not a substitute for a deeper, more participatory kind of democracy, but a foretaste of it.

Several representatives of the coalitions went on CBC radio's "Morningside" two days after the election to discuss the future of the popular movement against free trade. By the end of the discussion, host Peter Gzowski said with amazement, "I don't feel like I'm talking to people who have just been defeated!" Provincial coalition meetings held after the election were enthusiastic and well attended. There was no talk about whether to disband; the question didn't even arise. Everyone seemed to assume that the fight about free trade would continue, along with an enlarged campaign over the right-wing agenda the deal had always implied.

Some politicians appeared to feel the same fervour. "We lost the battle but the war is far from over," wrote Turner in a note. Royce ("Good morning, Senator") Frith sent a poem, with a nod to Noel Coward: "The kings and queens of business / How proud and tall they stand, / To prove the upper classes / Have still the upper hand." Frith added proudly, "The BCNI is having a celebratory black-tie dinner at the Rideau Club. (I'm not invited.)" As for myself, when I ran into friends who had participated in the fight, it was like meeting old war buddies. Others, who hadn't been involved, expressed amazement that I didn't seem gloomier — or gloomy at all.

Eventually, other phases of the mourning cycle set in: unbelief, anger, despair. Especially anger. There were numerous candidates for blame. Ed Broadbent and David Peterson, for example. What if Broadbent hadn't chosen to join Mulroney in attacking Turner for the second half of the campaign, turning the focus of the election toward Turner's credibility and away from the free trade deal? There was no way of calculating the effect on the outcome. What if Peterson had fought with a will, instead of showing real enthusiasm only for the campaign of his brother, Jim, in suburban Toronto? It could be argued that this election was decided in Ontario, not Quebec. One of the seats in London, Peterson's own home town, went to the Conservatives by eight votes — out of almost 50,000 cast. What about the federal Liberal party? What if they hadn't spent most of four years undermining Turner's leadership — continuing right into and through the campaign? There were also the Tories and the business organizations to loathe, but at least they stuck to their agenda: their object was to win the election. The NDP and the Liberals often behaved as if their goal was to lose it. One lifelong loyal NDP apparatchik pulled me aside and said, "Write the toughest, most vicious book you can. And don't tell anyone I said that."

It was also possible to blame the Canadian people. "The *oylam* is a *goylam*," said my mother, a secretary at the Clarke Institute of Psychiatry in Toronto. The phrase is Yiddish and means, roughly, "The world is a dummy" or just "People are stupid." Many involved in the coalition movement went through this phase and considered, for example, migrating to some other country in order to punish the Canadian people properly for their actions. Self-recrimination was also an option. What if we had published the cartoon booklet later — or earlier? Why hadn't we demanded a referendum? The coalitions had even made the major strategic error of not having $50 to $60 million to match the spending of business and government.

Finally, blame and anger settled into the more sustainable modes of gloom and despair. "I realized how much I cared," said a friend who hasn't ever been much involved in political activity, "when I saw Mulroney *dancing* on the platform election night and realized I was crying." Reality accomplished this mood shift in a great many people during the election aftermath, as Tories and business claimed their spoils by implementing, much more quickly than had been expected, the real agenda of free trade. Personally, I spent a lot of time listening to the blues in the weeks, then months, following the election. A lot.

Chronicle of an Aftermath

A brief account of the events following the free trade election of November 21, 1988, shows some of the real connections between our formal political system of elections and the actual world of power and government in our society.

On November 22, the day after the election, the *Globe and Mail* headline read, "Conservative majority; Voters back trade deal." A dubious conclusion. More than half of the Canadians who voted (52.3 percent) supported parties that were *against* the deal. Forty-three percent voted for the Tories. The other two elections in Canadian history on this issue, in 1891 and 1911, rejected free trade deals by *smaller* margins — 51 percent and 50.9 percent — but since those votes weren't split between two Opposition parties, they also returned majority governments against free trade. The *Globe*'s lead editorial that day after contained a fierce attack on writers Margaret Atwood and Timothy Findley for daring, a few days earlier, to question the appointment of outgoing Canadian ambassador to the U.S. Allan Gotlieb — a strong advocate of the trade deal — as new chairman of the Canada Council. It read like the proclamation of a Take No Hostages attitude toward those who had presumed to question business or government authority, and who almost overthrew it.

   The effects of the trade deal proper began to be felt immediately. On that same day — day one of the age of free trade — the president of Quebec's Chamber of Commerce congratulated the government on its free trade success, adding that it now had a mandate to cut spending, deregulate, privatize — and search out "imaginative formulas allowing an increase in possible choices for Canadians allowing those who desire recourse to private forms of social security like pension plans, private health insurance . . . ." So much for the many assurances of business during the campaign that social programs would be unaffected by free trade.

On that day too, Gillette Canada Inc. announced closure of its two Canadian plants, with loss of work for six hundred Canadians. Under the deal it could supply its Canadian customers from its U.S. plants. In what became a standard pattern, the company and the government denied any connection between the closings and the trade deal.

November 22 was also the day that Judy Brandow, editor of *Canadian Living* magazine, was fired. She had run for the NDP in the election and had been defeated by a Tory. Before running, she had received assurances that her job would not be in jeopardy if she stood for election.

On that day as well, the RCMP raided the offices of Tory MP Richard Grisé in Quebec, after a lengthy but unreported investigation. And a Tory adviser to a former Tory Cabinet minister from Quebec went to court, after many delays, on a charge that would have been embarrassing to the government had the case come up before the election. It was a busy day.

On November 24, three days after, the government announced it would not oppose a mammoth takeover of Selkirk Communications by Maclean-Hunter, a strong deal supporter. Takeovers and mergers began to blossom, along with shutdowns. David Culver, president of Alcan and of the pro-deal Canadian Alliance for Trade and Job Opportunities, explained something he and his comrades had failed to mention before the election: that there would be widespread job loss and, as it was often called, "readjustment" after the deal. "You can't have some growth in the garden without some death," said Culver. "Some flowers have to die for others to grow."

On November 25, four days after, a shoe company in Lachine, Quebec, announced it would close and put fifty people out of work. Footwear was always expected to be one of the big losers in the deal. That same day a U.S. company, Pittsburgh Paints, announced it was closing its Toronto plant, which employed 139 people. And a subsidiary of the American pharmaceuticals giant, Johnson &

Johnson, said it was moving a Toronto lab to New Jersey and eliminating sixteen jobs.

A similar willingness to press the advantage showed in the media. Dale Goldhawk, president of the performers and writers' union, ACTRA, had written an editorial opposing free trade in his union's newsletter. He was ordered by the CBC to resign either as union leader or as host of the national radio phone-in show, "Cross Country Checkup." He quit the union post. The *Globe and Mail* reported that current affairs producers at the CBC had been told by management to beware of covering stories about plant closings and job losses that were related to free trade. They were instructed to "keep in mind the long-term" benefits of the deal. In the months to come, there was scant coverage of such events, on the CBC or elsewhere.

Business Week, the U.S. newsmagazine, headed its December 5 story about the Canadian election "A Giant Step Closer to North America Inc." Estimates of what business had paid to snatch back the election began to appear. The Alliance said it had spent $1.5 million on its four-page insert — a retort to the cartoon booklet — plus another half million on ads. The National Citizens' Coalition said it had spent $0.5 million attacking Broadbent and another $200,000 on backing the deal. The Alberta government acknowledged dropping $600,000 to produce their pro-deal householder. These big spenders were only the tip of a propaganda iceberg. There were also the many ads placed by individual businesses and business associations that appeared everywhere in the country in the final days, and the workplace meetings, enclosures in pay packets and other interventions. Elmer MacKay, federal minister for Revenue Canada, indicated that *all* these costs would qualify as tax deductions because, as former revenue minister Perrin Beatty said, such expenses had "a lot to do with the very survival of their businesses." No deductions were allowed for anti-deal costs, even by businessmen like Mel Hurtig, honorary chair of the Council of Canadians. Investigative journalist Nick Fillmore, writing in *This*

Magazine, calculated that over $56.5 million had been spent promoting free trade in the two years leading up to the election, including more than $18 million by business and $32 million by the federal government.

Further candour came from Molson Breweries president, Mickey Cohen, former president of Olympia and York Enterprises Corporation and before that deputy-minister of finance. He explained, with regard to scaling Canadian social services and other programs down to American levels, "We will face greater pressure to harmonize, either because the Americans are asking for it or because our own businessmen are saying, 'If we're going to compete, we have to look more like the guys we're competing with.'" This sounded like a paraphrase of predictions made by those opposed to the trade deal. The Alliance insert, on the other hand, had asked, "Won't Canadian business lobby to reduce spending on social and other programs?" and answered, "Not at all." A consensus on the deal's effects was forming at last.

On December 6, the Catelli pasta business went up for sale, as a direct result of its inability to withstand U.S. competition that would arise because of the trade deal.

On December 7, former Quebec Tory MP Michel Gravel pleaded guilty to infuence peddling and fraud charges, after numerous legal tactics that had prevented the opening of his trial until after the election. A cynic might have wondered, If he was going to plead guilty anyway, why delay?

On December 13, Molson's confirmed its intention to cut salaried staff by 10 percent because the beer industry's exemption in the deal was "just a temporary reprieve," according to a senior vice-president. So even being left out of the deal didn't mean protection from its impact.

Under pressure to show some concern about these effects, Prime Minister Mulroney announced that a blue-ribbon advisory panel appointed almost a year earlier would report within the week on measures to alleviate damage done by the trade deal — though they had rarely met during the course of the year. One panel member said it was up to Canadians to "get off their butts" and win from the deal. In the end the panel recommended *no* measures directed toward victims of free trade, despite the fact that Mulroney had claimed such measures would be "the finest transition programs in the world."

The Canadian Manufacturers' Association called for cuts in social spending like unemployment insurance and other "non-wage compensation costs," in order to achieve competitiveness in the new economic reality, though the four-page Alliance insert had insisted that free trade would create "more wealth to improve government services such as daycare." By now job losses due to plant closings had occurred at Northern Telecom in Bramalea, Belleville and Aylmer (a total of 975 jobs), Storwal International Inc. in Pembroke (100 jobs), Canada Packers in Winnipeg (90 jobs) and Allergan Inc. in Pointe Claire, Quebec (62 jobs). Total job loss due to the trade deal within a month of the election, before the agreement was even in effect, was 4,000. The Canadian Labour Congress estimated that the prospect of free trade had resulted in the addition of fifteen jobs to the economy — at Windsor Aerospace.

Over Christmas the *Globe and Mail* of the pre–free trade era also fell. Editor-in-chief Norman Webster and managing editor Geoffrey Stevens were fired in a blatant and humiliating way. It seemed part of the new regime of free trade; Webster and Stevens had represented the older traditions of *noblesse oblige* and social responsibility among the Canadian elite. They also had certain quaint commitments to journalistic ideals like pluralism and informing the public. Publisher Roy Megarry, on the other hand, had stated that "by 1990, publishers of mass circulation daily newspapers will finally stop kidding themselves that they are in the newspaper business and admit that they are primarily in the business of carrying advertising messages." He made his deadline with a year to spare. He installed as editor William Thorsell, who had carried the business and government line on the free trade deal and other shibboleths of the new age. Thorsell immediately announced that more heads would roll at the *Globe*, as they soon did, while business writers moved into editorial positions. The *Globe* also announced the effective cancellation of its "labour" and "women's" beats, which seemed a little like neglecting stories about South Africa because you aren't all that keen on apartheid.

On January 1, 1989, the trade deal officially came into effect. That week the Canadian Council of Furniture Manufacturers estimated that at least 3,500 people would lose jobs in their industry in the coming five years, because of free trade. It had not participated in the debate prior to the election.

Employment and Immigration Canada announced it was "reviewing" a policy which required universities to try to find Canadians for teaching positions before considering Americans and other foreigners — because of provisions in the trade agreement.

An American trade journal reprinted a November letter from the National Association of Manufacturers — the most powerful industrial lobby in Washington, to the American secretary of the treasury, insisting that, under the trade deal, the U.S. should force Canada to raise the value of the Canadian dollar and thus eliminate an important trade advantage to Canada. In fact, the value of the Canadian dollar had been rising ever since the announcement of a negotiated deal a year before the election, and it had jumped sharply the day after Canadians voted. The chief economist of the Toronto-Dominion Bank said, "There is a belief in the United States that the Canadian dollar should be at par and that anything less is a subsidy." The chief economist of Midland Doherty Ltd., who calculated that the right level for the Canadian dollar to reflect reality in the two countries would be 77 cents, said that, at par, all Canadian manufacturers would be wiped out except those in forest products and steel. The Americans could probably count on the Canadian government to fulfill their wishes, but they also had the threat of retaliation against the Canadian rate as an unfair trade subsidy

— since the deal did nothing to protect Canada from such U.S. countermeasures.

By mid-January the United States government had completed a list of forty Canadian laws that would have to be changed during the next stage in the negotiation process, which concerned the definition of unfair subsidies. The new head of the U.S. trade negotiations office announced that her government wasn't finished with gaining concessions from Canada. "We must vigorously implement our free trade agreements with Canada and Israel . . . and seek appropriate expansions," she said. "In the case of Canada such expansions include — [disciplining] the use of subsidies." There was no comparable list on the Canadian side, perhaps because Canada had almost no leverage left to bargain with anyway.

In the third week of January, over a three-day period, three massive mergers occurred. On Wednesday the 18th, the second-largest beer company in the country, Molson's, merged with the third-largest, Carling O'Keefe. The next day, Wardair was gobbled up by PWA, the parent of Canadian Airlines. And on Friday, Imperial Oil took over Texaco. Business got bigger, but the benefits for everyone else were in doubt. Wardair announced almost immediately that its low fares would rise, and within the month stated it would be laying off a thousand employees. Molson and Carling O'Keefe said seven breweries across Canada would be closed and 1,400 jobs eliminated. Minister of State for Finance Tom Hockin's advice to brewery workers who lost their jobs was, "Just read the want ads."

A few days later, western grain farmers reacted with dismay to a federal move limiting the authority of the Canadian Wheat Board, which they called part of a "hidden agenda" of the free trade deal.

During the same week, Finance Minister Michael Wilson granted American Express permission to operate a Canadian bank, a major inroad into national control of Canada's banking system. The actual decision, in response to an application by American Express, had been ratified by Cabinet the very day of the election, November 21.

American Express had been the most prominent backer of the trade deal in the United States. The chairman of the Toronto-Dominion Bank stated flatly that this was a payoff to the head of American Express by the Mulroney government. A day later he said he'd been mistaken.

On January 26 it was announced that a U.S. corporation was buying Consolidated-Bathurst, one of the biggest and oldest pulp and paper companies in the country, from Paul Desmarais, who had said during the election, "It would be dangerous, very dangerous to reject free trade." He now announced, "There comes a time to take a profit." Minister of Regional Industrial Expansion Robert de Cotret said feebly that all the takeovers, mergers and shutdowns were a coincidence and had nothing to do with free trade. "It just happened," he said.

New U.S. President George Bush came to Ottawa in February, in what his staff described as a test run for his visits to real countries like Japan, China and Korea later in the month. "Except for the fact he is going across the border, this trip is really no different than the president travelling to St. Louis," said an official. "It gives the White House a chance to get used to working together on the road, and to get the bugs out before the big trips coming up." Bush also planned to thank Mulroney for approving the testing in Canada of a new and controversial version of the Cruise missile. According to Bob Hepburn of the *Toronto Star*, Americans were "pleasantly stunned that Mulroney okayed the request so quickly. They felt he would wait until the actual visit and possibly use it as a bargaining chip for U.S. concessions."

In Toronto in mid-February, Inglis Ltd. announced that it was closing its factory, putting 565 workers out of work, because of the free trade deal. There had been other recent closings at Maple Leaf Mills Ltd. and Rowntree MacKintosh chocolates.

The CBC continued to buckle. In mid-February, Roy Bonisteel, host of "Man Alive" for twenty-two years, quit because he was "fed up . . . I was not allowed to have opinions." He said management had been harassing him about expressing views for four years — i.e., since the arrival of the Tory government. CBC Vice-President Denis Harvey said, "Because 70 percent of our revenue comes from the taxpayers, we come under tremendous pressures to be balanced and fair." He seemed to have missed the distinction between taxpayers and the government. A few days later, for the first time in the history of the science program "The Nature of Things," an episode was cancelled because of pressure. The show was about nuclear energy. The CBC board of directors, at the urging of board member Bill Neville, a Tory strategist during the election, began its own review of the CBC's traditional review of balance in its election coverage.

The C. D. Howe Institute, a business-supported think tank, issued a call to panic about the deficit — the beginning of a long lead-in by business to the first free trade budget, scheduled for April. The deficit could be reduced by half over the coming four years, it said, "through improved targetting of social benefits" — that is, by eliminating universality of social programs, starting with unemployment insurance, old age pensions and family allowances. The Institute proposed selling off more Crown corporations like Air Canada and cutting back regional and agricultural programs. It also pressed for higher sales taxes and lower taxes on capital gains. Most of these measures appeared in the April federal budget. Aside from the trade deal, the Institute had little praise for the government's record, saying that the only other government achievements came in "areas in which there was no organized public resistance." The government obviously still had to learn to ignore the resistance of the public that had elected them. The Canadian Manufacturers' Association, the Canadian Chamber of Commerce and the Business Council on National Issues joined the call to cut the deficit by slashing social programs — exactly what they had said would be unnecessary if the free trade deal went ahead. CMA President Laurent Thibault stated, "The Canada-U.S. free trade agreement that we fought hard for creates great opportunities, but also makes it more urgent that we tackle the outstanding issues that affect our competitiveness." When Broadbent had quoted Thibault during the campaign to precisely this effect, Thibault attacked Broadbent because the words had been spoken in 1980. Now he obligingly repeated the thought. At the end of February, the U.S. Department of Commerce slapped a 103.5 percent duty on steel rails produced in Cape Breton — precisely the kind of penalty Canadians had been told they needed a free trade deal to avoid.

Through March, the government and its allies spoke incessantly of the perils of the deficit, a subject barely mentioned during the election campaign, but now apparently the top national priority. Canadians were told it was not the government's problem. It belonged, as Employment and Immigration Minister Barbara McDougall said, "to each and every Canadian." Yet it was not individual citizens who had thrown $399 million of public money at an oil upgrader project in Alberta, $150 million at a gas pipeline to Vancouver Island, or $300 million into a Quebec by-election, all in the run-up to the federal campaign. Finance Minister Wilson began backing away from promises the government had made during the election, which at the time he had called not mere promises, but "commitments."

In mid-March, Midas Canada announced that it was shutting a muffler plant in Scarborough, Ontario, and shifting production to the United States. The tariff on mufflers was due for elimination under the trade agreement. The president of Hayes-Dana Inc. warned that pay equity for women was impractical under the free trade agreement because it would make Canadian companies uncompetitive with American ones. The Ontario Employers Advocacy Council argued that improvements to the provincial Workers' Compensation Act would also endanger competitiveness under the trade agreement. In May in Toronto, management labour lawyer Barbara Humphries claimed that provisions in the Ontario Human Rights Code that aid the handicapped would, under free trade, encourage employers to leave the province for the United States.

By April it had become apparent that many Canadian manufacturers were moving, or considering moving, their operations not just to the U.S., but to Mexico, where the "Maquiladora" trade arrangements made it possible to count products as American-made, although wages and conditions were far lower than those in either Canada or the United States. Fleck Manufacturing Inc. near London, Ontario, had moved its plant south on October 1, 1988, the very day that the free trade election was announced. Custom Trim Ltd. of Waterloo, Ontario, opened two Mexican plants, leaving its Canadian operations in doubt, as did Kanata-based Mitel. "It's only a matter of time till tri-lateral negotiations begin" for a free trade zone including Mexico, said the vice-president for corporate relations of the Business Council of British Columbia.

Employers increasingly made threats related to the free trade agreement in order to force concessions from employees. At a food industry convention in December, the president of H. J. Heinz Co. of Canada had said that jobs and wages must be cut or the company would move its seven plants south of the border. The president of Nabisco Brands Ltd. said, "Nothing clears the mind so much as the spectre of being hung in the morning," and added that companies should "use free trade as a catalyst to mobilize employees to cut costs." In February a Toronto photo engraving company warned its workers that lower U.S. wages and longer working hours would have to be matched by Canadian workers. "We either change to become competitive in this new environment or we become a fatality," wrote J. R. Shaw, president of Photo Engravers and Electrotypers Ltd. At Bovie Manufacturing Inc. in Lindsay, Ontario, the plant manager wrote to employees in February, "The Mexicans are waiting. Your strike vote last night means as soon as you go out, the Mexicans will get your jobs immediately."

On April 11, Minister of Employment and Immigration

McDougall announced changes to the unemployment insurance system that would in almost every case "harmonize" it with the more niggardly American system. The government would cease to participate in the program, it would be harder to qualify for payments, and benefits would last a shorter time. During the election campaign, Minister for International Trade John Crosbie had said, "The prime minister has assured me that there will be no changes to unemployment insurance."

The April budget, the first "free trade budget," continued the harmonization process, though without acknowledgement. Regional development programs, considered unfair subsidies under U.S. trade law, were slashed by $2 billion, with further cuts promised. Freight rate equalization payments to farmers, which had been attacked by American protectionist lobbies, were chopped by over $100 million. In spite of Mulroney's campaign promise, "As long as I am prime minister, social programs, especially for the elderly, will be improved, not diminished, by our government," the budget introduced a "claw-back" provision that eliminated pensions for senior citizens with income above $50,000, and did much the same to family allowances. Since this provision was not fully indexed to inflation, it would include greater numbers at lower income levels over time. The major spending commitment to a national child care program made before the election was simply eliminated, and transfer payments to the provinces for health care and higher education were severely reduced. Via Rail was cut deeply, and what remained of Air Canada was put up for sale. Foreign aid was sharply curtailed. There were also very deep cuts in government grants to social advocacy groups such as the National Action Committee on the Status of Women, which had provided a source of democratic participation outside the electoral process. During the campaign, Finance Minister Wilson had said that "the economic benefits from the agreement will start to be realized shortly after its implementation on January 1, 1989." He now predicted a loss of 125,000 jobs by 1990.

Perhaps he meant the benefits to companies that moved to Mexico.

On May 25 Minister for International Trade John Crosbie appeared before the Standing Committee on External Affairs and International Trade of the House of Commons for the first time since the election. Asked by a Conservative member to cite examples of jobs created by the free trade agreement, he announced, after consulting with his aides, that no such examples were available. None. This stunning admission went unreported in the Canadian press and media.

For three years before the election, the government had insisted that it was devoted to Canada's "cultural sovereignty" and that cultural support programs would only be enhanced by the prosperity that would blossom under free trade. Then in April 1988 it had announced that the program of postal subsidies for Canadian magazines was safe for "at least the next five years." The budget of April '89 flew in the face of that claim, with a $10 million cut to the current year's subsidy and a $45 million cut for each subsequent year, thus improving the competitiveness of American magazines in Canadian markets. The budget also slashed the already devastated CBC budget, leading to the prospect of the effective dismantling of the corporation as a national cultural institution. An internal report by the federal industry department said the trade deal would "adversely affect" the recording industry. International Trade Minister Crosbie announced that the report, from his own government, wasn't worth the paper it was printed on. Culture had ostensibly been "exempt" under the terms of the trade agreement. The exemption appeared a formality.

In May, Canadian food magnate Galen Weston said that Canadians should not expect any reductions in food costs as a result of the free trade agreement. A government publication, often mentioned by ministers during the election campaign, had contained the promise that Canadian families would save $85 to $130 a year on groceries. It had also guaranteed lower appliance and home costs. The federal department of consumer affairs announced it was not even monitoring post-free trade price changes, since it was almost impossible to isolate the effects of the trade deal from other influences.

In June, Kimberly-Clark Canada Ltd. announced that it was going to purchase lab coats and overalls in Mexico rather than Canada, leading to the loss of sixty jobs at Bovie Manufacturing Inc. in Lindsay, Ontario. A Canadian maker of glass containers, Enfield Corp., announced closings of plants in central and western Canada involving about 900 jobs. A federal report had identified the glass industry as a problem area under the deal. K. T. Industries of Winnipeg laid off twenty people at the same time as it expanded its operations into the United States. Fiberglas Canada Inc. cut 180 jobs at its insulation plant in Mission, B.C. Albright and Wilson Americas closed a chemical plant in Newfoundland, laying off 300 workers and shifting production to North Carolina. Lawnmower manufacturer Toro Co. of Manitoba made plans to supply Canada from its American plant and laid off 60 workers. At Coleman Canada in Etobicoke, Ontario, 225 employees lost their jobs when the company shifted its production to Kansas. Bendix Safety Restraints Ltd. of Collingwood, Ontario, announced it would lay off 400 workers and move operations to Mexico and Alabama. "This has nothing to do with the Canada-U.S. free trade agreement," said a company spokesman at head office in Michigan. "It's strictly economic." The Canadian Labour Congress estimated that 25,000 good jobs had been lost during the first six months of free trade. In a different kind of harmonization, a report by Hay Management Consultants said free trade was likely to push up pay for senior Canadian executives by significant amounts. "Integration of our two economies . . . will increase the pressure to equalize compensation at the executive level," said the report's author.

I end this chronicle arbitrarily on Canada Day, July 1, 1989, six months after the free trade agreement came into effect.

This slim account makes a good case for the irrelevance of elections to politics in Canadian society, or at least for an impressive gulf between the formal electoral system and the actual process of government. The election of 1988 was about free trade and little else. The post-election period is remarkable not so much because the government can be seen to have lied consistently about free trade as because, according to the government and most media sources, almost everything following the November 21 vote was presented as having virtually no connection with free trade at all.

The explosion of public concern had compelled the government and its business backers to run, with some reluctance, on their support for the free trade agreement. They laid aside earlier, vaguer slogans and made extreme claims for free trade, as though nothing else even affected the fate of Canadian society. With free trade, the winds of prosperity would blow, as the prime minister put it; without free trade, he warned, two million jobs could disappear. But following the election, quite suddenly — dead silence on the subject. The government discovered other obsessions, among them the federal deficit and the need to retrench programs. True, these new obsessions jibed perfectly with the requirements of the free trade agreement, but the connection was never drawn. It was as though free trade had nothing to do with current dilemmas and no effect on decisions — in fact, it was as though there had never been a free trade deal. This is the sort of experience which, in the private sphere, can engender schizophrenia and doubts about one's sanity. Was there ever a free trade deal, or a national debate, or a free trade election?

The media colluded. They simply stopped commenting on free trade when the government and business stopped talking about it. In some cases, such as the CBC, this was the result of direct instruction from above. Occasionally, particularly in connection with plant closings, the statements of union officials or other critics attributing these to free trade would be reported, along with blanket denials by corporate and government spokesmen. But in most instances — such as cuts to social or cultural programs, mergers or privatization measures — the press simply took the government at its word and did not even point to free trade connections. There were few broad assessments of the deal's effects, or only very superficial ones. This treatment by the media effectively fulfilled the government's secret communications strategy of September 1985 on free trade: to ensure a state of "benign neglect" among the public on the subject. In fact, logic suggests that somewhere in post-election Ottawa there existed a second-generation secret communications strategy on how to handle the free trade issue, the gist of which was . . . benign neglect.

This remarkable transition to a free-tradeless politics illuminates the real function of elections in our society. The government and its business tutors wanted a free trade agreement. They did not want to have a broad democratic discussion about it, nor did they want an election over it. When public debate over the issue became unavoidable, they joined in, as though the whole thing was an unfortunate impediment to their plans, an obstacle to be overcome. Once the election had been won, they showed themselves entirely indifferent to the pledges they had made in order to win it.

They revealed a similar indifference toward future elections. They had their plans for the transformation of Canadian society and they bickered only over details and the speed with which they could implement those plans. They seemed unconcerned that the electorate had indicated it wanted the very opposite of what was being imposed, and confident that they could win next time as they just had: when it became necessary they would crank up the machine, do and spend what was required — but that was several years ahead. This kind of behaviour — the word arrogant comes to mind — suggests that something new has evolved in electoral politics. In the past, governments at least worried about voters between elections, and this affected their legislative programs.

They now seem to have a much higher degree of confidence in their ability to control voting behaviour at election time, regardless of what has happened during their time in office. This confidence is based on improvements in the technology of electioneering: rolling polls, image creation, media manipulation, selective voter targeting, negative campaigning, and similar "advances." Elections are now treated as little more than isolated exercises — though ones which must be mastered when their time comes round. In between comes the other exercise, that of real power, and the two seem hardly related. Arrogance is prone to surprises, however, and one almost occurred in Canada in 1988.

The New Age

The first person I ever heard speak about multinational corporations was Canadian economist Steve Hymer. Hymer, who died tragically in a highway accident in 1974, lived and taught in the United States, but he worked closely with economist Mel Watkins on the famed Watkins Report about foreign control of Canada's economy, published in 1968. Watkins says that once in those years long past he and Hymer went to interview a high official at the State Department in Washington about how the U.S. government viewed the changing nature of the world economy, particularly the rise of huge multinational, or as they are also called, transnational, corporations. Hymer asked about the fact that some businesses were becoming so powerful that they could become rivals to nation-states as we know them, and with their global reach even threatened to make the traditional nation-state obsolete. Did the official or his government feel that some day these huge enterprises might threaten the very existence of separate countries and governments? The State Department official answered coldly, "It never crosses my desk in that form." Watkins still chuckles when he recalls it.

The extended battle over free trade which culminated

in the 1988 election was not merely a renewal of the War of 1812 when the United States invaded Canada — even if it felt that way at times to some participants. There was more involved than two countries. There was the truly global force of international capital in its late-1980s form. The upper ranks of big business today — the relative handful of huge corporations — have effectively rolled back the worldwide challenge of socialism, which began in the Soviet Union in 1917. At the moment, there are no contenders against their control of the world's wealth, and their ability to organize and distribute it as they see fit. They have remade the face of the global economy in the form of their "free" markets — which they strive to control with great precision. There was a time when capitalists thought of dominating and using national governments and sometimes even of creating nations for their own purposes and profits. They are now so powerful and self-sufficient that they incline more to elbow governments and nations aside, preferring a different kind of territorial entity, free of the impediments and particularities of actual countries and with almost exclusively economic characteristics. In other words, free trade areas. In the face of these mighty global corporations, mere governments tend to cower and retreat. If the battle against free trade had an occasionally parochial quality, it was because those fighting it sometimes forgot the awesome nature of the forces on the other side, identifying them "only" with the American state and its far-flung empire.

The economic record of this mighty force is not beyond criticism. It has redistributed wealth upward, so that the tiny fraction at the top has far more than it had and those below far less. In the U.S., where its development has gone furthest, the top one-half of one percent of the population went from owning 25 percent of the nation's wealth in 1963 to owning 35 percent in 1983 while the bottom 90 percent slipped from 35 to 28 percent. From 1978 to 1987, the poorest fifth of American families became 8 percent poorer while the richest fifth became 13 percent richer. Real income and wages have declined for the working majority. Those living in poverty rose from 28.3 percent of the population in 1978 to 35.2 percent in 1986. Simple dreams are fading out of reach. U.S. home ownership levels during the past eight years declined for the first time since 1940. During the Reagan years, genuine Depression conditions re-emerged in the U.S., with homelessness, decline of education and destruction of inner cities. *Time* magazine, after Reagan's second term, challenged Americans with Reagan's own question of 1980: are you better off than you were when this government took power? *Time* replied curtly, for the majority, No.

Even after the implementation of the business agenda under Reagan in the U.S. and Thatcher in the U.K., basic economic problems remained unsolved. Britain had a balanced budget *and* a huge trade deficit. The U.S. had supply-side economics *and* the greatest debt in world history. Deregulation of American airlines led, after a brief burst of new companies and lower prices, to fewer airlines and higher fares than ever, along with unprecedented terror in the air — instead of hijackings, there were accidents, near-misses and planes that simply disintegrated en route.

Globally the triumph of raw multinational capitalism in the 1980s had similar questionable results. UNICEF reported that in the underdeveloped world, the slow progress of the past had become a thing of the past during the decade. "For almost 900 million people, approximately one-sixth of mankind, the march of human progress has now become a retreat . . . . After decades of steady economic advance, large areas of the world are sliding backwards into poverty." Average income in most of Africa and much of Latin America fell 10 to 25 percent in the 1980s. In the 37 poorest nations, spending on health declined by 50 percent and on education by 25 percent. In almost half of the developing countries, the proportion of young children enrolled in primary school fell. This was all a result of the debt which those countries had to pay endlessly and hopelessly to the bankers and financiers of the global corporations, according to UNICEF. Meanwhile, a parallel immiseration was occurring even in the developed countries, except for the wealthiest sections of those societies. The private Worldwatch Institute warned that the "looming threats we now face . . . have so much momentum that unless action begins now to reverse them they will inevitably lead to paralyzingly costly economic consequences and the collapse of social and political institutions." Canada shared in this global pattern of the 1980s: income was redistributed upward while real wages and salaries fell. Yet in some areas — privatization, deregulation, a completely free hand to transnational business — Canada had lagged. With free trade in place, the lag was gone.

This surge in the power of big business also has enormous political implications. If almost everything consequential in human life is owned and controlled by a few massive corporations, what is left for politics to be about? Governments of the Reagan, Thatcher and Mulroney stripe seem elected primarily to eliminate whatever is left that governments do, and to turn the action over to business. Much of what was once in the public domain and subject to public debate, is passing over to business through the processes of privatization: education, health care, garbage disposal, airports, and even, in the U.S., courts and prisons. Government increasingly becomes a kind of purchasing agent of business services, using public funds, while business, in the hands of so few, can easily make deals among its own to parcel out the work and the way the work is done. Governments could still regulate business activity, except that deregulation is as central to their program as privatization, and no party that seriously opposes either plank will be supported by business. Competing social institutions which might provide alternate visions to that of business are simultaneously undermined: the unions, for instance, through legislation and plant shutdowns or their threat; or the women's movement; or the arts, which have traditionally been capable of challenging conventional views. As government retreats from cultural support programs, it insists that the "private sector" take up the slack. To the extent that this happens, the business world increasingly imposes its own standards: corporate executives now sit in and vet dress rehearsals of publicly supported Canadian theatres before confirming their sponsorships. Even a concern like environmentalism is swept up by the corporations as something from which to profit, while they assure environmentalists and the public that they alone have the power to deal with the issue. The realm of political concern shrinks till it tends to focus only on matters of personal or symbolic behaviour. In the United States, politics today seems to be mostly about abortion and the right to burn the flag. Public issues are vanishing from the public realm. Why should a citizen bother with politics when nothing much seems to happen there? So voter participation declines.

This may be an aggravating situation, but it is full of historical logic. Democracy as a political form was probably invented in ancient Greece, but it made its modern appearance through the revolutions of the late eighteenth century in America and France. The most radical claim introduced by those revolutions was the assertion of human equality, expressed in practice through the political equality of citizens. Over coming years, those excluded from political rights — women or slaves, for example — gained the right to vote and hold office, but one problem remained. Citizens who were equal in the political realm were radically unequal in the economic and social realm. In fact, the right to private property affirmed by the same revolutions frequently led to increased inequality at the level on which people lived their lives. This undermined equality in the political realm too, since those with great economic power could easily convert it into political power, through the simple exercise of buying votes or more subtle versions of the same thing. Most radical thinkers and movements of the last two hundred years, including Karl Marx, aimed at resolving this contradiction between formal political equality and real social inequality. Equal should mean equal, was their view, and they proposed a variety of solutions, most of which came under the heading of "socialism." The fact that none of their proposed solutions has actually worked so far does not eliminate the perplexing issue they addressed. They didn't have the answer, but they had a hell of a good question.

It faces us squarely and unavoidably. The power of transnational corporations today makes that of feudal lords seem puny. There are fewer of them worldwide than there were fiefdoms in many mediaeval realms; they disagree and fight occasionally but, overall, they coordinate their interests; and because of scientific and technological developments, their resources are unprecedented. (In many ways the contemporary media play a role parallel to that of the mediaeval church: assuring people that all is well with the world and urging them to absorb their energies in private salvation, through devout consuming, fitness, self-actualization, etc.) These business institutions are not interested in damaging competition with each other, or in interference from governments. They are inherently anti-democratic, because they do not want any obstacles to the exercise of their power, even though their activities often affect people's lives more directly and intimately than those of governments do. The kind of free choice that interests them involves not voting, but buying: the "democracy" of consumers in the marketplace, severely restricted by the limited options offered by the corporations and highly manipulated by advertising. In 1989, two hundred years after the French Revolution's Declaration of the Rights of Man, the Canada-U.S. free trade agreement brought a virtual Declaration of the Rights of Transnational Business into the centre of Canadian political life. In March of that year, Saskatchewan premier Grant Devine announced a program of privatization while waving a copy of the American journal *Newsweek* with a cover story on "The Decline of the Left." It's a global trend, squealed the premier, as if he were talking about cellular telephones. He wanted the people of his province "to be part of this exciting new world."

Becoming a Citizen

Two months after the election, I spoke again with Lillian Shavalier and Ellen Riddell, the waitresses from the Holiday Inn I had met at the start of the final week of the campaign. We talked in a bar near the hotel.

Lillian said, "In the restaurant, the only question was, Who're you voting for? That's it. This time, even with people who never talked about the election, people were getting confused with free trade. They'd hear one, then another." Ellen said, "At the end, I decided we'd better vote Liberal, just to ensure the PC's wouldn't get in. But I'm still an NDPer at heart." Then Dave from room service came and sat down with us, and said he'd voted PC in the election, because "something has to be done about this mess," and he figured maybe free trade would "at least do something." This seems to me a very understandable motive.

He is a member of a generation for whom the prospects of economic advancement often seem to peak at the level of managing a McDonald's. They are pummelled with media incitements to a lifestyle which they know will never be theirs. Alongside this economic gloom, they have been aware all their lives that a nuclear disaster could descend at any moment, while the formerly joyous anticipations of youthful sexuality are ringed for them with deathly fear. Dave was not all that well informed about the negative potential of free trade, but for him, maintaining the status quo held little attraction, regardless of the alternatives. A man has got to dream.

In these respects, Dave is close to what you might call a pure case of a voter. Various concerns and frustrations tumble about in his life, seemingly unconnected to anything he can do about them. Then one day an election is called. Suddenly the whole mess is supposed to be resolved in the simple choice of a candidate, party or leader. He takes his vote seriously, like most voters in my experience, from Victor Nowicki in Vancouver to Bill Butt in Conception Bay, Newfoundland. But the election is still seven weeks away, and life's preoccupations continue — job, family, bills, personal crises. It's hard to shift gears, and campaigns usually offer little to latch on to. The parties are trying to win support rather than inform voters. Like most of life's momentous decisions, this one is on you before you are ready — you haven't given it the time you'd hoped. But you do your best. As election day approaches, you pay closer attention, yet you aren't quite sure what you're looking for. So you pick up on little things, and eventually something determines your final choice. You are a voter, but not quite a citizen. I don't know how Dave felt when the mess continued after the voting, and even worsened. Did he feel frustrated? Did he start to grow cynical?

Joan Prowse, on the other hand, moved across what you might call the voter-citizen continuum during the election of 1988. Joan is twenty-eight. She comes from Burlington, Ontario. She studied "research techniques" at a community college, then went to work for a company that did film evaluations, until one day she found herself thinking, "Why am I evaluating someone else's work when I have my own ideas?" She took a degree in radio and television at Ryerson Polytechnical Institute in Toronto and now works for a small company that makes industrial films and commercials, along with some documentaries and TV dramas. She told a tale of involvement.

"My friend John took me to a thing in May last year at the Steelworkers' Hall on Cecil St. For something to do. We just walked over. Politics and me, I'm not an active person. But the guy there was talking about energy, I was just — I felt — I can't believe that. And I also couldn't believe that it was going to happen and that *I* didn't even *know* about it. And John had been thinking about doing a video. To give to candidates and go door to door to show on their VCRs. So that got me motivated. I think the free trade issue brought out a lot of people who won't get into things. It did a lot for kind of defining what Canada was, whether you're for or against."

They and another friend formed a company called
Canada for Canadians, and produced a half-hour video
which they managed to get shown almost everywhere in
the country. She said, "It's amazing how people come together. We had someone write original music, and our
cameraman gave us at least $5,000 of his time. And my
boss gave us free editing time. I like what John said in an
interview: that we did everything we could, we were opposed to it, and we wanted to speak out on it." When a
friend took their video to the Maritimes (because he was
going there for a couple of weeks), he managed to get it
shown on some local stations and then "we got a little
money for him to go across the west."

They were intrepid and inexperienced, a fearsome
combination, and had remarkable success getting their
video aired, especially right after the election was called.
"Within three weeks into the election, people were really
open to it. They just didn't realize what free trade was.
We supplied information about what was at stake. But in
the last four weeks, we were shut out. People we took it to
said, It's biased, for example, at cable stations. In Ontario
. . . it was by far the hardest to get it on there, on cable or
independent stations. They said, No. They'd say, Your
tape is biased, and we offered to set up a debate after
showing it, or find something pro. But it was very hard."

She began discovering forms of political control she
hadn't suspected. "When I went to CBC national radio,
the reporters were coming over telling me free trade was
a good thing. It was amazing. People there were all for it.
I'd be watching Barbara Frum on "The Journal" when
they had the debate about free trade, and the way they
had the table set up. They had the government's information on the table. The opening shot opened on the
agreement and then zoomed out — *both nights*. Also, after
the debates, Barbara Frum immediately went over and
shook the pro sides' hands. Little subtle things like that,
that I notice because of my work. Later, near the end of
the campaign, I was watching her with Broadbent. God,
she didn't give him a chance.

"Every time I went out I talked about it, every time I went to a party. Or when I went to lunch. I got in a huge fight at the Wheat Sheaf, the bar on King Street. They gave you two stickers, green or red, if you were for free trade or against it. I went around inviting people with red stickers to come see our video and this guy who was For — he worked for Northern Telecom — was screaming.

"I think the government made you feel guilty for being against it. By saying the people against it didn't know what was good for the country, they weren't business-minded. They said we were radicals. For example, Crispo called us "left-wing pinko radicals" in Saint John. I went to a seminar there for business. It was really ridiculous and I was embarrassed. Calling us left-wing radical pinkos. And saying the reason we work for the CBC is that we can't make it in the real world."

She's talked with friends of hers who voted Tory. They said they just kept changing their minds. Her best friend works for an insurance company in customer relations. She told Joan, "I had your propaganda and then I had the PC's propaganda and when I went to vote, theirs was the last thing I had that stuck in my mind. It was the last thing I had." I mentioned to Joan that it would have taken a lot of money to match the material from business and government, and the coalitions against the deal were tapped out. Joan said it wouldn't have been necessary to match them but it would have been important to get a word in. After a while, the pro-deal barrage wore people down, because they saw nothing else.

A friend of Joan's who works in advertising said that at first she opposed free trade, but "at dinner after the election I found out she voted for free trade. She said, 'In my kind of business it makes sense because the ad companies are being taken over by the Americans. I'd be biting the hand that feeds me.' She's a very ambitious person. And she didn't want to come out and say, I'm against it. And I myself, at work — people at work didn't want to talk about it. People in the business community went along with what their bosses were telling them. Like getting a

letter in your pay packet from Stelco" — the huge steel
company based in Hamilton, Ontario. "Most people are in
business," says Joan, by which she means that most people
work for businesses and identify with them. "Everyone
looks at who is paying them, and if that person is in business, they don't want to bite the hand that feeds them."

Others she knew were affected as she was. "I had a
friend in Ottawa, the day of the election, who stood outside the poll with a sign that said, 'Remember this day, it
could be the last day you're voting as a Canadian.' I have a
twin sister and she's totally oblivious to politics. She's a designer in the fashion industry. She's kind of, 'Oh, I don't
like thinking about politics.' She had to go to work that
night in Oakville but her polling station was in Burlington
and she got stuck in traffic and said, 'I didn't care if I was
late for work, I just wanted to get there and stop that
deal.' " Will this kind of involvement carry on with Joan's
sister? "I don't think so. But she'd never even voted before." Joan herself went "down to the GO train station the
day of the election because we heard the Tories were out
in the morning giving out stuff."

Has she changed? "Oh yes. Now I watch the news just
about every night. It has made me more aware of how
politics really does affect our lives. And also, I had this belief, I'm such a naïve person. I thought if you were doing
the right thing, you really would win in the end. Even on
election night. And when we didn't, it really was a kind of
slap in the face and it also made me question how really
democratic our country is if the Canadian public can kind
of be bought."

How will this affect her in the future? "I don't know.
I'm not anti-American, I'm pro-Canadian. If the Americans start changing our country, I won't want to stay here
and watch our country change. I could go to the U.K., but
I don't want to. Or I could stay and fight to the bitter end.
But I don't want to see it happen. That night of the election, I actually cried. I went home and cried. I thought,
Now it could become reality, it actually *could* happen. Before, I just kind of didn't look at the government as

having any influence in my life. I was this entity that kind
of went about my life, but now I realize I really do have to
be aware. I only found out about it by chance, by going to
that meeting, and I'm glad Canadians will be paying attention." She and her friends now have their own
company and have already produced two videos, one on
the Meech Lake accord, and another on the shutdown of
the Summerside military base on Prince Edward Island as
a result of the April '89 federal budget.

She is like a laboratory example of politicization: its
unexpectedness, its slowness, the way it can build. She is
also vivid proof of how important it is for those in power
to keep citizens uninvolved: to keep voters from becoming citizens. If a few more people like Joan wandered over
to a few meetings just for something to do, everything in
this society would stop working the way it does.

Quebec and Other Heroes

For twenty or twenty-five years, starting in the 1960s,
Quebec functioned as a source of political inspiration for
many in English Canada, because of its fervent nationalism, its cultural creativity and its pride in its past, along
with the way it seemed to join its national yearnings to a
desire for social justice. In Quebec, for example, unions
played a central role in the fight for national independence and dignity. The issue of French language rights
was tied to the cause of human rights everywhere — as
brilliantly expressed in Michèle Lalonde's 1970 poem,
"Speak White." ("Speak white / tell us again about freedom and democracy / We know that liberty is a Black
word . . . .") There were conservative Canadian nationalists who rejected Quebec nationalism, but to others,
myself included, it seemed an undeniable force — even if
its result were to mean an independent Quebec, somehow
connected to an altered Canada. I wrote sympathetically
and often about Quebec nationalist politics, from the
time of the War Measures Act in 1970, through the

election of the Parti Québécois, the referendum on independence . . . .

This sense of connection terminated abruptly with the free trade election of 1988. It was as though the people of Quebec had tired of being, in Leonard Cohen's phrase, beautiful losers, and had decided to join the certifiable winners of the 1980s: business and corporate capital. The nationalist movement, with the exception of labour, embraced Brian Mulroney and his free trade deal. The many human and social resonances of Quebec nationalism seemed to dissipate.

In fact, the late 1980s have been a time of fallen idols, lost heroes and diminished models. An earlier generation of political radicals once looked to the Soviet Union for inspiration; a later one, nurtured in the 1960s, came to invest much hope in China, Cuba or Vietnam. For various reasons, none of these exemplars were capable of sustaining the politico-emotional investments made in them. Other noble nation-building efforts such as those in Mozambique or Nicaragua were brutally suppressed by outside forces and compelled to concentrate on sheer survival rather than innovation. Of course, none of the peoples of those beleaguered societies had ever asked to carry a burden of expectations from generations of political idealists in developed Western countries.

Besides, there is something to be said for smashed idols: they put you on your own. The trouble with heroes and models is they are bound to disappoint sooner or later; in the meantime, one tends to become absorbed with copying or adapting ways in which others appear to have succeeded, rather than creating one's own path. Some Canadian Maoists of the 1960s seriously urged Canadian activists to go to the "countryside" in order to "rally the peasantry." Political inspirations can be debilitating. Once foreign models have lost their allure, if one intends to continue working toward a radically better society, then an approach will have to be found more through the creative exercise of moral and political imagination than by taking a work-study trip to a socialist paradise. A certain value comes from knowing you're going to have to make progress mostly on your own. It gets you off your butt.

So for some of us in English Canada, it wasn't all bad, after twenty years of feeling comparatively unsophisticated in culture and politics, to finally get the Quebec monkey off our back. Maybe they could even learn something from us.

An Interesting Blip

One afternoon in December '88, I talked to Karen Strype, a former teacher who now lives in York region, a sort of parody of a free trade zone north of Toronto, where developers and other monied forces casually manipulate local governments. Talk turned to the federal election and the heady weeks of democratic chaos in the middle of it, during which it looked as if the normal forces of wealth and power in our society might be routed. "Yes," she said, "that was an interesting blip, wasn't it?"

It is not easy to evaluate the election of 1988 and especially the outbreak of public debate that made it unique. It is not hard to be discouraged by some of the questions it raises about our political system. Kari Dehli, the post-doctoral fellow at the Ontario Institute for Studies in Education who worked on Dan Heap's campaign in Toronto, moved to Canada from Norway sixteen years ago, just after a comparable political event. "In Norway, where I'm from, in 1972, there was a referendum on joining the Common Market, and the Labour party and Conservative party and major industries and unions were pro. And the coalition against was the same as it was here: environmental groups, cultural groups, youth and left sections of the Labour party, women's organizations, farmers, fishermen. They formed the No-Vote coalition and *won*, by about the exact percentage that voted for the Liberals and the NDP combined — that is, 53 to 47. And it remade Norwegian politics. Denmark joined at almost exactly the same time, and it was a disaster for their economy. And

Norway has maintained almost full employment and protected resources coming out of the North Sea."
Presumably, had Norwegians voted in a general election
with a three-party split rather than a referendum, the
whole event would have been an interesting blip rather
than a historic turning. The point was not missed in
Canada where, after the 1988 election, buttons appeared
which read "53–43 No Deal."

Other comparisons are also troubling — especially with
societies to which Canadians have long felt politically superior. Eugene Whelan, former minister of agriculture,
escorted Mikhail Gorbachev — then a Soviet vice-premier
— for ten days when Gorbachev visited Canada in 1981.
In April '89, Whelan reflected on the democratic reforms
being implemented in the Soviet Union under Gorbachev
at the same time that Canada was re-electing its Tory government. "Over there they need a majority to get elected,
you can cross out candidates if you don't like them and
they can't be elected unless they get 50 percent. Here
Mulroney gets 43 percent and he puts through free trade.
Our whole political system needs an overhaul."

The election also raised questions about the degree to
which money can buy success in our democratic system.
The experience ought to have boosted the stock of vulgar
Marxism, a theory which states that control of the economy entails control of every other aspect of society,
including politics and culture, and that fundamental
change is impossible while the property system remains in
place. Such conclusions were particularly apt with regard
to the press and media. They are now so concentrated
and so interlocked with other financial and industrial interests that they function in many ways as simply the
public relations arm of corporate wealth. The popular
movement against free trade tried myriad ways to get its
message into the Canadian media both before and during
the election, but it found only one successful method: buy
space. It's not foolproof: they can still reject the purchase
on spurious grounds, or bury the ad or insert it in the
travel section. Besides, the only forces in this society

wealthy enough to consistently buy that kind of space are the same corporations that also own or dominate most of the media at this point.

Personally, I am not sanguine about the Canadian future. If you were a betting person, I think you would be foolish to wager in favour of the survival of the country — unless you got very good odds. Broadbent was probably right when he said Canada would likely not last twenty-five years after a free trade deal, though he might have overestimated the time-frame.

On the other hand, politics — in the good old Greek sense — is not a game, or a betting matter. It is what you do about what you really are. In this light and despite the dour prospects, I think it would be foolish to be negative about recent Canadian political experience and especially the free trade election.

It would also be historically myopic. Other peoples of the world have lived through far more before they made even minimal gains against established wealth and power. In China, the people have been engaged in revolution against authority and privilege for eighty years, nonstop. Many other societies went through decades of defeat or limited victory before winning definable successes — and then were frequently driven back in coming years. What has the struggle cost us in Canada so far? Three years and a large number of exhausted, dispirited people? Piffle. Despite the intensity of the conflict and the high stakes involved, nobody was assassinated by death squads during the Canadian election of 1988. No one was abducted before the eyes of their family, or dropped dead and mutilated on their doorstep. There wasn't even blatant censorship; that was done with relative subtlety. Canadians interested in a more democratic and equitable society and in beating back some of the truly barbaric forces of our age have merely made a reasonable start.

The breadth and inclusiveness of the popular opposition against free trade was unprecedented in Canadian political history, but it was only a beginning. It never became a mass movement. Some of its constituent organizations — the labour movement and the women's movement in particular — did reach out and involve large chunks of their memberships, but other elements, like the churches, did less to actually activate their members. One sign of the limitation of the coalition movement is the fact that it never demanded a national referendum to settle the free trade issue, preferring the tortuous route of an election, in which chances of defeating the government and its deal appeared reasonable. The government would almost certainly have denied a referendum, yet the reluctance of the coalitions to go in that direction indicates a certain lack of willingness on their part to trust the fate of the country to its people.

This is ironic because the single most hopeful element in the entire election of 1988 was the role played by the Canadian people. If there is a hero to this tale, they are it. When they got a chance, when they were given a minimal amount of help, they responded with animation and intelligence.

This contradicts the widespread notion that people in our society have been stupefied by public relations manipulation and mass media mindlessness — an assumption found across the political spectrum and on which electioneering by all parties is premised. Remember that there never was a focused national debate on free trade, that the government never stopped doing a selling job and avoided direct confrontation and that the only relatively spontaneous moment in the entire three years — that is, a very brief exchange between Turner and Mulroney during the televised election debate — led to a massive shift in opinion and intention. Everything else, both before and during the election campaign, was a matter of public relations, advertising or staged campaign events. The only time the proponents of free trade got out in front of the people in an uncontrolled situation, everything changed. It's not people who are the problem. Their minds and their ability to judge haven't been destroyed by the best efforts of our tawdry age. They just need half a chance to make a relatively unmanipulated judgment. It seems to me that the most profound lesson of this experience has been: people are not stupid, despite the fact that many have tried to make them so.

It seems to me as well that there was a real victory for the anti-free trade forces in the election of 1988, but it did not concern free trade, it concerned democracy. The government and its business tutors had an explicit anti-democratic agenda, as stated in their secret communications strategy of 1985. They intended to stifle discussion on the subject, and where that was impossible, to sell rather than educate — in their own words. The anti-free trade movement did not stop the trade agreement; it did not defeat the government and stymie its right-wing agenda; it did, however, utterly smash the government's anti-democratic secret communications strategy for free trade. The discussion which took place was not as open and informative as it might have been, it was largely distorted by wealth and intimidation — but it occurred.

In almost everything I have written, I have faced what I think of as the problem of the ending, because the forces that deserved to win, as Laurell might say, almost never did. How are you to be honest about defeat and failure, yet at least minimally hopeful about the future? I've tended to think of this as a problem for Canadian writers, but it might apply to writing anywhere, on many themes, and certainly to what could be called the history of the democratic impulse. The defeats for that impulse have been many, the victories few, and those few victories were often subverted soon after, so that their democratic promise was largely betrayed — the case, I would argue, in both the American Revolution of 1776 and the Soviet Revolution of 1917. They were, in other words, interesting blips.

The question is, What is the value of a blip, and what is its significance compared to dominant trends, as identified by election results or the cover of *Newsweek*? There have been blips throughout history, and much of the time they have represented humanization, progress, the assertion of the real social nature of people instead of their diversion to the sidelines of history while the powerful play on the field. Spartacus was a blip, as was William Lyon Mackenzie — and many we will never hear about. They are the movement of the truly human and the truly interesting in history, as against the eternal reassertion of the status quo — a state causally related to benign neglect — and occasionally, glacially, laboriously, the blips refuse to fade, they link up with one another, and they attempt to define the shape of the future.

We are all implicated politically because of our social and historical interdependencies, so politics affects all of us all the time — as many kind people pointed out while I travelled during the election of 1988. That's not the same though, as being a citizen, which involves consciously acting back; doing what we can to affect what affects us. It is obviously possible to live a life without that active kind of politics. It might be a rich life, and possibly a happy one. It wouldn't though — if Aristotle and others were right — be a fully human life. That's all.